News in the Global Sphere
A Study of CNN and its Impact on Global
Communication

News in the Global Sphere

A Study of CNN and its Impact on Global Communication

Ingrid Volkmer

UNIVERSITY
OF LUTON

press

British Library Cataloguing in Publication Data
A catalogue record for this book is available from the British Library

ISBN: 1 86020 554 2

Published by
University of Luton Press
University of Luton
75 Castle Street
Luton
Bedfordshire LU1 3AJ
United Kingdom

Tel: +44 (0)1582 743297; Fax: +44 (0)1582 743298
e-mail: ulp@luton.ac.uk
www.ulp.org.uk

Cover Design by Gary Gravatt, Morgan and Gravatt Design Consultants
Typeset in Palatino
Printed in Great Britain by Whitstable Litho, Whitstable, Kent

Contents

Acknowledgements

Iowe thanks to many colleagues and friends, of whom I can only name a few here. I would like to thank David Thorburn, who has inspired my interest in CNN almost ten years ago. Back then, CNN was an innovative and promising news channel, however, in those years widely unknown in Europe. My first idea was to analyse CNN's coverage of European issues. The tremendous national and international expansion of CNN has shifted this research angle into the global arena. Particularly Roland Robertson's globalization theory in the context of the Anglo-American debate, widely initiated by the journal *Theory, Culture and Society*, supported an understanding of this obviously new global media, ie content-flow-environment. I thank Roland Robertson for his intellectual guidance, his comments and support. I also owe thanks to Dieter Baacke, who has as a colleague and friend always encouraged me.

I am grateful to many journalists of CNN, who took their valuable time for quite lengthy and insightful interviews. I thank Alyssa McElrone, who coordinated many research stays at CNN, Tom Johnson and Eason Jordan, Kay Delaney and Lou O. Curles, who discussed various aspects of my research from CNN's angle with me and always supported my research at CNN's Headquarters.

Other invaluable colleagues and friends have contributed to this project: Gary Melton and Jack Estes, Wolfgang Schweins, Maja Thomsen and Susan Bennett. I dedicate this book to my parents, Wally and Helmut Volkmer, who always taught me to think global.

Introduction

The current sociological debate on 'Globalization' may well constitute a change of paradigm in sociological theory. Within this debate, the categories conventionally used to define intersocietal relationships which focus on a 'unifying' social or economic construct of world society, and tend to homogenise the globe as a whole – from Kant's universality of human rights, through Weber to Wallerstein, 1974, Luhmann, 1975, and others – look very different from the new global perspectives.

These perspectives encompass theories of a diversified world, the 'discovery' of the co-existence and interdependence of 'globalism' and 'localism', or, in broader sociological terms of 'universalism' and 'particularism', as Robertson defined them in his theory of globalization. (Robertson, 1992) They pave the way to a reinterpretation of worldwide cultural phenomena as both multicultural and particular. Quite early on in the debate Featherstone (1990, 1991) gave a very convincing explanation of this development in postmodern terminology by advancing a 'consumer' culture theory.

In the architecture of sociological globalization theory, new links within the discipline of international communication appear. The media, in their function of shaping, sustaining and diversifying global stratification, influence a worldwide formation of 'communities', 'identities', 'democracy' and other forms of social organization. When we view the media as initiators and mediators of a multidimensional global communication process, the sociological theory of 'globalization' linked to the concept of global communication brings to the fore the most obvious global relationship between communication and politics. This new global political communication is still, today in 1998, in the age of Internet technology, powerfully shaped in many instances – the breaking of political crises in particular – by Cable News Network (CNN), which has become a classic model of a global news institution.

The launching of CNN's international news outlet Cable News Network International (CNNI) in 1985 brought about new forms of global political communication within a period of only a few years, affecting political action on many levels and on a worldwide scale by extending political

1

communication globally. CNNI has reshaped the conventional agenda of international or 'foreign' news and created a platform for worldwide communication. This journalistic initiative has altered the focus of global news in an interrelationship of changing political centres and peripheries, and has given a new meaning to news, journalistic values, the setting of a global agenda.

These multilevel developments point to the variety of dimensions in global communication which involve 'homogenising' simultaneously with 'heterogenising' effects. On neither a general, nor on a specific level have these been incorporated into contemporary communication theory. Although a few publications refer in a more general way to CNN's programming and involvement in the Gulf War, (Katz, 1991; Zelizer, 1992) neither the growing worldwide audience of CNNI nor its increasing global reputation as 'The World's News Leader' or the political role of CNNI in various world regions[1] has stimulated any significant thinking about the reformulation or reformatting of existing concepts of international communication. No new theoretical framework has emerged for interpreting this new level of 'global communication', including its worldwide impact on new cultural and political structures and journalistic standards.

Such a theory of 'global communication' could, however, be of great value for redefining or even replacing conventional concepts of international communication, which still refer mainly without any meta-theoretical specification to 'international' 'world' or 'global' communication and its 'order'.

A specific theory of global communication needs to be developed, on the meta-theoretical basis of this globalizing sociological approach, so as to describe the specific roles of these various global movements in shaping the diverse, and (particularly in the case of the Internet) continuously diversifying global communication processes. The political and cultural effects of global communication are still widely unexplored in communication studies. On the other hand, media conglomerates such as CNNI (or, to be even more precise, the Turner Broadcasting System, Inc. [TBS]) have already begun to structure global multilevel audiovisual communication by creating their own specific notions of the globe, in the interest of expanding their business. These include:

(1) segmenting the global market into markets for continental and regional programmes by exercising differentiated models of global journalism and of global marketing strategies;

(2) diversifying their global operations in other economically effective ways such as time-slot placement of 'carrier' programmes which are rebroadcast on national channels, and special-interest programmes;[2]

(3) producing new programmes and engaging in new patterns of international cooperation.

CNNI, as a globally operating media conglomerate – and on this general level MTV can be equally regarded as the initiator of similar phenomena –

tends not so much to 'homogenise' the globe as to diversify McLuhan's now clearly simplistic idea of a 'global village' into global villages, with their own network of main and side streets, ready to follow CNNI in establishing world-centres and peripheries that change daily.

CNNI has inaugurated a market-force-oriented process which shifts global communication onto a new level by mixing the conventional reference-system of national news presentation, with its 'home' and 'foreign' news (which in fact involves a 'domestication' of 'foreign-ness'; see Dahlgren and Sparks, 1991) with a global juxtaposition of the 'internal' and the 'external', a substantial new inter-relationship which can shape political action (as became most obvious in the involvement of international media in the democratic movements of Eastern Europe). This switch to global determinants builds worldwide political structures through new demands for the integration of political action into a worldwide consensus of 'democracy' which includes the co-existence of diverse 'realities' and values. In recent years various news channels similar to CNNI have been established, such as Euronews and BBC World Service Television, which focus on international distribution and provide a public arena whose importance should not be underestimated in a time of increasingly media-related world politics.

Another element that CNNI has brought to the growing complexity and disorder of conventional international political communication is stylistic: the introduction of a new journalistic language with 'sound bite' semiotics; (Gitlin, 1991) 'fact' journalism; 'breaking news' stories instantaneously and simultaneously transmitted around the globe via 24-hour satellite. Different worldwide societal definitions of the 'meaning' and 'importance' of specific political events, of news hierarchies and of political issues, are remixed in a global context. This new globally distributed mix supports the consciousness of diversified global communities, a process which is reinforced by a diverse worldwide program-schedule transmitted globally directly or indirectly via syndicated re-broadcast contracts and affiliated programming.

The following study interprets these emerging spheres of global political communication as various types of reciprocity – defined as the effects of re-broadcasting national political issues from a global viewpoint back into the political framework where they originated. One of these effects is the constitution of a worldwide homogeneously time-zoned *biòs politikon*, instantaneously affecting worldwide political action or interaction via press conferences or public resolutions transmitted around the world by CNNI. We consider these processes as *the* most important new configurations of global political communication, which, however, seem to be quite invisible from the perspective of conventional communication theories.

At present, approaches to international communication apply conventional theoretical constructs to disparate fields of international communication, such as:

(1) studies which reveal the imbalance in global media images and portrayals; (Galtung and Ruge, 1965; Stevenson and Shaw, 1984)

(2) analyses of the media imperialism of global conglomerates; (Schiller, 1976; Nordenstreng and Schiller, 1979; Sussman, 1991)

(3) investigations of the cultural effects of 'main-streaming' processes (Morgan, 1990) through internationally transmitted media productions;

(4) analyses of the varying role played by national news media in times of international crisis. (Cohen, Adoni and Bantz, 1990; Raboy and Dagenais, 1992)

On the surface these studies appear to be concerned with processes of global communication. A closer look, however, reveals a transnational (ie, bi- or multilateral) context rather than a specifically global one. If the 'globe' is brought seriously into focus, it is used either in a more general, unifying sense of the word, or it has more of an international – that is, bi or multilateral – meaning (see Merrill, 1983; Gerbner and Siefert, 1984) but without any reference to the antecedents of current sociological postulations on globalization. In general, it can be assumed that these concepts of international communication deal not so much with global as with transnational communication, primarily in relationship to 'traditional' metatheories of international communication, developed in the past by Parsons in his work on modern Western societies, and transformed into communication theory by Lerner's influential book on *The Passing of Traditional Society* (1958). There are, however, a very few recent writings on international communication which seem to express an increasing awareness that verified views on international communication phenomena are needed, (McQuail, 1987; Mattelart, 1992; Gurevitch, Levy, Roeh, 1991) or point to the methodological problems posed by the a new global, transnational communication status quo. (Negrine and Papathanassopoulos, 1990) Recent approaches interpret the global media flow from a very specific standpoint, ie as an 'intertextuality' with effects on a diversified global culture; (Barker, 1997) other studies analyse the transnationality of media images (Wilson and Dissanayake, 1996) in both global and local terms. (Dirlik, 1996, Polan, 1996)

By adopting the 'global culture' approach (as defined by Featherstone, 1990, and Robertson, 1992) this study aims to discuss a broad theoretical framework for global political communication. This undertaking focusses in particular on empirical findings which allows us to draw the picture of a global civil society, a term which we relate to Robertson's category of the 'global human condition' as a globally expanding consciousness of 'humankind', represented in issues of global political communication.

Within this broad conceptual framework, I argue that global political communication (as launched by CNNI) results in the construction of a *global public sphere*, which has various macro and microframed access modalities for worldwide broadcasters and news events beyond conventional 'gatekeeping' hierarchies. On the *macroframe* this global public sphere implies international co-operation, affiliation and syndication structures as well as news exchange systems (such as globally operating news agencies), on the *microframe* news language and presentation routines (avoidance of stereotypes, placing of news events in a larger regional, continental, multinational or global context). These macro and microframes of international political communication reach beyond traditional public sphere definitions (such as those submitted by Lippmann, 1922, 1954; Chomsky and Herman, 1988, or Habermas, 1992; and see for support of the arguments: Dahlgren, 1991). This assumption results in the construct of a global public sphere, positing a global human condition and a new field of political action through global institutions of an 'intersocietal and intercivilisational' kind, (Robertson, 1992:41) like the various legal and organizational instruments of the United Nations as well as in worldwide movements (represented by NGO's such as World Watch, Human Rights Watch, Women's Rights, Greenpeace). I shall argue that from this global public sphere, consisting of a worldwide available audiovisual, satellite-transmitted 'communication platform', *a global civil society* emerges which can be regarded as part of a global 'syncretization'. (Robertson, 1992:41)

The 'global civil society' concept is advanced here through the description and interpretation of recent developments in the function of news organizations, broadcasters and news agencies in editing, presenting, influencing, inaugurating and transmitting political processes. The framework of the argument is laid down by the specific employment of the classic philosophical categories of 'Universalism' and 'Particularism' – two qualitative poles between which global political communication seems to oscillate. They provide a macroframe for the classification of the global 'jungle' of available news programmes and a microframe classification of CNNI's news content. Under this scheme, global news events (ie transmitted by CNNI) are categorised qualitatively (topics, 'actors', angle of reporting, presentation of the global context and so on) and by their political references outside of the conventional government and national contexts. I argue that the provision of this global public sphere 'platform' specifically serves the communication requirements of the following:

(1) worldwide movements on a broad and (due to global communication) expanding variety of 'human' issues which have established their own news marketing concepts (Gitlin, 1991; Mancini, 1991) and find equal access to the global public sphere: for example, via various CNNI programme models;

(2) new worldwide types of political organization (cultural, religious or ethnic [Moynihan, 1993]) which constitute globally 'imagined' communities. (Anderson, 1983)

It also supports the emergence of new information channels providing political communication for a global civil society.

In terms of globally acting news media, I argue that the assumed emergence of a global civil society is communicated worldwide within the diverse levels of a 'global public sphere', heterogeneous in itself and with a differentiated scheme of universalism and particularism. For many reasons, this emerging global public sphere is currently still dominated by CNNI, which (1) affects global political action ('primetime politics'), (2) speeds up political interaction, and (3) influences journalistic values worldwide (Larsen, 1992; Foote and Amin, 1992), thus giving a homogeneous global shape to diverse news events.

It is argued that the theoretical construct of the 'global public sphere' implies an overall dimension of global political communication. This leads on to a discussion of global civil society, chiefly in terms of Hegel's concept of 'mediation', advanced as part of his concept of modern civil society, and meaning emerging social factors between operating between state and nation. (Hegel, 1820, 1967) The employment of this Hegelian category allows us to map the specific mediation role of global political entities, above and beyond state and/or nation references: namely, across larger multistate/national political action units towards the globe (and vice versa). We look at the increasing influence of multinational or even global political organisations' fields of action in their role as initiators of global mediation processes, not (as in Hegel's modern view) within but beyond statist and national levels. Whereas for Hegel, mediation was confronted with the problem of the duality of state and nation, in a global civil society the problem of duality occurs in the synchronism, balance and imbalance of universal and particular political developments being globally distributed beyond, between and back into traditional political boundaries (such as borders of political action and control, ideological, religious and cultural influences).

When examining CNNI I argue truly 'universal' communication targeting the globe as a whole are in decline whereas particular political interests are being propagated worldwide. This is due to having principle of general access to this global public sphere – for example via talk shows, press briefings and conferences via interactive television or the Internet, exclusive interviews and features produced by CNNI's international staff as well as by the various international news organizations. I discuss this hypothesis through further typification of a scheme of universality and particularity in the global public sphere, showing how global civil society is stratified into various types of global civil societies, communicating on different mediation levels within a worldwide public sphere. The enlargement of political geography thanks to the mediation of relevant universal and particular political communication contents within the global public sphere might lead to one to regard global civil society as a 'fourth' realm. This realm would be more than a third party, (Cohen and Arato, 1992) between the state/nation duality, insofar as state/nation politics are increasingly affected by a pure notion of the omnipresence of a global public sphere.

This theoretical approach provides a broad background for an analysis of CNN and its impact on global political communication as a system which (1) is connected on various levels with global news organizations and (2) has developed a variety of types of programme for specific mediation spheres of global communication. The results of a content analysis of the program *World Report* globally distributed simultaneously via CNN functions as empirical evidence of the previously developed hypotheses and allows parallels to be drawn with other internationally distributed news programmes. Besides these sets of data, results of qualitative interviews with professionals of different journalistic ranks at CNN's headquarters in Atlanta, Georgia, provide an inside view into everyday journalistic routines and the programme philosophy of the CNN news system.

As the fastest growing medium, the Internet can be regarded as an exemplary of a globalized media world which has shifted global communication to a new level. However, the myth of the Internet as a global medium is mainly embedded in Western industrialised media cultures. Terms like 'Cyberdemocracy' and 'Cybersociety' are constructions of a future potential, which is of no interest to various world regions, where the Internet, if available at all, serves different social, professional and political functions. The following study does not refer to the Internet as a networking technology but regards CNNI as a phenomenon which has constituted a new kind of global news programme flow and thus a new kind of global communication, with the ideal of equal representation of all cultures and nations. The theoretical model of global communication, the model of a global public sphere, consisting of the mediation of universal and particular elements can be further applied to the Internet (see Volkmer, 1997), however, the following study focusses primarily on the mass medium of global satellite television.

Notes

1 For the interdependence of universalism and particularism in ancient Judaism, see Long, 1991: pp.21.
2 Which he defines as "Print- und Bildmedien," "mündliche, schriftliche oder elektronische Kommunikation," "modernes Datenwissen," "klassisches Bildungswissen" (Spinner, 1994:34).

1

International Communication Flow and the Paradigm Change in Communication Theory

The terms 'international', 'transnational' and 'global' communication not only stand for different definitions of more or less the same phenomenon, but also suggest the history of worldwide communication structures as well as their current diversity. Global communication gives us an eyewitness view of events taking place in remote locations and in the commercial and political capitals of the world, enabling us to become informed about issues of global, regional or local relevance. It also allows us to participate in a globally disseminated world culture. These global processes, in which information and knowledge, values and ethics, aesthetics and lifestyles are exchanged, is becoming increasingly autonomous, creating a 'third culture'. (Featherstone, 1990:1) As Featherstone explains, this involves a 'generative frame of unity within which diversity can take place'. (Featherstone, 1990:2) Such a 'global world culture', as a substantial element of global 'systems' in the spheres of economics and politics, is dependent to a great extent on global communication.

Whereas in the seventeenth century communication systems were utilized to send coffee prices from Venice to London, or, in the nineteenth century, to transmit the names of presidential nominees from Washington to London, or, in this century to broadcast Armstrong's first steps on the moon to a nearly global television audience, nowadays they broadcast issues of a local, regional or global relevance around the globe. The moon-landing media experience, watched from China to Argentina, was indeed a large step for mankind: simply because for the first time Planet Earth was seen as the habitat of the whole human race, without regard to ethnic, national or other differences. The idea of the 'world' seemed to have switched all of a sudden from a metaphysical concept into a physical reality for a mass audience, from a diverse and conflict-laden living space to a global whole, whose inhabitants shared the fate of existing on a small planet in an undiscovered universe.

Since those days in 1967, the technical facilities, structures, and impact as well as the content of global communication have changed tremendously. Technical diversification and the advent of satellite technology have created interactive global circuits via audivisual and audio signals, digital telecommunication and Internet technology. New globally and internationally operating television networks have been established and have contributed to the near autonomy of global communication. This means that the new global media in particular – such as television, traditionally a national medium of communication – now not only function beyond state and national boundaries, but disseminate around the globe issues which influence policy-making, economics, culture and other forces. Because of these developments, global television affects the social agenda of societies, the composition of their 'public sphere'. But it also shapes ideas of a global 'reality' within the discipline of the sociology of knowledge: 'The change-within-being of the place where we stand' (Mannheim, 1964); re-evaluations of the individual world (Husserl's *Lebenswelt*). One example of such a re-evaluation is that suggested by Baacke (1987) with his socio-ecologocial models, in which fragments of global reality become central to the *Lebenswelt*.

However, it can be argued that fantasies and concepts of the 'world' have existed since Plato in his *Timaeus* defined the history of the world by the affiliation of the four elements to each other and to God and, writing as an astronomer, by the relationship of the planets; or since Aristotle defined the 'world state'; or since Francis Bacon distinguished between different world concepts, the *globus intellectualis* or *orbis scientarium*, identifying the world of science as distinct from the *globus terrestris* referring to new material 'worlds', the discoveries of new continents, and the view of an ever-changing world horizon.

During the Enlightenment, perception of the geography of the world spread dramatically, because of geographical discoveries and the desire for expansion into new political territories, and consequently led to the colonisation of new continents. The world was literally mapped through the discoveries of Portuguese, Spanish and British expeditions.

The idea of the 'world' as a universe of nature and reasoning, however, has become, since the Enlightenment, a profound element of modern thinking. Kant refers to a 'Cosmopolitan' as a patriotic citizen of his community. (Richter, 1992:17) He defines 'Cosmopolitanism' as follows: 'The character of the species, as can be ascertained from the experience of all times and all peoples is this: that taken collectively the human race as a whole is of a crowd of people living together, sequentially and contemporaneously, who cannot do without peaceful co-existence, yet cannot avoid constant mutual hostility. So through mutual compulsion exercised via laws which they have themselves devised, they live in a precarious but generally workable coalation as citizens of a world society, to which they feel themselves destined by nature.' (Kant, 1947) Cosmopolitanism is thus more a category of *Vernunft* (reason) than a political world domain, since Kant does not consider a republican world state as practicable. (Richter, 1992:52) In terms of this definition, world society consists of a global arena for public debate: 'All actions impinging on the rights of others and which are in principle incompatible with being made public, are unlawful'. (Kant 1947) This idea of truth in the sense of a 'publicly' approved validity involves a notion of 'the public' as the term is used in modern political and communication theory. Postmodern philosophy replaced 'reasoning' by 'simulation', and Hegel's term *Weltgeist* (world spirit) by an idea of 'instant' truth created by the media and conveying the image of a shrinking world. (Virilio, 1989:140)

These various philosophical theories imply an increasing concern with or focus on a globally expanded sphere of 'humankind' or the 'human condition' in specific relation to cosmological entities, to God as the creator of the universe, to reasoning as a natural human resource, but – in postmodern thinking – also to the influences of technological advances on the senses and aesthetics. They also imply a 'world order' and the interdependence of 'universalism' and 'particularism'.[1]

The issue of a diversified modern, (Giddens, 1990; Richter, 1992) postmodern or late modern globalization process, as defined by Robertson and Featherstone (1990), reveals a new situation in which world economy, world culture, world citizenry exist in parallel with strong 'tribal' collectivities (thus setting the terms for a new line of thought in sociology). In the view of these authors, 'globalization' means 'diversity' as well as 'parallelism'. There is much friction in this situation, which Barber (1994) illustrates in terms of the simultaneous realities of 'McWorld' (indicating commercial or pop-cultural cross-cultural homogenisation) and 'Jihad' (indicating the countermovement of fanatic localism). In Barber's concept, 'McWorld' consists of the economic global bond in which we all participate, be it by the consumption of global icons (Michael Jackson via MTV and movies like *Titanic*), accessories (Adidas and Swatch), culture (Mozart and Warhol), or information (Nelson Mandela and OJ Simpson via CNN). On the other hand, there is also the 'Jihad' side, where various renaissances and new kinds of nationalism and of emotion-led collectivities emerge, whether focussed on local territories, ethnic groups or political ideologies. This parallelism implies manifold political, cultural, educational, sociological, ethical and legal problems of a new kind. The characteristic dynamic of these interwoven as well as separate worlds shapes global 'reality' in short bursts. Both worlds have their philosophical and sociological fundamentals, their history.

However, since these two worlds are not constructed in a binary fashion, they carry a space between them – which Barber does not include in his picture – where neither 'McWorld' nor 'Jihad' exists. The space or vacuum between these two worlds is increasing. The assumption of such a widening gap eliminates not only Barber's concepts of 'McWorld' and 'Jihad', but even traditional ideas of 'society', 'state' and 'nation'.

11

Moreover, the parallel existence of various forms of 'universalism' and 'particularism' on the global scene calls for a new theoretical perspective to deal with the new social constructs and communities which traditional theories cannot encompass. Barber argues that his two worlds are less and less influenced by civil society because its basic concepts are based on nation/state structures. On the one hand, traditional institutions and participatory instruments are passed over and thus cease to function in a globalized political system. On the other, they are becoming worthless because their underlying concept is based on an international political system. In the global political system, new players, leaders emerge, outside of the totalitarian or democratic state leaderships which have gained global or interregional influence.

In terms of communication, globalization consists first of all in a dense new media infrastructure of satellite and cable systems of facsimile, Internet, e-mail and broadcast channels. System theorists assert that the growing density and complexity of communication are the sign of a growing 'world community'. Global communication is more than the expansion of modernization. It can be argued, as Luhmann does, that the universalism of worldwide communication dynamically develops autonomously operating systems. (Luhmann, 1982) These instant, permanent global communication networks have, however, increasingly exogenous effects on the shape of national and social realities. Western societies especially have an overload of information circulating within them and world society is constantly reconfiguring itself via information. (Luhmann, 1997:150)

Information flow in this global arena is not limited to the so-called information societies: it permits the simultaneous monitoring of economic and political developments worldwide. It also affects the way specific areas of knowledge are constructed, it gives shape to a global 'reality.' It also influences ideas of 'humanity', as Williams (1982) remarks.

> We are changing. Not just in our institutions, the automobiles we buy, nor the fashions we wear, but in how we behave as human beings. ... The contemporary explosion in communication technologies – computers, satellites, tape disc, microprocessors, and new telephone and radio services – are perceptively changing the nature of our human environment. (Williams, 1982:11)

These processes call for a profound concern about the quality of the information supplied, the knowledge underpinning it, and whether access to it is adequate for public participation. Information has become a commodity and information gathering, processing, storage and transmission over efficient telecommunication networks '...is the foundation upon which technologically advanced nations will close the twentieth century as "information societies": ie: 'societies that have become dependent upon complex electronic information and communication networks, and which allocate a major proportion of their resources to information and communication activities'. (Melody, 1990:26-27) Access to these international markets of knowledge and information increasingly becomes a tool for economic and social development. Melody suggests, for example, that indicators should be developed for measuring

> ...relations between citizen needs, availability and uses of public information; the accessibility and use of public information by major segments of the population; and the rate of diffusion of essential public information throughout the population. Indeed we know from existing research that only a small proportion of minority cultures and the poor of all cultures know their rights as citizens in democratic countries. (Melody, 1990:34)

Marvin argues that as information becomes a commodity its cultural value decreases. He claims that information should be 'regarded as an empirically and theoretically correct representation of imaginative life and activity instead of a highly culturally specific and even surprising abstraction from a world in which many views of meaning are possible' (Marvin, 1987:59). Marvin maintains that this is so because information is regarded as being digital rather than analog, which would 'focus on information as a constantly shifting and repatterned feature of every environment, past or present, a transaction between knowers and what is to be known'. (Marvin, 1987:59) So he believes that the information society does not produce more knowledge. Rather, it has altered knowledge as such so that it becomes increasingly a-historical, believing that history does not matter and that the new information-age technology is unique. (Marvin, 1986:59)

Other critics of the so-called information society consider this to be primarily an economic and technological concept which does not refer at all to collectively shared content and accumulated 'knowledge'. Information is therefore an economic concept which holds that the value of a given '...piece of information is dependent on whether particular others have it or not ... the value of information tends to diminish rapidly with diffusion, to zero it is a personal secret'. (Ekecrantz, 1987:88) Precisely for this reason the information society is not necessarily an informed society, because, as Ekecrantz claims, knowledge and/or information does not multiply freely and in spite of the maximum possible production of information for the market, society's information needs have not been satisified, and 'society has not changed much'. (Ekecrantz, 1987:80)

While several studies have investigated the effects of international communication flow on so-called 'developing' countries in order to define the influence of international media content on domestic cultures, this has not been broadly discussed within the 'information society' debate. Various approaches apply more to the internal effects of 'information' than to the international communication flow into these societies, their 'exogenous' influence on social knowledge agendas and their effects on societal construction. An important study in this field, however, was conducted by Helmut F Spinner, who developed the idea of a 'knowledge order' in information societies. Based on his definition of knowledge which simply stands for 'information',[2] Spinner distinguishes among several levels of order, which he discusses in terms of a global information flow. Referring to news, however, he says there should be an informational de-colonisation, an elimination of the separation between opinion and fact in journalism and in its place a separation of idea and interest.

The most prominent representative of the idea of a media-related 'global village' is without a doubt Marshall McLuhan. As the world's most popular 'globalist', McLuhan argued that the technical 'evolution' of media structures has extended the human nervous system. Marshall McLuhan's concept of the global village, although visionary in the late sixties, when international communication had just become an issue for communication theory and the American television audience had just experienced its first televised war (in Vietnam), is still incorrectly used to describe the current phenomenon of global communication whenever global media events occur. McLuhan's metaphor might be appropriate (and simple) to express a notion of global 'togetherness', of a global community *Gemeinschaft* in Tönnies's (1963) terminology, an 'imagined community' in Anderson's sense (Anderson, 1983), but it does not include any new developments. The global village has gained complexity. Its new network of side and main streets has traced its way around the globe. These channels transmit the 'reality' of media events, and produce global comprehension, of universal relevance but also of a particular 'scrambled' kind. Especially since new technologies have enabled us to increase simultaneous global dissemination as well as a globally transmitted narrowcasted special audience content, global communication has become more complex. McLuhan's idea of a global village, of a (shrunken) global reality, of information accessible in a similar fashion to an audience around the globe, was indeed visionary in the late sixties; however, although the concept continues to be employed, it is much less appropriate for today's global media structure. It can be increasingly questioned whether global media communication effects a global homogenisation. Quite the opposite. It can be argued that because of the dense global communication infrastructure, particular communication elements are increasing, while universal issues are decreasing in the global communication field. Criticism of the global village metaphor is therefore at least threefold.

(1) McLuhan's global village has created new global villages, new main and side streets of global communication. According to his hypothesis that every 'medium creates a new medium', satellite communication distributes the same images around the world. Indeed, some events such as the moon landing, Kennedy's assassination, the Gulf War, Nobel Prize ceremonies and other world events of a 'festive' kind (Dayan and Katz, 1992) perpetuate the myth of the global village. They have the effect of temporarily unifying a globally dispersed audience in a universal ideal sense. But the increasing diversity of globally distributed satellite communication content also increases the

specificity of content, effects a separation of the global 'mass' audience and shapes new globally disseminated 'knowledge' collectivities.

(2) Besides the development of an increasingly diversified, globally distributed media content, satellite communication itself has become technically diversified. New globally spread target audiences are reached via 'point-to-point' (directly from satellite to receiver, just as news agencies communicate with broadcasters), and 'point-to-multipoint' communication (broadcast signals which target a broader audience, equipped with satellite receivers). Although every medium involves a new medium, this new medium refines the idea of a global village in a new, more specified way.

(3) McLuhan's view refers only to the production logic of commercial media industries, where new products have to be constantly developed to meet changing market expectations. He, however, does not mention the fact that media content is becoming increasingly 'hot' and more and more defined in order to distinguish it from prior products. The tendency towards programme fragmentation, to sell programmes on increasingly specific issues, is part of this process.

McLuhan's idea of the satellite era is one which 'more and more people will enter the market of information exchange, lose their private identities in the process, but emerge with the ability to interact with any person on the face of the globe. Mass, spontaneous electronic referendums will sweep across continents. The concept of nationalism will fade and regional governments will fall as the political implications of spaceship earth create a world government'. (McLuhan and Powers, 1989:118) This vision can be interpreted in terms of a globally disseminated popular culture.[3]

> One can speak of a broadcast news industry much the same way as one refers to the music industry. The past two decades have seen rapid international integration in the structure of the so-called 'cultural industries ... and this is just one instance where the news and recorded music industries match.

McLuhan and Powers argue that global industrial expansion occurs in both horizontal and vertical integration processes. For Wallis and Baran, the only difference is the time span within which 'hits' or 'major stories' can be created. (Wallis and Baran, 1990:250) Although McLuhan remarks that the new technology makes ideologies impossible, he does not refer at all to media-transmitted content as such. As Mattelart remarks

> In this vision of the global village, everything came about by virtue of the technological imperative alone. From there it was only one step to rubbing out the complexity of the culture and societies where those messages landed and took effect. (Mattelart, 1992:148)

The idea of a global village involves for some a kind of 'impoverishment' which is particularly exemplified by mainstream (pop) cultural products. 'Like the "Disney version" of nature and society that has beguiled and misled movie audiences in Europe and Asia, as well as in America, for nearly half a century, the conventional television version of human nature and social conduct that is deemed most eligible for export is often that which has survived in the domestic market-place through the triumph of mediocrity and the principle of the lowest common denominator'. (Matson, 1976:260) This enlargement of a similar homogeneous consumer culture is the one McLuhan also refers to. This means that the standardisation of ideas creates a global collectivity and is therefore the basis for a global perception of information (McLuhan, 1964) which then shapes the reality of the global village.

Another interpretation of the enlargement of political geography by the media was submitted, interestingly enough, at the turn of the century by the sociologist Cooley. Cooley analysed the enlargement of the nineteenth century political sphere brought about by its massive technological advances in terms of the ideas of 'morale' and 'humankind'. Through employing and experiencing 'new' technologies in order to communicate globally, people had, by the end of the century, evolved new communication skills that affected Western civilization (eg the telegraph, worldwide news reporting). Cooley understands communication as the mechanism 'through which human relations exist and develop – all the symbols of the mind, together with the means of conveying them through space and preserving them in time. It includes the expression of the face, attitude and gesture, the tones of the voice, words, writing, printing, railways, telegraphs, telephones, and whatever else may be the latest achievement in the conquest of space and time'. (Cooley, 1900:86-87) Besides the advance of modern democracy, Cooley also associates with these different enlargements of the human mind an increase in the degree of international consciousness. He understands this in terms of literature, science and, finally, politics, 'which holds out a trustworthy promise of the indefinite enlargement of justice and amity'. (Cooley, 1900:87) It can be assumed that such a 'freer course of thought' (Cooley, 1900:87) widens the dimensions of the world horizontally, but it also expands it vertically – across time. This 'overcomes' space' by bringing the past into the present, and making every notable achievement of the race a possible factor in its current life – as when, by skillful reproduction the work of a medieval painter is brought home to people dwelling 500 years later on the other side of the globe'. (Cooley, 1900:87) In Cooley's perspective, horizontal and vertical enlargements involve 'not only thought but feeling, favoring the growth of a sense of common humanity, of moral unity, between nations, races and classes.' Cooley also takes into account the effects of communication 'without any mutual understanding' of 'indifference' (Cooley, 1900:88) and refers to the importance of making issues 'comprehensible' because the

> ...resources of modern communication are used in stimulating and gratifying our interest in every phase of human life. Russians, Japanese, Filipinos, fishermen, miners, millionaires, criminals,

tramps and opium-eaters are brought home to us. The press well understands that nothing human is alien to us if it is only made comprehensible. (Cooley, 1900:89)

In the eighteenth century, along with an increase in the range of issues available to the public, consciousness of other, 'alien', cultures increased.

> In the US at [the] close of the eighteenth century, public consciousness of any active kind was confined to small localities ... The newspapers ... were entirely lacking in what we should call news ... people are far more alive today to what is going on in China, if it happens to interest them, than they were then to events a hundred miles away. (Cooley, 1900:83)

Cooley also took notice of the newspaper's power which had already produced a 'fear of publicity'. (Cooley, 1900:85) It can be argued that the press had contributed a great deal to the idea of 'humankind' in this period of relativism, in which 'every culture had to be understood in its own term' (Friedman, 1994:69) by providing comprehensible, human issues that appealed to the public.

The current idea of a global village is characterized by a global concern for 'humankind' in terms of 'human rights', supported by audiovisual participation in the remotest areas of the world, from famine catastrophes in rural Africa sub Saharan regions to human-rights violations in Chinese prisons. This is associated with an increase in jet travel, which diminishes our perception of distance, because it can be traversed so easily. In this way we derive from symbolically experienced events a sensation of the utmost 'reality'.

'Globality' in modern communication theory

Although the concept of global universalism is already a part philosophical understanding, and other theories, such as that of the unified global village and the transformation of modern Western societies have contributed historically to a diverse conception of the subject, today's view is very different.[4] 'Globalization' is related to modernization as well as to postmodernization, and has to become part of various disciplines. As such it may become a new paradigmatic future 'intellectual play zone'. (Robertson, 1990:16) This more current concept points to emerging new structures of global expansion and diversification in culture, policy, economy, morality, and so on. Moreover, the type of globalization already discussed in sociological discourse consists in viewing these diverse processes from the global standpoint, requiring an approach that is the reverse of earlier global perspectives. In the new approach, traditions of sociological vocabulary as well as approved patterns of social reality and societal construction are eliminated, verified or refined.

Starting from this standpoint Robertson argues that previous political developments, especially since the early fifteenth century, can already be regarded as 'minimal' phases of the globalization process:

(1) The 'germinal phase', which lasted in Europe from the early fifteenth until the mid-eighteenth century. It is characterized by 'incipient growth of national communities' and the 'downplaying of the medieval 'transnational' system.' Concepts of humanity were specified and the synchronous time of the Gregorian calender was invented.

(2) The 'incipient phase', which lasted from the mid-eighteenth century until around 1870. Within this phase a shift towards the idea of the homogeneous, unitary state in conjunction with the 'crystallisation of conceptions of formalised international relations, of standardised citizenly individuals and a more concrete conception of humankind' was accentuated. It was also the time of the increase of agencies which were concerned with 'international and transnational regulations and communication'.

(3) 'The take off phase',which Robertson defines as the period from around 1870 until the mid-1920s, characterized by increasingly global conceptions as to the 'correct outline' of an 'acceptable national society'. This also includes some non-European societies in 'international society', an immense increase in the number and speed of global forms of communication, and the development of global competitions, such as the Olympics and the Nobel Prize. The world time of the Gregorian calendar is almost universally adopted and ideas of national and personal identities emerge.

(4) The 'struggle-for-hegemony phase', lasting from the early 1920s until the global international conflicts of the mid-1960s, is marked by worldwide ideological conflict and the establishment of the United Nations.

(5) The 'uncertainty phase', which began in the 1960s and still continues into the present, has seen the identification of the Third World and a 'heightening of global consciousness in the late 1960s which led to the realiation, that (Western) societies increasingly face problems of multiculturality and polyethnicity'. (see Robertson, 1990:26f)

Robertson argues that certain developments, especially in the constitution of nation/states, have added a global dimension to human identity. Although the above is only a brief description of selected worldwide developments, it points to key stages of political expansion and to the moral and individual consqeuences of living in an expanded world.

Robertson maintains that the prevalence of the nation/state in the twentieth century is a component in globalization (Robertson, 1990:26) and that the idea of the nation/state as a form of institutionalised social living (see also Lechner, 1989) was central to the accelerated globalization which began to occur just over 100 years ago. Robertson further adds (1987, 1989, 1990), that as well as the nation/state and the system of international relations, other major components of globablisation have been contextually-received conceptions of relationships between individuals and of humankind. 'It is in terms of the shifting relationships between and the upgrading of these reference points that globalization has occurred in recent centuries'. (Robertson, 1990:26) Robertson's critics object that what he defines as 'globalism' is already covered by the concepts of 'world systems' and 'world politics'. This is false: they are too closely linked to modern Eurocentric sociology to encompass globalism. (Robertson 1990:16ff) Robertson himself criticises current sociology as well as 'business, media and other circles' for failing to define the problem of globalization adequately. (Robertson, 1990:19)

Robertson's study of the increasing internationalization of the world at different periods and within diverse social structures does not, in his description of the 'minimal' phase include any communication technology. But the minimum phases of global communication did in fact involve developments in media technology, especially news distribution and journalism. Major evolutions took place in the nineteeth and twentieth centuries, primarily in Europe and the United States.

The distribution of knowledge and information by the media, the amplification of spheres of life from the private to the world perspective can be described historically as follows.

Distribution in specific circles

'News', defined as 'new information about a subject of some public interest that is shared with some portion of the public' and what is on a society's mind (Stephens, 1988:9), was orally shared, distributed and discussed in local contexts in the 'cosmopolitan' publics of Athens and Rome. With the economic internationalization and growth of major European cities (Venice, Amsterdam, London), news increasingly became internationalized as it was exchanged between these centres of commerce as well as across the Atlantic to the British colonies. In mediaeval times and during the Renaissance, royal pronouncements and commercial correspondence was distributed via couriers and messengers (who also spread news and gossip by word of mouth) in mercantile, courtly and monastic circles. In the fifteenth century, the first postal routes were established by the Tasso family (who later changed their name to Thurn und Taxis). In 1500 Franz von Taxis, appointed as *capitaine et maître de nos postes*, was authorized to transport official letters within the inter-'national' region of the Netherlands, Germany, France and Spain. The economic newsletter was invented some years later by one of the Fugger family. and helped to form an international financial community.

> Through the news they shared, the wheat traders of Venice, the silver traders of Antwerp, the merchants of Nuremberg, the financiers of Augsburg, and their trading partners around the world, were being drawn together into a society based on this new sensibility; on common interests – the fate of some ships sailing from India to Lisbon; on common values – a belief in the rights of capital. (Stephens, 1988:77)

Creation of public communication

During this phase, various technical advances led to an increase in media development, to a new media-related infrastructure as well as to specific news 'journalism'. Societal, technical and journalistic developments were instrumental in the creation of a public sphere in the 17th century. The rise of a citizen class characterizes the 17th, 18th and early 19th centuries in Europe. The first periodically published newspapers and the penny press were created. Newspapers were published regularly (monthly, weekly and later, around 1850 three times a week or daily); the world's oldest were published weekly for the first time in Germany in 1609: namely, *Aviso* in Wolfenbüttel and *Relation* in Strasbourg. (Wilke, 1984:78) *The Penny Press*, published as a printed 'news flash', contained information about current events and was sold in the streets. (Wilke, 1984) In 1690 the first American newspaper, *Publick Occurences* was published in Boston. In the United States, English newspapers, too, were widely circulated after they arrived in American harbours, 'and articles reprinted from their pages dominated early colonial newspapers'. (Stephens, 1988:185)

Newspapers of the 18th century already fell into current categories: they were published regularly, included a variety of stories, and displayed a consistent and recognizable title or format. (Stephens, 1988:149) Printers in Amsterdam re-published exported newspapers in English and French as early as 1620 (Stephens, 1988:150) 'with a Dutch merchant and newswriter stationed in Cologne'. (Stephens, 1988:155) By 1825 the United States had more newspapers circulating to more people than any other nation on earth. (Stephens, 1988:201)

By the end of the 19th century, freedom of the press had become an acknowledged civil right in France and the United States; it had become a right in England as early as 1642.

The invention of the steam engine in 1840 enabled printers to produce 4,000 copies at a time, and consequently circulation increased annually. With the broadened audience, newspapers were quickly commercialized and contained advertisements; the increase in cheap 'penny papers' for the masses shaped news and its headlines as a new commodity, in addition to the serious function of political reporting. The effects of this differentiation of the newspaper medium were a new style of journalism and a greater commercialization. It also made the editors more independent of the subscribers (though not of advertising firms).

This increasing commercialization, and wider circulation called for a new infrastructure in order to provide newspaper editors with the commodity 'news.' The news 'wholesale' agencies, such as Havas (the predecessor of today's Agence France Presse, Paris), as well as Wolff'sche Telegraphenbureau (the predecessor of today's dpa, Deutsche Presseagentur), and as Reuter's (London), which still operates under this name, were established.

In the United States the joint organization of East Coast newspaper publishers, the Associated Press, was founded, later renamed AP of America. In the second half of the 19th century, these agencies became most influential in the founding of other news agencies – for example in northern Europe. Although the agencies were originally founded in order to sell news to domestic newspaper publishers, they quite quickly entered specific continental market niches: the Wolff'sche Telegraphenbureau spread through northern Europe in countries such as Denmark, Finland, Sweden and Russia; Havas expanded into Portugal, Spain, Italy, Romania and Serbia; Reuter's moved into Belgium, the Netherlands, Bulgaria, the British Empire, Egypt, Australia, New Zealand, Japan, China and Malaysia. (Höhne, 1977:42f)

These developments led by the end of the 19th century to journalism acceding to the rank of a profession:

> ...journalism was given a place in the universities, and professional organizations of publishers and editors were formed. Journalists had formulated a 'service idea' – 'the people's right to know'' and their right to have access to facts. (Stephens, 1988:262)

Journalism established methods of observation and investigation as well as 'professional norms', such as 'news reports should be free from opinion or bias of any kind''. (Stephens, 1988:262) Newspaper publishers used reporters to send information from distant locations within their own countries and abroad: for example from the United States to France and Prussia. Stephens compares this information-gathering with that of scientists: the 'journalistic method' was born. News journalism was already considered an 'enterprise', especially in the nineteenth century when American local newspapers such as the *New York Herald* employed correspondents to cover events in Europe.

> Some American editors, with their omnipresent hunger for news from Europe, began by walking down to the docks to obtain news off the most recently arrived ships. Among the first to demonstrate such enterprise was Benjamin Russell of the *Massachusetts Centinel and Republican Journal*, who was gathering news on the docks of Boston by 1790. The next frontier was the harbour itself. In the early years of the nineteenth centruy, Henry Ingraham Blake, of the *Mercury and New England Palladium in Boston*, boarded a boat and began meeting the ships. (Stephens, 1988:230)

In May, 1844, Morse's telegraph sent the first news message from a railroad station near Baltimore to Washington.[5] The event reported was the political convention at which presidential and vice-presidential nominees were selected.

> Shortly after the convention had settled on its presidential and vice-presidential nominees, a train left Baltimore. It stopped briefly at Annapolis Junction, then arrived in Washington, buzzing with the news. However, by the time that train pulled in, the inventor Samuel Morse had already announced the composition of the ticket to the

sceptical crowd at the station. Morse had stationed a telegraph operator at Annapolis Junction to transmit the news to Washington on the completed section of the first extended telegraph line. It had taken the train an hour to cover the distance from Annapolis Junction to Washington. The world's first telegraphed news message – reporting as Morse announced, that 'the ticket is Clay and Frelinghuysen' had arrived almost instantaneously. (Stephens, 1988: 227)

With the invention of the telephone in 1876 by Elisha Gray and Alexander Graham Bell, the speed of news transmission increased, and timeliness became a new factor even in the international, cross-channel transmission of international news, possibly due to the newly established cable line from France to England. In order to regulate international traffic on telegraph lines (which up to this point was a matter of bilateral agreements such as that between Austria and Prussia), as well as the subsequent telephone traffic, the International Telegraph Union was formed (the precedessor of today's International Telecommunication Union [ITU]). In 1865, 20 European states met in Paris and signed the International Telegraph Convention, and soon thereafter 27 nations adopted its regulations at the International Radiotelegraph Conference. In 1932 the International Telecommunication Convention furnished the charter for the merging of the International Telegraph Union and the Radiotelegraph Union. (Bittner, 1982)

The history of global communication must take in the means whereby news events are distributed, internationally and globally. Stephens points out that while the American Civil War was a 'newspaper war', the Second World War was a 'radio war'.[6] (Stephens, 1988:278)

In Stephens' view this is a 'logical outgrowth' of the increased costs inherent in competing in the intensified race to obtain news. Even with the first appearence of news agencies in the nineteenth century, diversification emerged. The existing agencies expanded tremendously. US newspaper publishers on the East Coast founded the Associated Press agency and increased their co-operation (a contemporary example of such co-operation would be Eurovision, the news exchange operated by European public broadcasters). Associated Press members were first limited to New York papers, but later included other East Coast cities such as Boston in order to split the cost of news boats in the harbour in the 1820s (Stephens, 1988:259) and to expand their news coverage. The agency leased a steamer in order to meet ships from Europe at Halifax, Nova Scotia, and telegraphed the messages exclusively to its members.

The founders of Reuter's in London and the Wolff'sche Telegraphenbureau in Berlin had both worked for the French agency Havas. Reuter had started his news agency in London by 1848. The internationalization, greater commercialization and professionalism of news increased its value as a commodity and diminished its identity as powerful and influential form of political information.

Following the practice of the editors in Boston, those in New York began to use 'news boats.'

> Most of the major New York newspapers joined together to send a boat into the harbour in search of European newspapers and European news. When that cooperative venture split apart in 1828, it led to some intensely competitive races through New York harbour. Rowboats were soon replaced by schooners, and the schooners began venturing farther and farther out in the sea lanes to intercept ships. (Stephens, 1988:231)

Other races for news involved horses, trains and pigeons: 'journalists were not above hijacking each other's train or shooting down a rival's pigeons'. (Stephens, 1988:231)

While the media enterprises of these early years battled for up-to-date international news, they were able to pick up local news first hand. Editors hired reporters and sent them out to local events or to coffeehouses in order to pick up gossip and rumors. 'Persons are employed ... at so much a week, to haunt coffee-houses, and thrust themselves into Companies where they are not known; or plant themselves at a convenient Distance, to overhear what is said, in order to pick up Matter for the Papers'. (Stephens, 1988:234)

Colonial internationalism

This phase is marked by continual improvements in existing news technology, such as telegraphy. In 1856 David Edward Hughes introduced a telegraph which modified the arriving signals into letters, and the German Siemens Company developed a rapid telegraph in 1912 which carried up to 1,000 letters per minute. (Höhne, 1977:36)

World wire and cable systems were established in the late 19th and early 20th centuries by Britain and Germany. Their main purpose was to improve military communication, and communication with governments of colonised countries, as well as navigation. In 1857 the first attempt was made to connect Ireland and Newfoundland by underwater cable, but it never operated because of technical shortcomings. The second cable succeeded, and Queen Victoria and the American President, Andrew Johnson, exchanged greetings in 40 letters, which took one minute to be transmitted. After the third cable broke, the Atlantic Telegraph Company became bankrupt. (Höhne, 1977:35) The new Anglo-American Telegraph Company laid a cable between England and the United States in 13 days over a distance of 3,745 kilometres. It was inaugurated on 27 July, 1866, and there has been a line between the two continents ever since. The Ostdeutsche Telegraphen-Gesellschaft, founded by the German and Romanian governments, established a cable line from Constance to Constantinople to Asia, without involving Russian territory or British cable lines. The third cable company, founded by Germany and the Netherlands, crossed the Pacific Ocean, and Germany and France tried to compete with Great Britain on the South American and West African cable line. By 1912, Great Britain already controlled 53 per cent of the World Cable System.

The established news agencies expanded their international scope. Between 1904 and 1910, offset printing was developed, and in 1923 the news magazine *Time* was founded in the USA.

Transnational media organizations

The first news event simultaneously transmitted internationally by European television was the coronation of Queen Elizabeth II in 1953. This event was broadcast for the first time within Europe and the United States via television by the newly established Eurovision. Eurovision still operates today as a division of the European Broadcasting Union, which was founded in 1950 as a counterpart to the OIRT (Organization Internationale de Radiodiffusion et de Télévision) of the USSR. and socialist Eastern European states, established in 1946. Parallel to the founding of Eurovision as a joint exchange agency of public service television stations in Europe, the OIRT founded Intervision with a similar purpose in 1960. Because of new international television infrastructures, more and more news events of world interest, such as the moon landing in 1969, Nixon's visit to China and the Munich Olympics terrorist attacks in 1972, were broadcast to an international audience. The ITU expanded its regulative authority in 1977 in order to distribute UHF frequencies of satellites and to regulate geo-stationary satellite positions.

The first satellites launched were the United States' *Telstar* in 1962; *Early Bird* by the Intelsat organization, which already had one transponder which it leased for television distribution; the USSR's *Molnija* in 1969 and *Intersputnik* in 1975. The succeeding Intelsat satellite generation, *Intelsat 3*, was equipped with 40 television transponders. Indonesia launched *Palapa* in 1976, the Arab countries *Arabsat* in 1985, Japan *BS-2* in 1986, and the first *Astra* satellite was launched by the Société Européene des Satellites (SES) in 1988. Thus satellite footprints gradually spread over international regions. Today *Intelsat* is still the only globally operated satellite chain, whereas other satellite systems such as *Intersputnik* cover continents or international territories.

International and global commercial media systems

During this phase, media systems expanded internationally and globally and new worldwide models of broadcasting have been established. These include:

(1) Broadcasting stations began to operate internationally simply by leasing transponders. Some of these operations were conceived in international terms and programmed for an international audience. While commercial broadcasters focussed on as broad an audience as possible, public service broadcasters have increasingly targeted a regional as well as an international audience.

(2) Agencies, from the 'big five' Western broadcasters to the small ones, have shown increasing awareness of a wider range of international news.

(3) There has been an expansion of already existing syndication agreements (EBU, Eurovision, Asiavision, Intervision) by, for instance, the increase of exchange services.

(4) The international services of national broadcasting stations, such as BBC World Service, Deutsche Welle, and Worldnet have expanded into the field of television.

(5) Commercial channels such as CNNI and MTV have begun to fragment programming on special audience issues and establish worldwide narrowcasting and broadcasting round the clock. Other models such as the 'vertical integration' of publishing companies are expanding international, as in the case of *The Financial Times*. Globally operating media entrepreneurs (Rupert Murdoch and Ted Turner) have established worldwide programme networks.

Negrine and Papathanassopoulos remark that satellite channels especially have an extensive need for low-cost programmes in order to fill various time slots outside primetime and even to fill primetime attractively. (Negrine and Papathanassopoulos, 1990). For this reason, they rely heavily on low-cost programmes. The need for entertainment programmes for the transnational television market is fed by production in the United States. In Brazil and in India production for regional market demand is heavily related to entertainment content. Since increasing fragmentation and diversification have occurred globally during this phase, 'news' has also become a worldwide media 'product' in line with further narrowcasting developments. This sector allows publishing companies in particular to sell their products to a secondary audiovisual programme market. They, together with entrepreneurs with interests in news, and the related technological industries (such as Microsoft) have been prompted to step into the assumed 'gold mine' of television programming. Television organization, programming and journalism are being influenced by the new technology and organizational models in the same way that journalism was influenced by telegraph and cable technology at the turn of the century.

International or global satellite television does not have to take account of primetime in the same way that domestic broadcasters do. Because of the world's numerous time zones, 'the sun comes up somewhere all the time', as a CNN slogan aptly states. The elimination of a set primetime decreases the need for journalistic deadlines and increases on-the-spot journalism of a new satellite-newsgathering type. These satellite channels reach out to a global population, which can be informed of major happenings in the world without delay. (Kato, 1976:254) Through video technology, 'tourist' journalism is thereby established. (Wallis and Baran, 1990:219)

Internationalization of developing nations

The internationalization of media in developing nations has increased since the early seventies. This involves satellite operations but also the establishment of news organizations targeting a global narrowcasted audience with religious-ideological programming, like Islamvision (Lent, 1991:173) or regional affiliation such as Asiavision. URTNA (the Union des Radios et Télévisions Nationales Africaines) was founded in 1962, ASBU, the Arab States Broadcasting Union in 1969, and CBU, the Caribbean Broadcasting Union in 1970. ABU (the Asia Pacific Broadcasting Union) was established by 34 countries in 1971 as were the ASCO (Arab Satellite Communication Organization) and OTI (Organización de la Televisión Iberoamericana) or Latin America.

Although the history of the founding of global or international media organizations or agencies in developed nations (not to mention developing ones) has not yet been theoretically analysed, there has been, traditionally, some study of issues dealing with communication between advanced nations and those in the process of developing. Many studies on international communication focus on the analysis of 'foreign' programmes in a national context where, for example, the structure, topics and origin of news become focuses of concern.

The communication developments described above are substantial parts of a globalization process which extends from inter-local to inter-national information distribution. Globalization refers today to phenomena ranging from the worldwide distribution of identical programme content or globally interchangeable programme formats to the worldwide distribution of 'special interest' information targeting a globally dispersed 'minority' audience. In the context of these developments, the term 'international' becomes obsolete, since national borders determine the flow of information to a far lesser degree. Instead the awareness of a collectively defined 'reality' is a function of satellite footprints.[7]

Communication concepts of traditional modernity

When communication theory deals with media phenomena which cross borders, the terms 'international', 'transborder' or 'transnational' communication have been employed, and in many cases have been replaced by the term 'global' communication, in order to describe the now worldwide, continental or regional flow of media content. Although this varied terminology describes different and distinct ideological concepts, only a few studies imply specific definitions. The underlying concepts of these terms are based on early cross-national or cross-statist media content dynamics.

In communication theory globality can be understood as communicating around and across the globe. Whereas the transmission of the music channel MTV and of news via CNN includes local programme segments and establishes local markets in competition with domestic programmes, films such as *Starship Enterprise*, or recently *Titanic* are distributed across the globe. Science Fiction films also involve a pop cultural fiction of the planetary system, stereotypes of the 'alien' and the 'familiar', and, through this, a concept of 'humankind' in its spaceship-like habitat, be it *Starship Enterprise* or 'Spaceship Earth' in a universe of infinity. Globality can further be understood in a broader sense as an analysis and description of new social, cultural and communication patterns which emerge from the fact that (mass) media programmes are distributed worldwide.

For an analysis of the theoretical framework underlying current communication theory, it is important to identify the effects which its historical antecedents have had on the international flow of programmes. We shall pay greater attention than has previously been given to the international flow of communication models and distribution patterns, and their social and cultural effects on the shape of worldwide audiences as a global community. These processes and effects are not sufficiently reflected in current theoretical terms nor in discussions of communication theory.

The idea of 'modernization' as a starting point for international development communication

International communication as a tool for modernization and political re-education was discovered after World War II when such efforts were geared towards Europe. Large-scale economic aid went hand in hand with communication programmes designed to re-educate citizens about political propaganda (Rogers, 1969:10) and also to support economic growth. These undertakings, which met with considerable success at the time, were then transferred to general efforts to support and sustain 'economic' (as the equivalent of 'cultural' and 'societal') development in countries of the Third World. This idea of the spread of modernization as a development goal inspired economic development projects. A process which was considered as one of 'reviving cultures, emerging nations, and new states' in turn increasingly effected a 'revolution of rising expectations', such that people throughout the 'backward' and 'impoverished areas of the world suddenly acquired the sense that a better life was possible for them'. (Lerner, 1963:330)

Broad international 'communication aid programs', however, began with the United Nations Conference in 1948. At this conference a resolution was passed that 'freedom of information is one of the basic freedoms' and furthermore that 'free' and 'adequate' information should be broadly considered among the participants as the 'touchstone of all the freedoms to which the United Nations is dedicated'. (Schramm, 1964) This idea was then turned into a programme of 'concrete action' by UNESCO, to 'build up press, radio broadcasting, film, and television facilities in countries in process of economic and social development'. (Schramm, 1964)

Communication was understood – and this was also the UNESCO approach of those days – as a 'tool', an 'instrument' to develop societies by changing their traditional communication environment to modern structures. In this way the 1948 UN conference can be considered as the ideological and conceptual starting point of the notion of international communication which has to a great degree survived until now.

As some developing countries such as Brazil, Mexico, and India have achieved tremendous developments in terms of communication and launched their own satellites or have co-operated, as have several Arab States, in a satellite consortium, two formerly connected economic areas – the social and that of communication are drawing apart. The motor for this has been the commercialization of broadcasting as a separate 'economy' and the establishment of secondary markets for television (and media such as film) where medium-income countries sell to other developing countries.[8] Although these satellites are still under-utilised and face many difficulties (various 'last mile' problems such as those of telephone circuits and lack of software) they are clearly an attempt for independence in terms of communication. The Intelsat organization, as the first global inter-governmental satellite system, has established several communication programmes in order to support the specific communication needs of economically developing countries.

The underlying 'metatheory' of UNESCO activities was a concept of 'modernization' modelled on the European tradition, but lacking the social, philosophical, ethical and other interlinked elements specific to the process in Europe. The pragmatic view of this externally created modernization process was simply to utilise media as a tool for societal transitions from traditional to modern societies. The historical process of European modernization implied a national principle and thus a specific nationalism, a democratisation process which has taken diverse roads even within Western countries. Greenfeld explicitly describes processes of modernization in five European countries: England, France, Russia and Germany plus the US. She distinguishes in her general remarks between 'civic' and 'ethnic' nationalism. This 'civic' process consisted in the following:

> The national principle that emerged was individualistic: sovereignty of the people was the implication of the actual sovereignty of individuals; it was because these individuals (of the people) actually exercised sovereignty that they were members of a nation. (Greenfeld, 1992:11)

This concept of the collective sovereignty of modern nations was interpreted in such a way that the relationship of economic and social or democratic development was over-emphasised; furthermore, this process was assumed, once having been initiated from the outside, to proceed further within the society in question. So this theory of international communication does not so much describe the direct influence of internationally distributed programmes (which are available through satellite technology today in audiovisual and auditive form and also in print) but conceptualises internal (technical) stages of the diffusion of the idea of modernising processes. These stages were based on the sociological framework of modernization enshrined in Max Weber's and Talcott Parsons's (1961) theories. These theories were helpful since they implied patterns such as 'endogenous' and 'exogenous' 'sources of change'. (Parsons, 1961)

'Globality' as such or the process of globalization has, in the contemporary era of modernization, been synonymous with the idea of the universality of the paradigm of modernity. For this reason it was assumed that the current concept applies universally to social development.

Although the processes initiated by UNESCO for modernising the infrastructure of domestic communication systems tended to generalise in their theoretical approach, their practical implications were surprisingly distinct. The major differentiations were made, as Eisenstadt argues, between 'internal' development, referring to social life and culture, and 'external' development, referring to technology and the economy. Traditional societies were thus '...perceived as basically very limited in their capacity to cope with problems or master their environment, while modern societies were seen as coping with a continuously wider range of internal and external problems and environments. (Eisenstadt, 1975:31-32)

During the late 1940s, 1950s and early 1960s, most development theorists argued that the problem of 'underdevelopment' or 'backwardness' could be solved by a more or less mechanical application of the economic and political system in the West to countries in the Third World'. (Servaes, 1991:54) It is the metaphor of growth which was assumed to proceed in a unilinear fashion. These early models of communication modernization result from the two-step-flow communication models which were developed in the US during studies of the political campaigns of opinion leaders and followers. The findings of Katz and Lazarsfeld's 'Erie County Study' (1969) in particular revealed that communication processes entail more personal communication than was originally assumed.[9] According to this theory, personal communication functions as a 'gatekeeper' on political issues and enforces the media-initiated agenda within a community. In development communication, however, this finding was transferred into the assumption that '...mass communication is important in spreading awareness of new possibilities and practices, but at the stage where decisions are being made about adopting these new practices, personal communication is far more likely to be influential. (Servaes, 1991:56)

Social change to modernization was also associated with the diffusion of new technology within a society. Parsons's theory was considered very helpful in understanding these complex interwoven processes. The influence of interaction at different levels of social development and the idea of technological diffusion within a society seemed to be an appropriate concept to implement technological changes in developing countries. De Fleur suggests six definitions of central terms of social system diffusion studies, such as 'new item' (which can come to the attention of the relevant group or society through borrowing or invention), 'invention' (ie, the act of forming some new combinations of culture traits), 'innovation' (ie, the change in patterns of conduct or action), 'obsolescence' (a concomitant of innovation), 'diffusion curve' (ie, the quantitative function describing the proportion of members of a group who have acquired a given new item or have changed their action patterns with respect to it over some period of time). 'Institutionalisation' finally refers to the last step in the stabilising of widespread patterns of action. (De Fleur, 1970:63f) These concepts, evolved and experienced in developed nations such as the US were transferred, with further criteria for modernity, into the development-communication approach. Four concepts of modernization can be distinguished.

The stage/convergence concept

Proponents of this concept claim that similar stages of development can be discovered in various societies. (Eisenstadt, 1975:32) This 'convergence' implies that 'ultimately all modern industrial systems will develop similar major institutional features'. According to this view, the greater its characteristics of 'structural specialisation', 'the higher the society is ranked on various disintegration of traditional elements' and 'the more able a society would be to develop a continously expanding institutional structure'. (Eisenstadt, 1975:33) This means that societies at this stage of development are able to increase the capacity 'to absorb change' and develop additional adjunct characteristics of modern societies 'such as rationality, efficiency, and a predilection to liberty'. (Eisenstadt, 1975:33)

Theory of sustained growth

This modernization stage focusses on the initial 'take off' process. Whenever this has been initiated, the development process proceeds in its own dynamic and does not need further outside motivation.

Theory of institutional development

This concept of modernization refers narrowly to the implementation of communication infrastructures. Societal modernization is strongly related to the two major forces of social dynamics: mobilisation and institution-building. The role of communication within these societal organizational structures has been analysed from various viewpoints. 'Social change' has to be initiated by mass media in order to enhance 'individual change' as well as 'social system change'. (Rogers, 1969:8) Consequently, these ideas define development communication as 'a type of social change in which new ideas are introduced into a social system in order to produce higher per capita incomes and levels of living through more modern methods and improved social organizations'. (Rogers, 1969:8) This is a view which can easily be related to Parsons' functionalist model of specific interdependence of social institutions within a society whereby an influence on some societal institutions is automatically related to a change in others.

Communication in traditional societies is not differentiated as a system from other social processes, given the lack of professional communicators, and information flows along lines of social hierarchy or according to the particular patterns of social relations in each community. Thus the process in traditional societies is not independent either from the order of social relationships or the content of communication. Concepts of development communication assumed not only technological and thus economic diffusion into developing nations, but also the initiation of a democratisation process: ideas which emerged from the mere assumption that political articulation involves political communication through the media. What has not been considered, however, is that, although developing nations or states are communities, they cannot be regarded as the same sort of community (*Gemeinschaft*) as the societies of the modern Western world, in which the paradigm of public sphere and political communication was developed. Transitional, traditional and modern societies cannot be distinguished from each other by the structure of the media system and the degree of linkage of public and political communication, simply because not only do cultural differences have to be carefully distinguished but also the specific historically developed shape of political communication works in conjunction with a specific model of a 'traditional' society.

The 'old' paradigm of modernization was replaced by a more relative one which consisted in the discovery that the

> ...mere destruction of traditional forms did not necessarily assure the development of a new, viable, modern society. Often the disruption of traditional settings – the family, the community or even the political order – led to disorganization, delinquency, and chaos rather than to a viable modern order. (Eisenstadt, 1975:35)

The old paradigm began to break down in the 1950s because of its '...inability to explain the variable patterns of traditional societies, their internal dynamics, as well as their independent development of different political and economic complexes'. (Eisenstadt, 1975:37)

Lerner's model of development communication as part of the old paradigm emerged from the ideology of the 'take-off', which would followed by self-sustaining growth in the dimensions of economy measured by growth in the Gross National Product (GNP), social indices such as urbanisation, and the development of political participation. (Schramm, 1975:45) 'The essential point was that growth in one of these spheres stimulates growth in others, and all spheres of society move forward together toward modernization'. (Schramm, 1975:47). Lerner argues for 'regularities' in the human condition and for a redefinition of 'development' in terms of culture-interactive rather

31

than of culture-specific. (Lerner, 1975:61) Within this paradigm, various paths to modernity were developed in the context of different cultures.

Transition theory

This new paradigm proposes that the western influences on modernization in a previously traditional system tend to develop a new type of social and political system. This new system, often described as 'transitional', then develops characteristics of its own by advancing its own mechanisms of 'stability' and 'self-perpetuation'. (Eisenstadt, 1975:37)

Eisenstadt describes two further criticisms of the modernization idea. The first consists in the argument that modernization '...does not always have any definite, universal, systemic, symbolic and/or structural characteristics; it is basically a specific one-time historical process that spread Western culture throughout the world and induced latecomers to emulate these Western models of industrialisation, political unification, and the like'. (Eisenstadt, 1975:39) The second judgement is the Marxist view of the expansion of capitalism, imperialism, colonialism, exploitation and thus – 'dependency'. (Eisenstadt, 1975:39) Both these concepts assumed that since 'modernization' could not become the general model for change, a wider variety of sociopolitical forms would exist, such as the 'absolute', 'estate', 'nation-state', 'patriarchal', and 'neopatriarchal' models. (Eisenstadt, 1975:42) These models of what would happen after traditional regimes had been superseded do not imply that societies remain at a given developmental stage. The transitional society, it is argued, is specifically fragmented and urban-centreed, and outside intitiatives from Western societies therefore automatically reach the already Westernized segments of the population. Pye questions whether one communication system (and approach) is sufficient to reach these different separated populations within transitional societies. (Pye, 1963:26)

Profound criticism of these ideas of Western-initiated modernization has been expressed by Western as well as Latin American social theorists. They are concerned not only about the pragmatic conceptualisation of an artificial idea of 'modernization', but also about the evolutionary and functionalist tradition which it implies. (Servaes, 1991:56) Their new paradigm is also based on the concept of modernization, but not in terms of a unilinear synchronous and homogenous process. Modernization has to be seen, so proponents of this model claim, 'as a process or series of processes with a common core that generates common or similar problems'. (Eisenstadt, 1975:41)

This conceptual advance implies that a theory of development communication must take cognizance of the following issues: it must reflect a relativity which involves a greater awareness of societal and cultural contexts, and it must incorororate a degree of variability in order to avoid stereotypes and clichés. The term 'relativity' also suggests that a 'new awareness of the extent to which all perception is culture-bound and selective and all knowledge is socially produced ... is producing deeper understanding of the idea that there are many ways of construing reality.' (Jamieson, 1991:29) The new paradigm also involves a world view which does not refer to terms like 'evolution', 'progress' and 'development' as the 'cumulative' invention of new and 'intrinsically better ways of doing things'. (Jamieson, 1991:30) Other basic elements of the new paradigm are:

(1) involvement of local people 'in the selection, design, planning, implementation of all programmes that affect them'; (Jamieson, 1991:30)

(2) concentration on 'solving the problems in existing systems that affect the people living in them instead of seeking to impose new and allegedly superior systems';

(3) creation of more and better feedback and 'the capacity to respond to it'. (Jamieson, 1991:33)

These general issues, based on fundamental criticism of the old paradigm, reveal the basic aim as still being one of stimulating development by communication skills and projects – a far from unproblematic matter.

UNESCO's so-called MacBride Report tackles the central issues of this new paradigm through the proposal of further projects in the development of communication, each country to decide what kind of development it wants before determining its communication policies. Servaes considers this objection as quite misleading because the gap between the developed countries and developing countries in terms of communication policy and structure is wide: "by looking at the real situation of national communication policies in the so-called Third World, I have learned that in nearly all nations, operational policies govern communication on an apparently ad hoc basis without any conceptual, organizational, or structural framework". (Servaes, 1991:52)

Communication and the transition from traditional to modern societies: Communication and national development

The term 'international communication' is associated to a great degree with development communication within the modernising processes described above.[10] It is broadly assumed that industrial development as well as urbanisation is the basic principle of all these modernization concepts.[11]

An important insight into the degree to which communication can be employed to support development was revealed by Lerner, who first considered media use as relevant for urbanisation. He saw a close relationship between the degree of urbanisation and the literacy rate. Only after 'a country reaches 10 per cent of urbanisation does its literacy rate begin to rise significantly'. (Lerner, 1958:59) In this survey, conducted in seven countries in 1950[12] and published in *The Passing of Traditional Society* (1958), Lerner defined the fundamental categories of 'modernising' nations by means of media.[13] On the basis of approximately 2,000 interviews, he developed the idea of the 'transitional communication process'. (Pye, 1963:26) Lerner regards the stages of communication within transitional societies as urbanisation, literacy, mass media exposure, income and political participation.[14]

These categories contain the building blocks of Lerner's theory. The individual virtue of 'empathy' enables people to learn and be motivated to copy Western lifestyles which they have experienced via the media. Empathy is, in Lerner's view, the fundamental virtue of Western modernization. Empathy enables people to take on roles, to create opinions, and to learn morality. This hypothesis was drawn from the fact that great social mobility (which is assumed to be an indicator of a transitional process) corresponded with media exposure. 'The importance of media exposure, in our theory, is that it enlarges a person's view of the world ... by increasing his capacity to imagine himself in new and strange situations'. (Lerner, 1958:96) Lerner argues that the degree of modernization of each of the seven countries can be characterized by the relation of transitional to traditional values. One of the questions which was assumed to indicate mobility was 'If you were made editor of a newspaper, what kind of a paper would you run?'. Lerner interpreted the results as follows:

> Underlying the variety of responses, there was a certain cluster of attitudes that came closest to the approved modern attitude. This stressed 'independence, impartiality, objectivity' as primary attributes of newspapers.

Lerner and his team 'tabulated the proportion of respondents, by type and country, who stressed these three attributes'. Lerner's interpretation of what is specific to different nationalities reveals

> ...a consistently higher proportion of Turks across the three types. In both of the advanced countries, Turkey and Lebanon, it is among the newly-participant Transitionals and many Traditionals that the importance of an 'independent, impartial, objective' press has been widely diffused... In Egypt, Syria, Jordan the lower regard for modern press standards among the Moderns seems related to a more profound malaise. In these countries, a substantial segment of Moderns is the radical young intelligentsia dedicated to deep and rapid social change.[15] (Lerner, 1958:97)

Both Lerner and Schramm employ Parsons's social-system approach to define various communication systems. These imply the 'interactive behavioural system', a 'style of life' of which the components are 'interactive' insofar as the efficient functioning of any one of them requires the efficient functioning of all the others. The components are 'behavioural' because they 'operate' only through the activity of individual human beings. 'They form a system in the sense that significant variation in the activity of one component will be associated with significant variation in the activity of all other components'. (Lerner, 1963:329) Schramm shares Parsons's view of an overall societal development in terms of a relationship of parts 'in which anything happening to one component of a system affects, no matter how slightly, the balance and relationship of the whole system'. Individuals as well as organised groups are regarded as systems. (Schramm, 1963:30) In this sense Schramm refers to a nation system within the 'partly developed' world system. This view explains the relationship between the nation, the media and individuals as a system and because of this inter-system relationship the 'behaviour of a newspaper is part of the nation's communication behaviour'. (Schramm, 1963:31). According to this approach, the functions of the media in development processes are (1) the watchman and informing function, (2) the decision-making function and (3) the teaching function. (Schramm, 1964:126) The increase of mass media reception enables people to share ideas

> ...as to who is important, who is dangerous, what is interesting ... The newspaper, radio, magazine, serving as a watchman on the hill, must decide what to report back. This act of choice ... determines in large degree what people know and talk about. (Schramm, 1964:129)

Media as part of a national development process are effective when they disseminate a 'homogeneity of culture and geography within a society'. (Schramm, 1963:34)

Schramm employs Lerner's term of 'national empathy' to define the tasks of communication as:

(1) contributing to 'the feeling of nation-ness', implying the 'widening' of the horizon from being a 'citizen of the village' to now being a 'citizen of the nation';[16]

(2) functioning as the 'voice of national planning' (for example, the national news service which gathers news systematically and shares it with the rest of the country);

(3) being used to 'help teach the necessary skills', meaning skills for agricultural production;

(4) helping to 'extend the effective market' (foreign trade);

(5) preparing 'people to play their new parts';

(6) helping people play their 'role as a nation among nations'.

Communication as a substantial part of society is connected with economic growth and political discourse: '...it is something society does. It is a way society lives'. (Schramm, 1963:35) People in rural areas are concerned with local policy matters, making them issues of face-to-face communication. The village is usually not much interested in 'policy at higher levels, and the higher levels are not much interested in sharing policy with the village'. However, when a country develops,

> ...it has an urgent need to widen the theatre of political discussion and policy making. The ordinary people need to overhear the national policy debates so that they can form opinions and, at the proper time, act on their opinions. The policy makers need to understand, more clearly than before, the needs and wishes of the villages, so that they can take account of them in making their larger policies. (Schramm, 1963:136)

Mass media are tools which widen the angle of political action and participation: for example numeracy or learning to read. Such an acquired degree of higher literacy provides a reason for having more and better newspapers.

> The more that people feel able to take part in political activities, the more they feel the need of education and information.The more information they get, the more they are interested in political developments. The more education they have, the more they seek information. (Schramm, 1963:36)

It was a decade later that these approaches were subject to criticism which either questioned whether these exports of media and infrastructure actually promoted economic development because they were simply adopted, or which complained that the goal of 'modernization' does not specify differences between developed and developing countries. Some of the arguments were influenced by the debate on media imperialism. These claimed that the influence of American advertising money generates

> ...public identification with consumption values, whereas economic development requires an emphasis on production values. Production values are similar to those incorporated by the concept of 'protestant ethic' and include a high propensity to invest accumulated gains and a corresponding antagonism to immediate gratification for its own sake. (Boyd-Barrett, 1977:134)

Concepts of initiating or supporting the national growth of developing countries have been substantial elements of United Nations Communication Programmes. The 'International Programme for the Development of Communication' (IPDC) was established in 1980 in order to increase 'co-operation and assistance for the development of communication infrastructures, and to reduce the gaps existing between various countries in the communication field'.[17] (Hancock, 1992) Its goals are:

(1) 'To assist developing countries (by the provision of consultative services where necessary) to prepare and implement information and communication development plans, and to create communication infrastructures;'

(2) 'To improve consultation and co-ordination among all parties interested in the development of communication (including United Nations agencies), and to promote regional co-operation among communication

institutions, to analyse national and international needs and resources and to prepare studies on international co-operation in the field of information and communication development;'

(3) 'To promote awareness of the role of communication in development and to improve international exchange of information' and finally to coordinate the funding of such projects. (Hancock, 1992:67/68)

IPDC orientations include the strengthening of infrastructure and access to the latest communication technology (satellites and data banks) as well as the implementation of national policies, 'plans for the development of communication' and a 'free flow of information at international as well as national levels, and a wider and better balanced dissemination of news and cultural products, without any obstacle to the freedom of expression'. (Hancock, 1992:75) These contribute to the freedom of the press and to the

> ...principles of independence, pluralism and diversity of the media. An increase in domestic and regional exchanges of information: in particular in the capacity of developing nations to participate effectively in the international exchange of information. Regional and subregional co-operation, particularly at the early stages of project development. (Hancock, 1992:75)

Besides the IPDC, the UN division called COMNET (Network of Documentation Centres on Communication Research and Policy) was established in 1969/1970, for the support of research activities in the field of communication by publishing a mass communication thesaurus. Regional communication research centres (such as Carimac in the Caribbean region) make up the membership of this organization.

The Non-Aligned News Agency Pool (NANAP) was inaugurated in 1975 shortly before the MacBride Commission began its work in 1977. Fundamental changes have taken place in UNESCO policy regarding the flow of communication. UNESCO organised intergovernmental conferences on communication policies and planning, established the MacBride Commission, and publicly supported the *Declaration on the Media* and the call for a *New World Information and Communication Order*. These activities caused a shift to a new direction in international communication policy.

Between 1969 and 1981, UNESCO was a principal actor in a rising international communication debate, many of whose features originated from the proposals of the international conferences that had been initiated. In the 1970s the United Nations became the major forum for the political discussion of international communication policy and developmental communication aid projects. The so-called New World Information and Communication Order (NWICO) was first discussed in the Non-Aligned Movement. (Hancock, 1992:139)

> ...The influence of the 1971 international panel continued to be strong for several years, until the creation of the MacBride

Commission reduced its influence. ... But the normative approach adopted by the panel foreshadowed the Commission's interest in dependency theory, images of cultural imperialism and selected socio-cultural or politico-economic perspective. (Hancock, 1992:140)

The prinicple of NWICO

...remains to this day the most concrete expression of the new order concept, and it reflects a mix of approaches: endorsing pluralism, press freedom, and respect for human rights alongside the elimination of the negative effects of monopolies, the responsibility of media professionals, respect for cultural identity and so on'. (Hancock, 1992:140)

UNESCO's policy was confronted with a twin-concept dilemma of either 'free flow' or 'balance': liberalism, involving the principle of pluralism and the unrestricted flow of information, or neo-Marxism, with roots in dependency theory and culturalist approaches. (Hancock, 1992:141) UNESCO's new strategy was finally defined in 1989.

The core of the 'new strategy', apart from its avoidance of all reference to NWICO, was to be the acceptance of a new equation for free flow and wider and better balanced dissemination ... On the one hand, free flow was seen as an absolute concept; something that ... could not be deliminated. On the other hand, the idea of improved dissemination was positively associated with the reinforcement of communication infrastructures in the developing world, which should, when fully mature, ensure the dialogue on equal terms with the industrialized countries, and an exchange between partners. (Hancock, 1992:147)

Criticism about development has been raised from the perspective of dependency theory, Marxism and structuralism. Beyond these underlying theories, the effect of transnationalisation has also increasingly become an issue. Development communication focusses on the transference of infrastructural elements and content from 'outside' into the country in question, yet only a few studies analyse the disintegration of national culture caused by communication habits, styles and contexts, like the adoption of transnational media content and icons by the 'elite' classes of a given society.[18]

Communication and international development: From propaganda to persuasion

Whereas the studies of development communication described above look at the transfer of communication as a societal system from Western to developing countries, 'propaganda' focusses more on the political content of international communication. This approach orginated out of the enforcement of US foreign policy through the use of media.

The fact that propaganda has become an issue can be seen as an effect of development communication. Since various countries with diverse political ideologies have established and expanded mass communication systems, new political communicators have emerged. According to the 'catching-up' thesis, a media apparatus has been established in transitional societies and skills for its operation have been acquired. This new, advanced stage of media development has become the focus of various US studies intended to detect the specific professionalisation of Third World communicators.

Propaganda and persuasion models have also been applied to international communication from political 'super powers' into developing countries and others. These nations had the resources – both technical and professional – for international or even global broadcasting. Boyd-Barrett remarks that during the 1970s, the Soviet Union ranked as the second largest international broadcaster, and between 1969 and 1972 it put out more programme hours than the United States. However, the international audience share was disproportionately smaller. Boyd-Barrett refers to a study of radio listening in Kenya, Tanzania, Uganda and Ghana in 1970 which revealed that

> ...at least in this region the BBC was the only foreign station apart from those in neighbouring countries ever likely to be tuned into by more than 50 per cent of the listeners, and that such stations as Radio Moscow, Radio Peking, Radio Cairo, Deutsche Welle and Radio Berlin International were listened to by no more than 10 per cent (and usually far less) of the radio listening population even on an occasional basis'. (Boyd-Barrett, 1977:133)

While programmes from Western countries had covert propaganda, programmes from Communist countries had overt propaganda. (Boyd-Barrett, 1977:133)

Communication concepts of relativistic modernity

Since the mid-seventies the concepts of development communication have been critically reviewed not only by western but also by Third World communication experts. Traditional concepts soon became the subject of re-definition or modification. These point out a profound ambiguity even in the term 'Third World' since it sets up divisions or barriers '...which only obfuscate rather that facilitate the analysis of the countries of Africa, Asia, Latin America and the Middle East'. (Stevenson, 1993:7) Increasing complaints did not result in a redefinition of 'old' approaches; in fact, especially in recent years, a serious case has been made for treating the whole concept of modernity in communication as a relative one, taking account of different kinds of knowledge and world views. Whereas criticism based on the notion of dependency argues in terms of economics, criticism based on the notion of imperialism see a threat to individual cultures from any relativist redefinition of their status, when the result is a blanket condemnation of the whole modernization concept as such, since development is an 'integral, multidimensional, and dialectical process which can differ from one society to another'. (Servaes, 1983:63) Concepts of dependency, culture, imperialism and relativism will be summarised here because they involve a critical view of the modernization concept and imply new issues of international communication.

Dependency concepts

Dependency theories oppose the paradigm of early modernization. Both approaches have in common that they focus first of all on economy as central for societal development. Proponents of dependency theory claim that fundamental contradictions exist in the world between 'central' and 'peripheral' economies. These approaches focus on international capital flow but do not differentiate between capitalist and feudal modes. The belief that Western ideas of modernization can and should be transferred into diverse economic environments implies the unquestioned universalism of the modernization project, while dependency theories bring in the concept of particularism, which had already paved the way for well-founded communication models in formerly 'peripheral' regions. Servaes argues that

> ...the greatest weakness of dependency communication research is the lack of an analysis of the nature of the class forces and the position of the nation state in peripheral countries... Dependistas put too much emphasis on the contradictions at the international level, and thus overlook the existing contradictions at the local level between the interests of the state and the media owners on the one hand, and between the government and the population on the other. (Servaes, 1983:60)

This argument can be supported by the fact that national communication policy is subject to planning, governmental intervention and strict internal regulation, whereas internationally the same governments support the free flow of communication. Political contradictions like this are practised in South American as well as Asian countries (such as Singapore). The varied new access to global communication brings these contradictions to the fore since local regulated particularities of peripheral countries enter the global communication sphere.[19]

Whereas originally dependency issues were raised in order to pinpoint economic interests in developing countries, recent approaches transfer this concept to various issues such as new dependencies emerging within developed, though imbalanced, media settings of communication flow. According to Kivikuru the main modes of foreign dependency for media are import (media content, processing structures, technical equipment) and adoption or absorption which consist for example in

> ...modes of operation or administration from abroad. The emergence of 'mini-BBC's' in former British colonies is a fairly typical example of adoption. Absorption means 'gliding' into new structures and practices without deliberate desision-making'. (Kivikuru, 1988:12)

'Dependency' refers also to the importation of cultural goods through media and thus to the increase of cultural conflicts within a developing nation which implies, according to Servaes, contradictory processes.

> On the one hand there is a tendency to import cultural content and develop local imitations. On the other hand, many Third World communicators and organizations are using the imported media technologies to attempt to forge a more autonomous culture. (Servaes, 1983:70)

Local media (theatre, oral media) which are used for educational purposes are considered as the last remaining sets of 'countercultural' projects. The parallelism of Western media and local ones create 'dualistic communication structures'. (Servaes, 1983:69) In Kivikuru's view, this process replaces a direct importation of mass communication content. He defines this adoption as 'modelling' which implies a strong refererence to those forms of mass communication which most easily become stereotyped, because of either structure or content. (Kivikuru, 1988:13)

The dependency debate has widened to take account of the media structure or media economy of peripheral Western countries. Kivikuru applies it to peripheral countries in general, not just to those which are involved in an economic and societal development process, thus bringing in Western peripheral countries like Finland. Though 'today belonging to the well-to-do elite of countries' Finland, he says, is 'still economically bearing marks of peripheral development and, culturally, many signs of the 600-year colonial bond to Sweden, as well as some of the century-long linkage with Czarist Russia'. (Kivikuru, 1988:16)

Whereas peripheral countries (and their local media organizations) have gained opportunities to increase their global dissemination, the emergence of satellite communication implies new dependencies and imbalances in Western developed nations. For this reason the focus on economic dependency has to be modified to one which assesses the communication structures of a country also in terms of its implicit access to, and representation on, a global market. In this view, issues of culture and cultural identity of particularities also apply not only to small developed countries, such as Finland, but also to Portugal, Ireland and others.

It is obvious to Kivikuru that '...options open to small industrialised countries such as Finland diminish in the same way, though not on the same scale, as in developing countries. The media system is linked, bit by bit, with the transnational production and distribution system'. (Kivikuru, 1988:20) Kivikuru sees other similarities to developing countries in the fact that there is no possibility of retreat after having made a basic choice.

> Another phenomenon combining Finland with developing countries is journalistic culture. The journalistic culture often operates as a filter for new professional practices, usually strongly promoting anything new in the name of progress; professionalism operates as a

carrier of dependency in much the same forms as in developing countries. (Kivikuru, 1988:20)

Journalistic culture works for the adoption of 'international practices' in as much as the mainstream of mass communication 'creates a mainstream ideology of professionalism'. (Kivikuru, 1988:21) News journalism in particular is strongly influenced by international news agencies especially in crisis situations when up-to-date material on political world conflicts is available only from international – that is national – news agencies, as the Gulf War clearly illustrated. It can be argued that today this information flow process is the only remaining imbalance to which the concept of dependency can be applied, though not in an economic or cultural fashion but in view of information bias.[20]

Such a concept can be advanced by replacing economic dependency with a structural analysis of world-wide information (and media content) flow in terms of 'periphery' and 'centre.' By this refinement it would be possible to eliminate some concepts of development communication and instead integrate phenomena of transnational media into a broad worldwide interdependent context.[21]

International cultivation

The term 'international cultivation' does not explicitly refer to the worldwide context of developing or developed nations and their inter-systemic communication structure. It implies elements of relativistic modernization, since this theory argues that a synchronous internationally distributed media content initiates a cultural mainstreaming process. George Gerbner's approach is based on the assumption that media are a single system, which is not greatly integrated into societies and which disseminates universal images across cultures. The original concept was based on American televison culture:

> TV penetrates every home of the land. Its seasonal, cyclical, and perpetual patterns organically related fact and fiction (all woven into an entertainment fabric producing publics of consumers for sale to advertisers) again encompass essential elements of art, science, technology, statecraft and public (as well as most family) story telling. The information-poor (children and less educated adults) are again the entertainment-rich held in thrall by the myths and legends of a new electronic priesthood. (Gerbner and Gross, 1976:175f)

Gerbner assumed that all societies have evolved 'ways of explaining the world to themselves and to their children'. This socially constructed 'reality' transmits ideas, values of 'what is important, what is related to what, and what is right'. (Gerbner and Gross, 1976:176) This process is defined as cultivation.

The assumed 'nearly universal', 'non-selective', and 'habitual use of television fits the ritualistic pattern of its programming'. (Gerbner and

Gross, 1976:176) Television in this sense is more than a distributor of cultural products; it has become a religious concept which unites an otherwise diverse multicultural society. The central underlying question in cultivation theory is finding types of common consciousness. Cultivation in this sense 'inquires into the assumptions television cultivates about the facts, norms and values of society'. (Gerbner and Gross, 1976:182) It thus constructs the values and norms as well as morals (like religion) of 'social reality'. A media-related cultivation-effect is found when comparing two groups of heavy viewers and light viewers. Although it is obvious that heavy viewers already have different values and lifestyles to light viewers, differences still persist such as the tendency to give 'television answers'.

International cultivation is also linked conceptually with debates focussing on cultural, media-initiated imperialism. This approach is concerned with the mainstreaming of cultivation processes within international 'symbolic environments'. It identifies specific value changes due to the flow of international (ie, US) programmes into various cultures. While no two cultures are identical, US programmes may 'fit' better or less well in different cultural contexts. Thus, US programmes may seem much more 'alien' in Asian and Latin American countries than in Western European countries or in countries such as Australia'. (Morgan, 1990:229) As Morgan argues, cultural indicators are differently interpreted: 'a kiss is not "just a kiss" everywhere in the world, or even for all people and groups within a single culture'. (Morgan, 1990:228)

International cultivation thus reveals the change which American programmes affect in diverse cultures on public consciousness of gender roles and 'Western lifestyle' stereotypes. This approach is focussed on the actual changes in habits and attitudes towards a pop-cultural or Western mainstream value system.[22] It includes the effects of 'the age of consumption' within the global consumer culture '...in which mainstreaming middle-class values are presented on the screen, regardless of the type of programme; the actors are surrounded by durable commodities, material conveniences, and many aspects of the "affluent society". (Kato, 1976:255) These programmes legitimate action and conventions and publicly shared knowledge of the 'wide world [which] is what this nervous system transmits to us'. (Gerbner and Gross, 1976)

Although international cultivation analysis involves entertainment as well as news programmes and their transmission not only of American-defined middle-class mainstreaming but of a mainstreaming and stereotyping of the 'real world', its application to the presentation of news in the centres and periphery would be particularly revealing. Here the global approach can be used to evolve an advanced cultivation theory which will be able to pinpoint the values, ethics and 'reality' of a world society and the reconstruction of political reality.

43

Media criticism in terms of imperialism

While cultivation analysis is concerned with the messages of internationally disseminated programmes, imperialist theories criticise the global programme flow as something which moved into the centre of US foreign policy and its declared responsibility for global communication in the late 60s. Technical innovations such as the early phases of the satellite market, which increased the flow of mass-oriented communication content across national borders, form the background for imperialism theory.

In the first phase of non-military satellite broadcasting, initiated by the United States in the early 1960s, President Kennedy said in defining the central goal of the new communication era, that all nations should '...participate in a communication satellite system, in the interest of world peace and a close brotherhood among peoples throughout the world'. (quoted in Hudson, 1990:21) The goals of this plan were fourfold: US leadership, rapid implementation of the system, the establishment of a truly global system, and benefits for all mankind from satellite communication. (Hudson, 1990:22) Edward Murrow, as director of the United States Information Agency, saw in these goals a 'dramatic demonstration of our concern for the peaceful uses of outer space and our willingness and indeed our eagerness to use that communication system in the tradition of free reporting in this country'. (quoted in Hudson, 1990:22) As Hudson further describes, the Senate Space Committee's *Communication Satellite Report* called '...space communication an entirely new concept of worldwide communication ... that would afford a unique potential as an instrument of international affairs'. (Hudson, 1990:22) Hudson remarks that this report 'saw the greatest growth in demand for satellite links to Europe, followed by the Caribbean and Latin America' whereas 'demand for communication with Asia was predicted to grow much more slowly'. (Hudson, 1990:22) The goal of the United States which also caused a tremendous amount of research as well as many communication projects in the Third World was defined by the Senate Space Commitee as follows:

> These new nations are certain to desire independent communication systems as part of their programme of self-government. A single space relay over Africa has entertaining possibilities as a link between all African nations and may prove attractive regardless of purely economic considerations. The United States may thus have a unique opportunity to assist these nations in their goals of self-realisation. (quoted in Hudson, 1990:22)

In 1961, the US proposed a United Nations satellite policy, which should 'forge new bonds of mutual knowledge and understanding between people everywhere', 'offer a powerful tool to improve literacy and education in developing areas' and 'enable leaders of nations to talk face-to-face on a convenient and reliable basis'. (quoted in Hudson, 1990:23)

The United Nations unanimously adopted the General Assembly Resolution 1721 (XVI), which stated that 'communication by means of satellite should be available to the nations of the world as soon as practicable on a global and nondiscriminatory basis'. On this basis COMSAT was established (Hudson, 1990:27) and soon afterwards, *Intelsat 1*, the so-called Early Bird, was launched.

Because of these technical innovations and an increased awareness, during the Cold War period, of the possible use of new global communication structures as an instrument of US foreign policy, imperialism theory came into being, concentrating on the increased use of these technologies by US-based broadcasters and the fast expansion of US programmes.

This theory, which consists of a fundamental criticism of cultural synchronisation and domination, focussed on issues of programme flow and media organizations. Galtung and Ruge's concept of the four mechanisms of imperialism: 'exploitation', 'penetration', 'fragmentation' and 'marginalisation' provoked debate on imperialism in the 1960s when 'relativism' became the dominant paradigm in international communication theory. This relativism was the subject of an early news-flow study undertaken by Galtung and Ruge (1965). These Norwegian researchers distinguished between different modes of 'imperialism', such as the economic, political, military, communicative, and cultural. Their study, entitled 'Foreign News' revealed for the first time an unbalanced news flow and pointed to the domination of Western news agencies and their specific centre-periphery-news exchange. In the light of this study, Galtung and Ruge regarded imperialism as an anti-development influence. The findings of this classic study of news values in the printed media, which is still used today as a bias model of new organizations, reveal six levels:

(1) 'The more similar the frequency of the event is to the frequency of the news medium, the more probable that it will be recorded as news by that news medium.' Criticism of this factor often fails to reckon with the diverse frequencies of new print and electronic news media. This finding does not hold as a general 'rule' but has to be applied separately to the different media and their organizational background.

(2) 'There is a threshold that the event will have to pass before it is recorded at all.' Especially in recent years the production of 'news' has tremendously increased to the point where more than the usual five per cent of all incoming news is actually transmitted (Wilke and Rosenberger, 1991). This finding applies not only to foreign but also to domestic news. The increase of international news agencies has to some degree balanced domestic and international news items so that the 'threshold' still exists, but exists in different media for different reasons. While channels providing a full range of content define the 'threshold' in terms of economic time frames and target audiences, fragmented channels define it in terms of diverse programme goals within a strategy of news diversification.

(3) 'An event with a clear interpretation, free from ambiguities in its meaning, is preferred to the highly ambiguous event, from which many and inconsistent implications can and will be made.' Because of pressure from an increased pace within news journalism and the change in 'reporting', it is obvious that ambiguous events may not be considered for primetime, but possibly for other information programmes.

(4) 'The more unexpected incidents have the highest chances.' This finding is especially relevant for commercial news organizations who want to increase their share of the market with exclusive reports. It has also be considered that increasing competition on the news market leads to channels vying with each other to be first with the news.

(5) 'The more negative the event, the more probable that it will become a news item.' In times of increased commercialization of broadcasting, negative events are viewed as critical journalism.

(6) 'Mental pre-images cause the news gatherer or news receiver to interpret news according to the pre-image more readily than other news.' These mental pre-images are shaped by an international agency network.

Additional factors specifically apply to international news:

(7) 'The more the event concerns elite or centre nations, the more probable that it will become a news item.' Peripheral countries increase their own news networks and increase news items about their national affairs.

(8) 'The more the event can be seen in personal terms, as due to the action of specific individuals, the more probable that it will become a news item'.

(9) 'The more the event concerns elite or centre people, the more probable that it will become a news item and there is some measure of ethnocentrism or cultural proximity operative.'

Although the Galtung and Ruge study has been extremely influential, critical objections have been raised, such as that their model and the methodology were too narrow and that it is necessary to bring in extra media data. A further objection was that it is not enough to look at the news factors which determine selective gatekeeping; the audience's perception of the media within a given society should also be integrated into the model. Furthermore, the model is insufficient for the analysis of current media structures such as commercial, public or governmental news systems and also cannot be employed in order to determine what is deemed newsworthy by full or fragmented news channels.

The peripheral nations do not write or read much about each other, '...especially not across bloc borders, and they read more about "their" centre than about other centres, because the press is written and read by the centre in the periphery who want to know more about the most "relevant" part of the world – for them'. (Servaes, 1983:28)

Galtung and Ruge's model of international newsworthiness also reveals the flow of news from developing peripheral to central countries and vice versa. But the analysis also uncovers the fact that peripheral countries do not communicate with each other directly but via a three-step-communication flow from a peripheral country to a centre country and to another peripheral country. They do not, however, propose the idea of a 'semi-periphery' serving as a buffer between peripheral and centre countries. (Wallerstein, 1984) This category came later, with imperialist media theory. These semi-peripheral countries have developed an elite class which uses a Western and American lifestyle, as described by Sussman and Lent in the Caribbean and Central American region, where US broadcast signals were receivable by satellite in the early 1980s. 'By 1982, many hotels and restaurants in Barbados and elsewhere had begun to import satellite dishes' for foreign TV; the lifestyle also became accessible via VCRs. 'Most major hotels were topped with satellite dishes, and video became an important acitivity of the elite classes, and a constant topic of conversation'. (Sussman and Lent, 1991:267).

> The first videoshops catered to an exclusive clientele and stocked mostly classic feature films and American network television programs. Over the years, the social class of video consumers moved downward, so that by the end of the decade video had become common in households of all classes. For those who cannot afford VCR's, there are entrepreneurs who rent tapes and charge admission to view them. (Sussman, 1992:268)

It can be argued that the term 'semi-periphery' should apply not only to the economic status of a given country but should also be associated with a specific degree of international media programme flow. Judging by this criterion, the number of semi-peripheral media countries in the world has increased, since because of the latest technological developments, more and more countries are part of a global programme flow.

The internationalization of the Western entertainment industry – the *Kulturindustrie* (Adorno, 1967), especially its media side – has become the central thesis of imperialism theory. 'Imperialism' refers to the process whereby the ownership, distribution and content of the media in any one country, singly or together, are subject 'to substantial external pressures from the media interests of any other country or countries without proportionate reciprocation of influence by the country so affected'. (Boyd-Barrett, 1977:117) These influences imply 'overt' as well as 'covert' infiltration of Western values. The term 'imperialism' also involves a one-way direction and the absence of reciprocal responses. These two elements of invasion justify the use of the term 'imperialism'. The study of imperialism as a general political and economic phenomenon typically relates it to the structural and economic requirements of the imperial powers, and as such provides a framework for the understanding of all international relationships in which those powers engage. Similarly the study of media imperialism is concerned 'with all aspects of relationships between media systems, not simply between those of the developed and of the developing world'. (Boyd-Barrett, 1977:118) Imperialism consists of two processes: the country which originates an international media influence either exports this influence as a 'deliberate commercial or political strategy', or 'simply disseminates' this influence 'unintentionally' or 'without deliberation' in a more general process of political, social or economic influence'. The country which receives this 'adopts' this influence as a deliberate commercial or political strategy, or simply 'absorbs' it 'unreflectively as the result of the contact'. (Boyd-Barrett, 1977:119)

These concentration structures are not characteristic of the postwar media age (that of television) alone. As described above, the commercialization of news media (such as news agencies) began in the 19th century. However, because of the sharp increase in media technology and the diversity of media markets (in conjunction with different media), new corporate structures have emerged which gained shares of as many market segments as possible. These corporations have built up vertically-integrated international company-structures and concentrated ownership more and more in their own hands. Schiller argues that the '...production of movies, television programmes, games, records, magazines and books is consolidated in a few corporate superstructures and made part of multiproduct lines of profit-maximising combines'. (Schiller, 1979:25) In the writings of Schiller and other proponents of the imperialism theory, the totality of these media conglomerates transforms national media structures '...into conduits of the corporate business system, and the heavy international traffic of commercial media products flowing from the centre to the periphery, are the most prominent means by which weaker societies are absorbed culturally into the modern world system'. (Schiller, 1979:25)

The shortcoming of this imperialism approach consists in its failure to integrate worldwide media developments, which establish new sub-regional markets. Schiller argues that because these media markets in Brazil, India and elsewhere are organised along commercial lines, American influence must be present, because these nations have to compete within a certain market segment with American products and thus they imitate them. They also cater to a demand for media content which is already shaped by low-quality US products. What Schiller and others overlook is the fact that in the context of very recent media developments such as the expansion of satellites as well as the telecommunication industry, formerly disadvantaged 'victims' of American programmes increasingly participate in a global programme flow. Further, imperialist theory views all media products in the same light.

They overlook the fact that arguments that may be relevant for movies like *Police Academy*, or television dramas such as *Beverly Hills 90210* cannot be applied to other media communication. The latter would include the international flow of news (such as CNN's), of music (such as MTV's) and sports (such as ESPN's) and subdivisions within these categories. 'News' can be political, economic, environmental; 'Music' may include reggae, soul, blues, rock; 'Sports' cover football, soccer, basketball, golf. Schiller argues that news is manipulated 'to a situation of political domination' and 'the reality presented to the region and from the region tends to be distorted according to political positions of the United States'. (Schiller, 1979:59) I maintain that programme markets have to be considered under regional market specifications. The global distribution of programmes such as those of CNN and MTV have shaped new regional markets which fragment and diversify and thus reveal diverse levels of internationalization. As regards news, this phenomenon can be observed in various markets where new international broadcasters are already taking part alongside American networks (NBC, CNN) and have initiated regional phases of internationalization. Among these new players are, for example, CCTV (Chinese Television) and TRT (Turkish Television).

The diversification of the news market (and this can be applied accordingly to other programme markets) has tremendously increased the international news flow as such, so a movement from 'concentration' to a wide range of news programmes on more and more balanced markets can be observed. Because of this changed situation, the thesis of 'imperialism' has at least to be modified to deal differently with entertainment programmes and formats (such as drama, soap, quiz or videoclip) and information and news programmes. The thesis should also be modified in terms of media in general, because print, audiovisual and electronic media have different global reception patterns. In order to reflect current media developments, the theory of imperialism – because of the global parallelism of universal and particular levels – must not only focus on the world wide and the few transnational media organizations but must also specify new 'imperialist' developments, such as bilateral transborder programme flow, which should also be applied to developed countries. This leads to a fundamental redefinition of the relationship of the media and national economy since imperialist theory traditionally concentrates on developing countries. By widening the viewpoint towards any unbalanced programme flow, which itself has to be subject of redefinition in the context of new 'global communication', various new patterns of imperialist influence would be detected: for example, not only between Eastern and Western Europe but also in terms of an unbalanced flow from large, powerful countries into the territory of small neighbouring states. An analysis of these new imbalances would reveal different types of transnational, international programme flow, for example in Finland, Portugal, and Austria.[23]

The traditional assumption that imperialist corporations are dominated by the United States is simply false, since today's multinational organizations include American, European, and Asian as well as Latin American investments. Moreover, because of satellite technology there are tendencies for new international alliances to be shaped in terms of common cultural as well as language bonds (for example, the progressive merging of Spanish and Portuguese and Latin American media, made possible by the *Hispasat* satellite, which transmits channels such as the Spanish Hispavision to Latin America). Of course it can be argued that satellite technology reshapes or celebrates a renaissance of old colonial bonds, but the situation is more complex than that.

From a national point of view, since the protection of national culture is also a fundamental subject of imperialist theory, Boyd-Barrett maintains that 'everyday experience of the media on the other hand reveals a highly visible international dimension' (Boyd-Barrett, 1977:116), to which even Schiller admits that there '...is no doubt that foreign propaganda broadcasting can be, and is, effective under some conditions. One condition for effectiveness is that the recipient population does not trust its own domestic broadcasts'. (Schiller, 1979:141) This international flow is also of political importance in totalitarian countries.[24] Moreover, official declarations about protecting national culture are a two-sided coin, especially in developing nations, since governments' public expressions about cultural protection may translate internally into protection of the government itself.

Boyd-Barrett distinguishes between two types of international media flow. The first is the one of exported media products

> ...from the US to Asian countries, (where) there is only a very slight trickle of Asian media products to the US. Even where there may appear to be a substantial return flow, as is sometimes the case in news, the apparent reciprocity merely disguises the fact that those who handle or manage this return flow are primarily the agents of major western media systems, whose criteria and choice are determined above all by their domestic market needs.

The second flow resides in the influence exerted by the very small number of

> ...source countries accounting for a very substantial share of all international media influences around the world, such as America, Britain, France, West Germany, Russia followed a long way behind by relatively minor centres of international media influence including Italy and Japan. (Boyd-Barrettt, 1977:117)

This 'dominant source' argument refers to the international media flow system of the early 1970s where, indeed, the Western media (also the 'big four' news agencies) dominated the world. Media imperialism describes both of these flows.

Imitation of the US media organization has also become a model for other countries and is directly implied in imperialism theory. In consequence, deregulation, such as that of previous public service markets in view of a media 'liberalisation', which consists in the licencing of commercialized media, has also recently become the subject of imperialism critique: 'National industries still exist, but the preponderant share of global production now is accounted for by giant companies, operating in scores of countries and headquartered in a few European, North American and East Asian sites'. (Schiller, 1992:21) Schiller argues that the new mode of global production and distribution has led to an almost complete commercialization of television and has fostered a concentration of television program production in a few international centres.

> Visit almost any country and you will find the same products and the same sponsors and the same programming on the local screens. These are brought into the home by global companies whose logos, through incessant promotion, have become household icons. (Schiller, 1992:21)

Relativistic modernity and communication

Although the approaches described above indicate the relativism of the concept of modernization, very recently a new view of the subject has become a substantial element in the debate on international communication theory. This new thinking is primarily represented by Hamid Mowlana, who argues that the global expansion of the western information society concept opens up a specific conflict-laden parallelism between the information society paradigm and the Islamic Community paradigm. He reflects on diverse cultures of modernization and Islam, in view of the importance and meaning of 'information' within different concepts of society. Referring to Wallerstein, he proposes: 'It now seems more imperative than ever to discuss global tensions not only in terms of explicitly economic, geopolitical and military structures, but also equally in the context of cultural, communication and information struggles'. (Mowlana, 1993:23) Mowlana suggests in this context an ecological model, dividing up various global environments into ecologies. Thus there is an ecology of goods and commodities, of services and education, of warfare, of information, cultural industries and mass media, of habitat and of ethics and morality. (Mowlana, 1993:24) His innovative concept views the globe in its diversity by rejecting traditional thinking about 'developing' or 'developed' economies, or the involvement of states in peripheral or central international communication imbalances. Mowlana proposes a cultural approach which does not reduce culture to national heritage, but sees it as more of a transnational operation. Both modern and Islamic states have a transnational tendency, each with its own fundamentally different concept of a global communication community. The difference between modern and Islamic models of collectivity are those already defined by Tonnies. Whereas Mowlana's term

Gesellschaft (society) indicates the modern view, *Gemeinschaft* (community) implies a transnational community model of Islam. Mowlana's communication concept (which is specifically targeted towards Lerner as the foremost modernization proponent) attempts to supersede the concept of modernity by looking at international communication and its national impact from a cultural point of view.

The concepts of dependency, cultivation and imperialism criticise modernization by distinguishing between urban and rural modern communication developments, and by describing exogenous and endogenous cultural effects. These views became the substantial conceptual element of UNESCO's communication policy, resulting, for example, in the appointment of the MacBride Commission. Mowlana submits not only a critical view of earlier communication meta-theories but a new theory of a truly relativistic modernity.

Globalization: towards a paradigm change in communication theory

In terms of the varied phenomena of current global communication, a differentiated view is necessary in order to reveal new and specific structures. This is quite a difficult undertaking since the conventional categories of 'imbalances' and 'expansion' do not seem to be appropriate for the new global communication flow. This new world order calls for something other than the conventional parameters of global communication, eg revealing the parallelism of 'universal' and 'particular' elements which involve global modes as well as local modes of communication which are globally distributed. Modernization can be interpreted as the dominant theoretical paradigm behind early approaches to international communication. Lerner's book, *The Passing of Traditional Society*, provided the theoretical framework for communication theory until the early eighties, when the UNESCO commission again criticised this approach because of its slant towards a Western information flow around the world.

As Robertson argues, the main task today is to consider the ways in which the world 'moved' from being merely 'in itself' to the problem of its possibly being 'for itself'. (Robertson, 1990:23) This means, in Robertson's view, a need for 'systematic comprehension of the macro-structuralisation of world order', which is 'essential to the viability of any form of contemporary theory and that such comprehension must involve analytical separation of the factors which have facilitated the shift towards a single world'. (Robertson, 1990:22) Communication theory seems not to have responded to the new demands of the global scope which are already being discussed in sociological debates.

While modernization implies a society constructed along nation/state lines, globalization involves the new structures of nation-state but also extra-societal worldwide communities.[25] Kant referred to 'cosmopolitanism' as a particular state of mind: that of being a citizen of the world; globalization has brought to the fore various forms of participation which developed not only through the global interconnectedness of world cities but also through a new cosmopolitan-local relationship. As Hannerz remarks, the 'willingness to become involved with the other, and the concern with achieving competence in cultures which are initially alien, relate to considerations of self as well. Cosmopolitanism often has a narcissistic streak; the self is constructed in the space where cultures mirror one another'; (Hannerz, 1990:240) and thus it involves different goals and intentions, different values. Globalization is therefore not a programme, a 'project', like that which was developed in the past to promote societal 'evolution' by linking economic and democratic development. Globalism is a theoretical approach which views the globe in its totality in order to reveal global diversifaction. This concept is already quite advanced in terms of global culture.

'Culture' as discussed above, was seen as an element of 'cultivation': the cultural 'indicators' supporting a (pop) cultural 'mainstream' process. The latest debates consider it as part of global developments in which media reception analysis has contributed to an 'ethnography of media audiences'. (Ang, 1990:243) Ang argues that it is necessary to distinguish between audiences by employing ethnography. Doing this would involve a concept of media reception as an integral part of popular cultural practices that articulate both 'subjective' and 'objective', both 'micro' and 'macro' processes. Reception should be appraised as one field of the 'complex and contradictory term, the multi-dimensional context, within which people live out their everyday lives'. (Ang, 1990:244)

This approach therefore demands that we differentiate on a broad scale between diverse media developments in various world regions, such as hegemonic forces versus ideology in Central America, or culturally-embedded types of information revolution in other regions.

Ang's approach is based on the co-existence 'of the monopoly of messages by the big networks and of the increasingly narrow codes of local micro-cultures around their parochial cable TV's'. (Ang, 1990:251) She also suggests that the generalized concept of a 'homogenising' international communication flow proposed by imperialist theory should be replaced by that of 'cultural synchronisation' since in 'the increasingly integrated world system there is no such thing as an independent cultural identity; every identity must define and position itself in relation to the cultural frames affirmed by the world system'. (Ang, 1990:253)

> The circulation and consumption of ethnically specific information and entertainment on video services serves to construct and maintain cross-national 'electronic communities' of geographically dispersed peoples who would otherwise lose their ties with tradition and its active perpetuation'. (Ang, 1990:257)

In Ang's view it is 'easy for us to talk about the "age of world popular culture", saying that the Beatles, Elvis Presley, James Bond, and many other popular heroes are universal heroes'. (Ang, 1990:257) And this observation may be quite correct. However, the existence of these universal heroes implies that there may be a danger of an 'instant globalism' in which national identity is played down. Globalization does involve the universality of pop culture. Such phenomena undermine the concept of nationalism as something simple, and demand that we refine it. A process of balancing nationalism and internationalism has also been an element in the development of European nationalism. Kato argues that 'globalism today is only another name for internationalism, and internationalism presupposes solid national integrity and nationalism'. (Kato, 1976:256)

Along with this change of paradigm, comes a clear recognition of the way in which international communication is now functioning: the differentiation of communication channels, a new view of 'the world', its cultural interconnectedness, its networks of channels of political communication. The media of international communication have been multiplied, the political impact of messages has been diversified. We experience new modes of political communication which have recently been developed, such as specific ways to 'present' news, new formats and a new global news language with its icons of 'freedom', of authenticity and global identity.

McQuail describes the transnationalisation of media content as follows:

> Transnationalisation was slow to be defined as a cultural problem because mass media were, from the start, organised on a national basis: media served their own (national) society first and usually reinforced the idea and reality of nationalism. Before the Second World War, it was also regarded as normal that great powers should try to disseminate their culture and religion in the wake of armies and trade. International flow of media content was, until mid-century, generally only seen as problematic in the context of competing ideologies and nation states – a matter of international politics rather than culture. This limited definition of the problem was altered after the Second World War by several circumstances: the much increased international flow of media content; the even more dominant position of the United States in this flow; the independence and nationalist movements of former colonies; and the global competition between the ideologies of communism and capitalism fought out in debates about international communication flow in UNESCO and other forums. (McQuail, 1992:292)

Because of new technologies, the new levels of international news flow have developed beyond the national context into a communication sphere which deals with larger 'entities', be they regional, ideological or whatever.

McQuail brings in new 'transnational' formats:

Much television and other media content has been effectively internationalized in terms of genre or format, even when it is locally produced. Typical of such 'international formats' are quizzes, games shows, many soap operas, telenovellas and other dramatic fiction genres, the news itself, sporting events, chat shows, etc'. (McQuail, 1992:293)

Although McQuail can be regarded as one of the first to argue in favour of new international communication levels, his analysis remains on a general level. In addition to the internationalization of programme formats and genres, there have also been tremendous changes in the organization of broadcasting and its modes of reception, due to an international expansion of media. This has given a new meaning to national and indeed international broadcasting. Whereas the original national focus of broadcasting emerged from a 'modern' point of view of national identity, which was distributed inter-nationally, the global viewpoint involves more protection of individual national cultures from 'foreign' influences.

The suggested global viewpoint takes account of the co-existence of all these different phenomena with their different histories, and analyses and interprets their diverse inter-relationships and their influences on different global regions. Besides these, we should also include new organizational models of globally vertically integrated media systems, such as Time Warner, Disney, Murdoch, TBS and others. (see McQuail, 1992:308)

The theoretical consequences of moving from modern views on international communication towards a concept of global communication are:

(1) Modernization is linked with mass media exposure as a uni-directional media flow from one nation to another. Globalization implies participation in programme segments which are internationally / globally distributed from various countries.

(2) 'Empathy' is a keyword of development communication. It implies '...the capacity to place oneself in the roles of others. A traditional individual without the ability to empathize with the roles of others (as might be represented in the mass media, for example) would perhaps be entertained, but his attitudes would not be changed, by radio, film, or newspapers'. (Rogers, 1969:45) Globalization also refers to authenticity of media content, identifying oneself with others within a common global community.

(3) Modernization is defined as a goal (referring to Schramm, 1963). Global communication 'systems' refer more to hyper-national communication systems, with global concerns of different kinds (ethnic, religious, political, ecological, economic) which are located beyond national interests, and target special communities around the world.

(4) Modernization refers to nations and states, globalization to communities of an extra-societal kind.

(5) Modernization refers to inter-nationalisation, globalization to the interconnectedness of different universal and particular elements.

The globalized market and the paradigm change in communication theory

New issues of global/international communication

During recent decades the development of communication technology has increased the internationalization of communication. The foremost technology in this field: satellite, cable and internet technology, has led to new organization models of broadcasting, new programme types, new global audiences and new types of global audience segmentation. Seen from our new perspective the international development of a so called 'free flow' of communication appears as a complex of differentiated markets within a totality of global mass media systems, and not a global system reaching out to various markets. Due to tremendous industrial developments in media production in Western-oriented nations, which have given rise new international-continental and international-global media markets, this new transborder flow reveals new international media 'content' (beyond propaganda and persuasion) in both presentation styles, aesthetics and formats. McQuail argues that 'television and other media content has been effectively internationalized in terms of genre or format, even when it is locally produced, quoting such formats as quizzes, game shows, etc'. (McQuail, 1992:293) McQuail suggests the following levels of transborder flow:

(1) National: What is offered within a national system by way of domestic media channels;

(2) Bilateral: what is offered in one system and received across the frontier directly (eg from USA by Canada, from Britain by Ireland, from Germany by Holland);

(3) Multilateral: what is offered internationally for reception in many countries; for instance, much of what is offered by pan-European satellite and cable systems in Europe, or by the international distribution of US films or popular music'.

This differentiation indicates an increasing complexity of international communication levels, far beyond mere supply, and contributes to a new awareness of 'transnational'– continental communication. Sepstrup (1990) proposes the term 'transnationalisation' as a dependant variable of 'internationalization' to relate this term to a specific 'area' such as a country, to a group of countries or to an international group of TV viewers. (Sepstrup, 1990:11) 'According to these distinctions, television supply is divided into the national supply of multilaterally-distributed television, bilaterally-distributed television, and nationally-distributed television'. (Sepstrup, 1990:11) Sepstrup defines 'transnational communication' in its significance for continental markets in the following terms:

(1) 'Nationally-distributed television', which implies a 'national dimension of supply and consumption' and thus 'refers to television distributed by domestic media;'

(2) 'Bilaterally-distributed television programmes', originating from 'specific, foreign domestic media, which can be received by other countries simulatenously and unedited, transmitted over the air, or by some other technical means;'

(3) 'Multilaterally-distributed television originating from outside the country, with no single intended direction of flow'. (Sepstrup, 1990:12)

Although Sepstrup's model implies variations and specifications of the one-dimensional view of 'transnational' communication, his terminology seems, however, to be inappropriate for a definition or further circumscription of current media developments simply because these categories are strongly related to terrestrial broadcasting. For this reason such an approach cannot reveal the new effects of 'international' communication which are inaugurated by satellite broadcasting. Satellite broadcasting has shaped a communication context in which trans-nationality seems to lose its meaning because of the decrease of state borders in the context of broadcasting. New programme types are related to specified channels, such as those made by the vertically integrated media 'systems' which produce programmes for international channels. Sepstrup's categories seem to be inappropriate to classify degrees of 'internationality' in the sense that national boundaries are less influential. It is the global diversity of 'life styles', music tastes, shopping habits, entertainment preferences, age groups, political and religious orientation which have become the determinants of a new global media market. Also the same broadcasting companies quite often launch different channels with varying international reach and place the same programme content on these different markets (3 Sat, BBC World Service).

In the light of the above, the traditional categories of international communication need re-thinking. International-continental markets are:

(1) increasingly shaped not so much by national borders as by satellite footprints providing 'information' across nations (these satellite programmes, moreover, segment national markets);

(2) influenced in terms of McQuail's communication flow levels as described above;

(3) in competition with international-global or other international-continental programmes and channels. From this point of view, global communication involves international-continental programmes (bilateral and multilateral) which are distributed within a continental flow, as well as international-continental programmes (continental programmes such as Disney Club, or Spanish programs) which are distributed on inter-continental markets, and globally distributed programmes with continental slots (a 'reverse' form of regionalisation).

In this perspective, international communication can be defined as the 'transborder flow' of communication from nation to nation which is distributed via terrestrial air waves in the conventional term of broadcasting. Transnational communication indicates communication across nations and reveals new audience types of the community *Gemeinschaft* type. (Tönnies, 1963) Global communication covers those programmess which are distributed worldwide. Beyond these general definitions of media flow, more specific approaches are necessary to reveal the new shape of the various inter-national market models in news and information media related communication. In order to reveal the characteristics of the changing and developing global television news and information market, regarded in its totality, and to analyse its continental influence in terms of merging markets, I suggest three categories: 'fragmentation', 'diversification' and 'segmentation'.

Due to diversification processes, more and more satellite broadcasters demand programmes which are produced in what are, from a Western point of view, 'secondary markets'. These are about to become new central markets for media production. In Latin America, Brazil is expanding its influence as a dominant media market for the film and television industry with commercial channels such as those run by TV Globo and Telemundo etc. In Asia, India has a major stake in production facilities.

In order to erect a conceptual structure that will take in this wide field of new issues of global communication, we also have to take account of recent developments in satellite systems, the internationalization of media regulation, and the way in which international/global programming involves fragmentation, diversification and segmentation within different media markets. Such an integrative view involves a macroframe as well as a microframe approach. Whereas conventional theories of international communication primarily refer either to programme organization or content, we consider it essential, in order to tackle the new issues of global communication, to include new global macroframe structures, the broad framework for global programme organization, giving an overview of extra-societal broadcasting developments. Macroframe elements of global television communication consist in satellite systems and international regulation; microframe description involves new programme models and programme content.

Satellite systems

Although satellite systems do not primarily provide programme services, they have established technical facilities as well as legal regulations for a worldwide programme exchange. Whereas Wilhelm distinguishes between the following satellite systems: (a) *Intelsat* as the global satellite system, (b) the Soviet satellite system, (c) *Inmarsat* as the maritime satellite system and (d) regional satellite systems, (Wilhelm, 1990:43) the following breakdown is based on the view of national participation in international/global television communication and also involves the three major developments in satellite system organization.

Intergovernmental systems

The first phase of satellite transmitted international/global communication consisted in intergovernmental satellite systems. Although Western nations were among the initiators of these joint corporations, very early on developing countries were equally involved.

Intelsat

On 20 August 1964, the Intelsat organization was established as an international intergovernmental organization of 19 Western nations: Australia, Austria, Belgium, Canada, Denmark, France, West Germany, Ireland, Italy, Japan, the Netherlands, Norway, Portugal, Spain, Sweden, Switzerland, United Kingdom, United States, Vatican City. Comsat served as the managing organization. The initial ownership was '...based on international usage: the United States 61 per cent, Western Europe 30.5 per cent, Canada, Japan and Australia 8.5 per cent. These quotas could be adjusted to enable developing countries to participate in up to 17 per cent of the total ...'US share would never fall below 50.6 per cent'. (Hudson, 1990:31) Any nation can become a member of Intelsat and/or take advantage of its broadcast or telecommunication services. Intelsat membership countries have increased to around 140 (in 1998).[26] The International Telecommunications Union (ITU), founded in 1865 and since 1948 operating as an agency of the United Nations, is in charge of orbital allocation management and licensing. During recent decades, since the World Administrative Radio Conference (WARC) in 1977, the ITU has experienced some particularly controversial discussions as the developing countries take an increasing part in formulating ITU policy, where they often adopt a critical stance (see also Gerbner and Sieffert, 1984). Due to the limited number of geosynchronous satellite slots, developing countries fear that the increasing use of the orbit/spectrum resource will be occupied by developed countries which 'heralds a potential congestion of the arc and spectrum which could prohibit their gaining access to these resources'.[27] (Kavanaugh, 1986:95) Intelsat is a self-regulatory and co-operative model of owners and users.

> The most important background to the current situation of Intelsat is Article XIV of the present Intelsat Agreement, which provides that public international (but not domestic) satellite systems established by Intelsat members outside of the Intelsat framework shall be such as to avoid 'significant economic harm' to Intelsat. (Snow, 1984)

Intelsat's 'spacefleet' consists of twenty satellites in various geosynchronous equatorial orbits, centred over the Atlantic, Pacific and Indian oceans. (Wilhelm, 1990:44) Intelsat's satellite system provides global distribution for major broadcasters: BBC, CNN the European Broadcasting Union, the Asian Broadcasting Union, and other news agencies, telephone services, communication services for airlines, banks, global industries, for international newspapers (*Herald Tribune, Financial Times*) as well as providing Internet access (since 1995). Intelsat has recently, like other intergovernmental systems (Intersputnik, Eutelsat) been reformed as a partly commercial company, while remaining a unique share-user model with obligations for technologically less developed world regions.

Table 1: Satellite Systems

Intergovernmental Systems:
Arabsat
Asiasat
Eutelsat
Intersputnik[28]
Global System:
Intelsat

Table 2: Intelsat Membership (1988)[29]

OECD Countries: 24 = 70.27% share
Non OECD Countries: 88 = 29.73% share

Eutelsat

The Eutelsat satellite system was established in 1977. It is modelled on Intelsat in respect of its management structure (it is managed by an intergovernmental council and has defined public service objectives). Eutelsat provides the European region with the following services: transmission of 12 television networks to 18 countries for cable distribution, transmission of Eurovision programmes, intra-European telephone and telegraph, multiservice data communication for computer networking, facsimile, remote printing of newspapers, teleconferencing. (Hudson, 1990:111) As television broadcasters, public service and private/commercial broadcasters compete for specific market shares in attractive international television regions, this 'commercial' competition has also reached the satellite market. Eutelsat as a publicly organised, intergovernmental body is currently reshaping its service in the context of an increasingly competitive market in television transponder lease (especially on the Astra dominated European market) but it has also developed strategies for the not as yet particulary competitive market in special satellite-transmitted services (such as teleconferencing, personal electronic interaction, data transmission of EBU, interlink of the Satellite News-Gathering [SNG] system for European Broadcasters, telecommunication for 21 nations in Europe as well as 'Euteltracs System' a vehicle allocation system for trucks and ships).

Eutelsat is currently operating seven satellites and leases transponders to national and international as well as global television channels. Eutelsat transmitted its first television signals in 1983. Today, Eutelsat is equipped with three different beam widths, a 'Superbeam' which focuses on Central Europe with high population density (this is comparable to the footprint of the five Astra satellites), the 'Widebeam' and 'Hot-Bird' footprint which targets Central Europe in a wider angle. Eutelsat's consortium consists of 40 member states.

Table 3: Eutelsat's 40 Member Countries:

Austria, Belgium, Cyprus, Denmark, Finland, France, Federal Republic of Germany, United Kingdom, Greece, Holland, Iceland, Italy, Liechtenstein, Luxembourg, Malta, Monaco, Portugal, San Marino, Spain, Sweden, Switzerland, Turkey, Vatican City, Yugoslavia

Intersputnik

Intersputnik was established in 1971 as an equivalent to Intelsat and consists of 14 member countries: Afghanistan, Bulgaria, Cuba, Czechoslovakia, German Democratic Republic, Hungary, Korean People's Democratic Republic, Laos, Mongolia, Poland, Romania, the Soviet Union, the Socialist Republic of Vietnam and the People's Republic of Yemen. 'In addition non-members such as Algeria, Iraq, Libya, Nicaragua, Syria sometimes use the Intersputnik network for communication with member countries' (Wilhelm, 1990:44) since Intersputnik can beam to any location on the planet but does not cover the world as Intelsat does. Intersputnik is the second global satellite network. As early as 1985, Intersputnik signed a co-operation agreement with Turner Broadcasting of the United States. (Wilhelm, 1990:45) The Soviet Union established an earth station 'for the sole purpose of linking into the Intelsat network'.[30] (Wilhelm, 1990:45) Intersputnik was entirely rearranged in 1997 when it formed a joint venture with Lockheed Martin to provide worldwide communication services. This new company which has its headquarters in London, is developing a new range of satellite products. Today, Intersputnik has 22 member states (the majority of which are located in Eastern Europe). The new company, however, targets the world market and plans to distribute satellite communication, direct-to-home video and audio, tele-communications and mobile services not only into Eastern Europe but also across South Asia, Afria and the CIS countries.

Arabsat

The Arabian Satellite communication Organization was founded in 1976 and is co-operatively organised. Arabsat is the Arab's League regional satellite system. Its footprint reaches from the West African Atlantic coast across the Indian Ocean. Arabsat provides two television channels, telephone, mobile and data communications. This satellite system comprises three satellites: *Arabsat 1*, launched in February, 1985, *Arabsat 2*, launched in June 1985 and *Arabsat 3*, placed in orbit in 1987. The uplink stations are located in Riyadh and Tunis. After some months of Arabsat operation, the news exchange system Arabvision was established 'to encourage daily exchange of television programmes and information among the different Arab television stations'. (UNESCO 1989)

Table 4: Arabsat's 21 Member Countries

Algeria, Bahrain, Djibouti, Iraq, Jordan, Kuwait, Lebanon, Libya, Mauritania, Morocco, Oman, Palestine, Qatar, Saudi Arabia, Somalia, Sudan, Syria, Tunisia, Yemen Arab Republic, People's Democratic Republic of Yemen, United Arab Emirates.

Palapa

Founded in 1976, Palapa was one of the first nationally operated satellite systems in Asia. Because of its huge territorial expanse and its high population density, Indonesia decided to establish a comprehensive domestic satellite system, becoming the fourth country in the world to do so. The Palapa system transmits television, voice and high-speed data for the government and business community as well as for the general public. Palapa can be regarded as a 'truly' regional as well as international system since it provides television channels and other telecommunications services for Thailand, Malaysia and Singapore. Intelsat and Palapa have agreed to use Palapa satellites for communication between countries.[31]

Whereas these intergovernmental satellite systems represent a first international satellite generation, the second generation consists of state operated satellite systems which were launched by India (Indiasat), Brazil (Brazilsat) in order to transmit data to remote regions of the nation.

The commercial satellite era

The third generation of satellite systems began in the United States in the early seventies and internationally, however, in the early eighties. This third generation can be described as a 'commercial satellite era'. Due to new technologies, the former broadcasting satellites have been replaced by satellites which provide direct broadcasting (DBS) technology, the so called 'Hybrid' satellites[32] which have the advantage of being equipped with more television transponders. These can be used for television distribution and require, due to their technical standards, less complicated licensing procedures than other satellite types. The attraction of these satellites for commercial organizations consists in the high amount of television transponders and the two flow directions such as 'point-to-point' communication for audiovisual data transmission (for example, among members of the European Broadcasting Union) as well as to broadcast stations or multisystem operators (such as cable systems) and 'point-to-multi-point' distribution to homes equipped with satellite dishes.

These technologies established worldwide new audiovisual market forces and economies which have promoted the continuing launch of commercial satellite channels. Some commercial satellite systems (such as Astra in Europe, Echostar, DirecTV and Primestar in the USA.) are specifically designed for television distribution

The two satellite systems described above provide for the distribution of national programmes (television and radio), programme exchange (such as EBU material, satellite news-gathering), the distribution of programmes within and into technically undeveloped countries of the so-called 'Third World', telecommunication transmission, and interactive system services.

Whereas most of today's commercial satellite organizations operate in one particular world region, providing one or more fragemented satellite service, only PanAmSat can be regarded as a global commercially operating satellite company. PanAmSat on the one hand delivers broadcast signals for global, regional and domestic channels around the world, on the other it enables international broadcasters to reach the highly desirable US television audience by delivering signals to cable systems and cooperating programmers. PanAmSat carries for example not only international television signals such as BBC, HBO, ESPN, Disney but also regional channels, such as China Central Television, India's Doordashan, and NHK Japan and financial news services such as Bloomberg, Dow Jones and Reuters. PanAmSat is therefore an interesting global satellite model, which competes with Intelsat (and has obviously forced Intelsat to renew its company structure) and also moves into regional markets (Latin America, South Africa, India), besides the US, where it has established DBS platforms, and competes with regional satellite corporations such as Brazilsat and Asiasat. PanAmSat operates currently a global network of 17 satellites. In the US PanAmSat is associated with DirecTV a domestic DBS satellite system run on a subscription basis.

Regulatory bodies of international communication: From endogenous to exogenous regulation

The ITU and UNESCO are the only intergovernmental councils and organizations with a world communication policy. UNESCO is in charge of communication projects designed to promote a free and balanced flow of information and international programme exchange. UNESCO is concerned with 'appreciation of the process and role of communication in society, high professional standards, policies, infrastructure, and training in the field of communications, and the use of the media for social ends'. (Rahim, 1984:394)

The ITU's function is to regulate world and regional telecommunication frequencies.

> The planning function consists basically of forecasting demands and supplies, studying technical problems, and coordinating national plans. Allocation of radio frequencies is another planning function. The 1979 general WARC authorized ITU to convene special WARC's on ... planning high frequency allocation, and the use of the

geostationary satellite orbit and the planning of space services utilising it. (Rahim, 1984:395)

The ideology of these intergovernmental organizations is to ensure that the mass media promote

> ...a fair and wide distribution of information on the goals, aspirations, and needs of all nations and cultural groups, particularly those oppressed peoples who are struggling against imperialism, neocolonialism, and racism. A new information order is necessary to insure individual, group, and national access to diverse sources of information. (Rahim, 1984:393)

Whereas three decades ago, US foreign communication policy tended to focus on issues of international development where the US had cause for concern, subsequent intergovernmental regulation has studied development problems from an international point of view. 'ITU's "first-come, first-served" principle was challenged by the developing nations. (Rahim, 1984:393) who increasingly raised their critical voice on ITU matters. The current ITU satellite regulation consists in the principle that each country has access to two satellite slots for which the government issues licences.

As the only global communication regulatory board, the ITU defines its areas of responsibility as the exploitation, allocation, registration, and utilisation of telecommunication resources. (Rahim, 1984) ITU's policy of first-come, first-served, became an internal political issue for developing and developed nations within the organization:

> Whereas developed nations sought a regulation for satellite allocation, developing nations considered this as a disadvantage because the first come-first-served rule did not apply to their needs. The WARC conference in 1979 stated the need for equitable access to the 'spectrum and orbital' resources. (Rahim, 1984)

The priority and increasing influence of international broadcast regulation on national legislation is also remarked by McQuail and Siune: 'When considering the role of international organisations in the formation of mass media policy in Europe, it is important to bear in mind that international agreements generally function only to the extent that individual states ratify them and incorporate them into their own laws and regulations'. (McQuail and Siune, 1986:28) The view on international communication of these organizations is one which involves satellite communication but from the perspective of nations communicating with each other by programme inspill or transborder flow. The few globally operating organizations, such as UNESCO, critically analysed the global imbalance of communication capital, and programme flow from the West to the developing world, and concluded that a certain degree of regulation was required. (*World Communication Report*, 1989) This perspective does not take any account of the most recent global communication developments, such as the establishment of new communication markets in developing countries (India and Brazil). The New

Information and Communication World Order debate of the UN also neglects the degree of urban, media related and connected cultures in world cities. The urban classes of the world invest in communication markets such as in Ghana, Nigeria, in Asian markets and other developing countries, where the media industry has become an important economic force. It can be argued that the globally operating regulatory bodies as well as other international legislative commissions, such as the ITU and European Union are gaining in influence over the organization of international/transnational communication as well as (indirectly) over that of national domestic communication. I describe this process as endogenous regulation, meaning one where national domestic markets are organized from an exterior, ie international (European) or global perspective. Exogenous regulation, on the other hand deals with international communication from a national/domestic point of view, for example in countries which exercise a centralist broadcasting policy, and defends state interests in an international community.

Today, intergovernmental agencies are subject to the two opposing concepts of international programme regulation, and are also, because of the way satellite allocation and ownership are organised, increasingly involved in a competitive commercial satellite market. Besides these regulatory problems, the term 'transnational/international' comm-unication now has implications beyond those conventionally covered by communication theory. These new channels have to be related to new modes of political communication within the global and the national 'public sphere'. They involve new participatory structures on a macro- as well as microframe level. Regulatory control of international communication is transferred from national sovereignities to international regulatory organizations, such as the European Council, the WARC and the ITU. The dilution and eroding of state authority with regard to communication policy indicates the shift of authority for broadcasting onto the world community which regulates the communication flow. Although these developments are currently most profound in industrialised nations, they also affect transitional and developing nations.

> As international economic integration is expanded, the impact of domestic public policies is reduced. Control over the domestic economy by national governments is weakened. These developments are forcing governments to recognize the need for a full range of international trade policies, addressed not only to direct trade in information and communication equipment and services, but also to acknowledge the implications of global information and communication networks and services for other industries. For example, these considerations are central to current discussions at the International Telecommunications Union as well as Gatt. (Melody, 1990:27)

The internationalization of television regulation, which includes satellite distribution, is restricted to generalised, mass market programming and does not include new programme distribution sectors such as international out-of-home-markets.

Until recently at least it was assumed that each nation/state could operate its broadcasting entirely as it wished according to widely varying cultural and political norms. There is nothing novel about the export marketing of cultural goods or about transnational media operations in general, but the 'gates' of national television systems and markets were formerly controlled by a small number of institutionalised actors able to sort out problems of access, egress and any associated property rights of owners, writers and performers. Moreover there are powerful private media groups probing the system in search of new and possibly profitable fields of operation. The changed situation is thus much more than a matter of technological innovation. (McQuail and Siune, 1986:27)

Table 5: Different Types of Actors and their Logics with Examples from Transnational, National and Local Levels *

Level of activity	Type of actor	Examples of actors found in Europe	Logic expected to be behind policy
All levels	Media industry	Software as well as hardware	Economy, profit/survival development of know-how
Transnational	Political system	EEC	Economic growth employment: European integration
	Institution	UNESCO	International education and culture
		Council of Europe	European culture
	Broadcasting	EBU	Professional cooperation
	Technological/ technical	European Space Agency	Technology development
		ITU/CEPT	Technical standardization
National	Political system	State/Parliament/ governments	Economic growth/export, employment, culture
		Ministries	Administrative logic
		Political parties	Power/political ideology
	Institution	Churches	Ideological influence
	Broadcasting	PTT	Continuation of monopoly
		Radio & TV	Defence of public service
	Organization	Newspaper publishers' associations	Breaking monopolies
		Advertisers	Commercialization
		News agencies	Public service
		Labour unions	Employment
Local/regional	Political system	Administrative boards	Administrative logic: local integrity
	Broadcasting	Radio/TV stations	Decentralization
	Organization	Grass roots	Local democratization

* Table from McQuail and Siune, 1986:23

This table indicates different types of actors on the transnational, national and local/regional level in Europe. According to this table, the transnational regulatory body in Europe is the EEC. The only regulatory body on the global level, beyond continental or national regulation, is the ITU (which is primarily concerned with the organization of satellite broadcasting and issues concerning developing countries) for the regulation of global broadcasting.[33]

Whereas McQuail and Siune list so-called 'grass roots' organizations at the local/regional level, these are not listed on the transnational level where they also exist as public relations agencies for political organizations which operate globally via carrier programme channels. 'Media industry' is listed on all levels, though this term covers all recent variations and new broadcast developments.

Fragmentation, diversification and segmentation: New developments of transnationalisation of news programming in diverse markets

The developments described above have been influential in terms of the increasing internationalization of television channels. Recent expansion models are the following.

Transcontinental expansion of channels which carry news and information programme slots

Due to the limited opportunities on the home market, several US cable channels have expanded internationally into Europe, Southeast Asia and Latin America. Among these are NBC/MSNBC as the first international branch of a US network, CNNI, Bloomberg, CNBC. These channels include commercial or private enterprises as well as public service channels, both cabled and terrestrial.

Re-broadcasting of selected programmes

This expansion model is for example exercised by ABC, CNBC, BBC and can be regarded as an advanced 'by-product' of the above mentioned channels. This model also dominates the internationalization of television in East European markets (Nova) but also on Southeast Asian Markets (Star TV). It involves the production of pre-packaged programmes exclusively for the international market, but also magazine-type programmes for highly regulated markets, such as Europe, which permit the insertion of 'regional' issues in order to meet continental/regional regulations or political restrictions.

Expansion of programme systems

This model is primarily exercised by Rupert Murdoch's News Corporation on the Asian Market. By the lease and sublease of the satellite transponders of Star TV, News Corporation established a system with a variety of international programming. It also provides a 'jigsaw' programme, consisting of attractive items from international channels (such as BBC, CNN, MTV) which are rebroadcast in a carrier-type programme. The Asian Star TV system can be regarded as a 'concentrated' version of BSkyB, which offers a selection of eight channels as a pay TV system[34] in Great Britain.

Carrier programmes and vertical integration

This expansion model applies to news agencies (such as ITN) as well as publishing companies. It can be regarded as a new programme model in a diversified market which increasingly requires specified target group programming.

These transcontinental developments have had a fragmenting influence on diverse 'regional' television markets. In Western Europe, satellite technology has been most influential in the re-organization of broadcasting systems. Commercially/privately organised television channels have emerged and shaped new markets. The commercialization of television has also brought about the reshaping of public broadcasting and refined what public service functions on a competitive television market are about.[35] These television channels have introduced a new communication era to Europe and have diminished the traditional structure and programme concepts of national broadcasting stations. Within only 10 years of commercial/private television channels in Europe, several developments of international television programming can be clearly delineated.

The effects of this satellite era can be globally analysed by looking at the television markets which are not defined by state, nation or cultural borders but by satellite footprints. Murdock and Golding (1977) argue that in the 1960s two developments seemed to be most profound in 'advanced capitalist countries':

> The first is the long-term trend towards concentration which has led to an increasing number of sectors being dominated by a handful of large companies. The second is the more recent increase in diversification which has produced conglomerates with significant stakes in several sectors of the communication and leisure industries.

Murdock and Golding describe these economic strategies within the media industry as gathering 'control': 'How far this potential for control is actually realized in practice, how exactly it operates and in whose ultimate interest, are however, empirical questions'. (Murdock and Golding, 1977:28) They also argue that

> ...the traditional company structure in which the founder and his family held the majority of the shares are parcelled out into relatively small holdings, none of which provides a sufficient basis

for effective control over the allocation of resources. In addition, the founding families have progressively withdrawn from their traditional entrepreneurial and executive roles with the result that operational control of the large corporations has passed into the hands of the new elite of professional managers who are the only group with the necessary specialized knowledge and expertise to run the increasingly complex operations of the modern business enterprise. Hence, command over the means of administration has decisively replaced ownership of the means of production as the basis for effective control over the contemporary corporation'. (Murdock and Golding, 1977:29)

'Fragmentation', 'diversification' and 'segmentation' can be found in continental as well as global media structures which are strongly related to each other: global fragmentation influences continental and even national programme developments and shapes new market competitions. The diversification of global programming reveals a variety of programme content in the context of a single programme-area (eg news, music or sport) on continental markets. Segmentation finally implies new programme structures on continental markets within the reach of specific satellite footprints. Segmentation processes are originally initiated by an international/global programme flow into a specific region and subsequently modify the original programme market. This modification can also be described as 'the merging of markets', a term which refers to the national and international programme developments as an interrelated network within diverse world markets. As markets merge, fragmentation, diversification and segmentation play a part not only in programme development (broadcast strategies, market forces, the expansion and specification of target audience programming) but also in the shaping of regional programme cultures.

Whereas traditional theories on international communication take the interrelationship between developed and developing nations into consideration, the proposed broad terminology helps to identify not just an interrelated global broadcasting structure, but also the integration of national, transnational and international programming in specific regional/continental markets. This description could also reveal reception patterns of international programming. However, the few studies which focus on the reception of international programmes undertaken in Western Europe reveal that in this region international programmes are primarily selected for entertainment, whereas domestic channels serve for information purposes. This means that in a world region with a strong public service broadcasting tradition, international programmes have, at best, a supplementary function, simply because of the strong reputation of public service broadcasters in terms of news and the additional variety of informational programmes provided by commercial/private organizations. It can also be argued that in a global broadcasting context the search for high domestic/national audience shares is misleading. The concept of programme 'success' is inadequate to cover the influential role of an international or global programme on a domestic and regional market and casts no light on the meaning of minimal domestic audience ratings achieved by an 'authentic' international programme which gains internationally respectable market shares. For these reasons, the ratings of international and national programmes have to be differently interpreted within a domestic environment.

Fragmentation

Fragmentation is defined as a narrowcast carrier programme or channel market. Global fragmentation was invented with the launch of the first internationally distributed commercial channels, CNN and MTV. Although we are today facing a wide variety of internationally distributed television programmes, these two television channels can well be regarded as the 'entrepreneurs of a new global satellite age'. While these channels implemented the new satellite television era,[36] the international expansion of narrowcast programmes as well as channels has developed six fragmentation models which can be regarded as characteristic for today's international programme organization:

(1) *The internationalization of domestic commercial channels*

This type applies to nationally-organised commercial channels which offer a full programme service (such as RTL Plus, SAT 1, PRO 7, Sky News, NTV).

(2) *The internationalization of carrier programme channels*

Channels which are organised by an international consortium (Star TV, Super Channel/NBC, MBC, TVAsia, NBC Latino) and offer a full programme service consisting mainly of carrier programme segments are part of this model.

(3) *The internationalization of programme diversification*

This model refers to the internationalization of diversified programming (MTV; CNN, Sky, Nickelodoen, ABN, CNBC). It leads to fragmentation: thematic channels arise focussing on such areas as 'music', 'news', 'children's entertainment' and 'sport'.

(4) *The internationalization of domestic public service broadcasting*

Due to satellite technology as well as the dualism of domestic broadcast markets, public service stations redefined their goal of serving a 'public'. Original public service stations are distributed via cable and satellite technology (such as PTT Nederland).

(5) *The internationalization of national channels serving a global audience*

This model covers national channels which are inaugurated to serve a worldwide expatriate audience but also a general global audience. This is the traditional model of truly inter-national broadcasting, represented by AFN (USA), Worldnet (USA), RNTV (the Netherlands), Deutsche Welle and BBC World Service.

(6) The internationalization of private channels

This model applies to those channels, which are privately, as distinct from commercially, organised. These are for example the Catholic church news programme and also Islamvision.

These models serve as examples of a new development in international broadcasting. This development leads to a global fragmentation of not only domestic but also of international and worldwide interconnected programme markets.

Diversification of 'news' and 'information'

The internationalization of the news and information segment of broadcasting has also been subject to what might be described as 'vertical' and 'horizontal' integration. The term 'vertical integration' originally reflected the involvement of media entrepreneurs in other media segments than their original one within a given local market. By extension this technical, economic term can be applied to the new type of national and international broadcasting organization which invests into various media levels and resells a substantial part of the programmes produced in a vertical (global) market. On the local level, vertical integration, according to US broadcast regulation, was subject to legal restriction because it was assumed that the ownership of several media systems within a local market would be a threat to the diversity of public opinion. For this reason, the local market has been legally protected in the USA, so far as political programming is concerned. Elsewhere the national and specifically the international version of vertical integration has become a subject of concern as regards advertising and the importation of Hollywood entertainment. However, neither on the continental nor the international level, has the regulation of political and news broadcasting in favour of a guarantee of diversity of political content been a live issue.

Whereas vertical integration indicates the increasing tendency of media companies to invest in other areas than their original one, the term 'horizontal integration' refers to a 'geographical' expansion of news programming. Models of vertical integration are:

(a) Ethnic or religious channels like the 'Catholic News Network'.

(b) Thematic channels, such as business/financial news (Bloomberg) or *Die Zeit*. These produce carrier programmes which reach international audiences via channels which were either created to be international, or which are internationally-distributed national channels (RTL, SAT 1)

(c) ABN, Asian Business News is a special case. It was founded in May 1994 and attracts a regional, not merely local audience. It broadcasts, by satellite, 18 hours a day of news and analysis in English and a short segment in Mandarin. It can be received in Japan, China, all of SouthEast Asia and Australia as well as eastern India. The channel is available in Taiwan and in Singapore via cable. Due to state legislation, it can only be received in Singapore one hour per day (although Singapore holds a 10 per cent share in the channel). Advertising has been thin for CNNI and Star TV and NBC which just started a satellite service, featuring CNBC programmes from midnight until 8 am. (Gargan, 1994)

Segmentation in different media environments: international case studies

The conventional view of international communication theory is to study communication developments in conjunction with economic growth in semi-peripheral or peripheral capitalist systems. This, however does not take into account different economic developments within low-income regions of the world and makes no reference to, or comparison with, high-income countries. Moreover, it can be argued that the emergence of media industries in diverse parts of the world and countries in various stages of economic development, such as India, Egypt, Indonesia and Brazil cannot be regarded as a new kind of industrial progress or cultural production. These recent developments are not to be viewed as development communication or as media imperialism simply because they reproduce Western media formats and content. However, these media industries do in fact produce their own programmes for domestic use as well as for other international subcontinental markets which copy successful international (for example, US) programme genres, presentation-styles and formats, in order to establish a communication industry of their own. Schiller claims, 'Now we don't see wealthy Anglos any more, but rich white Brazilians enjoying standards of living that would make any middle class American envious'. (Schiller, 1991:22) But these observations do not reflect the increase of worldwide satellite communication where new programmes, new target groups and new types of media communication have already been established and the culture of the 'Third' as well as the 'First' world has been involved. Within this new global communication market 'development communication', 'propaganda' and 'imperialism' can be regarded as issues of previous decades when different technical and political contexts were still in place.

Even across Europe, East and West, households have different types of access to the new technology, since satellite and cable penetration varies from area to area, though television programmes are simultaneously distributed via both technologies and could potentially reach most European households. Audience acceptance of 'foreign' programming is also variously developed within Europe.

Looking in particular at the structure of television news markets on the world scale, and taking account of the great diversity of channels now existing internationally, the following model is proposed. It attempts to reveal a general tendency towards programme internationalization and globalization across different markets, and to describe what is becoming a global television market. This environmental model opposes those approaches which regard developed countries and developing countries simply in terms of various degrees and types of commercialism. For example, McQuail and Siune define such models by employing a broad and general term of 'commercialism'. They developed this term in the late 1980's when European national broadcast monopolies were increasingly undermined by commercial broadcasting systems. McQuail and Siune thus distinguished between European countries with 'relatively "high" commercialism' (Britain, Italy and Luxemburg), '"medium" commercialism' (France, West Germany, The Netherlands, Finland, Spain), and '"low" commercialism' (Denmark, Sweden, Norway, Belgium). Their differentiation of 'high', 'medium', and 'low' commercialism relates to what they saw as the characteristic structure for the late 1980's in Western Europe. Accordingly, they saw the reasons for these different developments in the following forces: '...a historical association between limits to commercialisms and northerliness, protestantism, socialism, and possibly, cultural and educational level of development. In some countries more than others, the press has come to be regarded as a "spiritual" asset for linguistic, cultural, political or regional reasons'; other reasons are seen in small countries with separate languages (more resistant to commercialism). (McQuail and Siune, 1986:163)

The following models of different broadcast environments characterise the specific degree of internationalization and globalization in different worldwide media markets. These markets are described as media 'environments'. This term indicates that they are not defined on the basis of state and national borders but in relation to specific given international broadcast structures of which domestic broadcasting is increasingly a part. These environments in which global as well as international channels operate, reveal the specific function and effect of global channels like CNN.

Although quite obviously these environments are of great diversity even within a continent, it can be argued that these differences are in the process of disappearing because of a global merger of markets, a process which, as we have shown, encourages the diversification of a sector like news within the footprint area of major satellite traffic. The term 'segmentation' is used to describe a particular sector of the global market, in this case that of news, viewed in terms of the international structure of the television industry and patterns of broadcasting structures, a totality in which international/global broadcasting models merge.[37] The following environments are exemplary for this approach. They serve as case studies of five world wide broadcasting regions, seen in terms of the internationalization of news and information programmes.

'Overspill' environment

'Overspill' applies to an uplanned international programme flow occurring because of already established satellite technology. This overspill environment is characterized by a comparatively low degree of regulation of international programme flow and by a low degree of target audiences. The term 'overspill' does not so much refer to active state intervention in order to restrict broadcasting but describes the low attraction of a region from the perspective of international broadcasting. This is not simply the attitude of international broadcasters when approaching this environment, but arises from the environment itself. Whereas in other markets a high density of international programme flow can be observed, and regulation, where exercised, is endogenous, the overspill environment restricts primarily domestic broadcasting and domestic journalism.

Wide areas of the African continent can thus be regarded as exemplary overspill environments with a certain low level of programme inflow from satellite relay stations which are necessary for the global transmission of programme traffic. State regulated broadcasting is widely exercised, international broadcasting is of minor importance. The availability of international channels is limited because three satellite footprints target the African continent. Two Arabsat satellites beam into the Arab northern part of the continent and one, (Intelsat VI) with a wide beam, covers almost the whole continent. Although these satellite footprints divide the continent into two regions (a northern Arab and a southern African), the continent can be divided into three regions: a northern industrialised Europeanised and Arab part; Black Africa in the sub-Saharan region, and South Africa, an industrialized country with strong links to Europe and other Western regions of the world.

Whereas in the regions of the developed world there is internationalization in a global sense but also in the sense that neighbouring countries commonly share a satellite transponder for common inter-national channels, African internationalization is still tied to overspill communication with Europe and the US which are in a position to afford this type of communication.

African broadcasting regulation is not subject of African Congress policy but (as compared to Europe) is regulated by individual governments. State-run broadcasting monopolies therefore exist, with the effect that some governments limit the entry of international broadcasting and others restrict domestic broadcasting for political reasons and censor and strongly restrict journalism. Therefore, governments in overspill environments do not pay attention to the entry of international and global channels because they assume that only a small audience has access to these television programmes (as opposed to the more popular medium of radio, which cannot be technically restricted) and that the programmes have a low degree of political relevance for domestic policy.

Whereas internationalization is regarded in other regions as a lively exchange between countries within one continent, African internationalisation is still (again in comparison to other environments) defined as communication with Europe and the USA. As Ansah remarks

> The last few years have witnessed the drawing up of agreements between some African countries and industrialised nations for the transmission of television programmes via satellite. Such is the case with France's Canal France International, Canal Horizon and TV5-Afrique which packaged programmes under certain mutually-agreed conditions. There is also the classic case of CNN, as well as BBC World Television. (Ansah, 1992)

Communication within the continent is still technically undeveloped. 'In news terms, Africa is viewed as a vast black hole fringed by Libya and South Africa. With the exception of these two countries, it is not a player in the great global power game'. (Fitzgerald, 1989:59) Journalists have been arrested and as a result, 'Africans rely on the foreign media for reliable reports of what is happening on their doorstep'. (Fitzgerald, 1989:59) It is argued that the foreign press takes over the watchdog role of a Fourth Estate for the continent. (Fitzgerald, 1989:61) In order to exemplify two characteristic overspill environments, the following case studies of Nigeria and Ghana may serve as illustrations.

Nigeria can be regarded as an example of an African country having, in terms of that continent, a high degree of press freedom. Nigeria has a daily circulation of 23 newspapers, 54 magazines, 29 radio stations and 32 television stations. 'It is without doubt the freest anywhere in Africa, and it compares favourably in terms of freedom of expression with the standard of even the freest presses of the Western world' (*West Africa*, 1987b:301), though it seems unclear for Nigerian journalists in what this freedom consists. The nation's interest is defined as development journalism since journalism has to relate to the system of which it is a part. (*West Africa*, 1987b:302) Other plans to privatise broadcasting have been discussed in Nigeria. (*West Africa*, 1987b:302) TV carries in Nigeria not only entertainment but also social, political and educational responsibilities. (*West Africa*, 1989, 4) Since then international broadcasters such as Canal Horizons have begun Pay TV broadcasting 19 hours daily for Senegal. (*Medien Bulletin*, 4/1992):8)

Broadcast media increase not only the knowledge gap between the well educated urban and the less well or uneducated rural population. They also widen gaps in life-style by increasing the international orientation of the urban population. Whereas in other environments internationalization brings a widening in the scope of what is broadcast both in outlook and programming (for instance through the re-broadcasting of carrier programmes) in this environment it simply provides a replacement for bad quality domestic programming, caused by self-censorship due to government influence on journalism.

Consequences for audience segmentation are such that the societal élite of the overspill audience prefer international programmes (BBC World Service, CNNI in African countries, US programme in Caribbean areas) to their own programming.

Table 6: CNN Distribution in Africa

Country	Broadcast	Cable*	Hotel/Other	Start Date
Africa: 28				
Algeria			X	1990
Angola	X		X	1991
Benin			X	
Bophuthatswana	X		X	1990
Botswana			X	1992
Cameroon	X			1989
Djibouti			X	1991
Gabon		X	X	1991
Ethiopia			X	1991
Ghana	X	X	X	1991
Keyna		X	X	1990
Liberia			X	1988
Malawi			X	1991
Mauritius	X			1992
Morocco			X	1990
Namibia	X		X	1991
Nigeria	X		X	1988
Reunion	X			1991
Senegal			X	1992
Sierra Leone			X	1991
Swaziland	X			1991
Sudan		X		1992

Source: Africa CNN Country and Territory Client List

Whereas Nigeria is an example of African press freedom, Ghana can be considered as a model for a regulated, though diversified media country. Broadcast media in Ghana are controlled by the government. The Ghana Broadcasting Company (GBC), founded in 1935, operates two nationwide radio services, and four regional stations. The television branch of GBC started in 1965 and provides 46 hours of programming a week.[38]

Ghana's press is among the most diversified, according to a BBC study. The number of papers and circulation figures grew during 1991 and 1992. Foreign papers and magazines are available, provided they have a licence from the Secretariat of Information. The government owns the two major newspaper groups, the editors of which are appointed by the head of state

Table 7: Sources of Information[39]

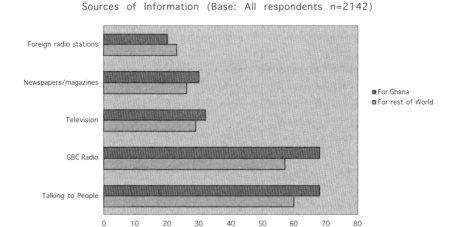

Sources of Information (Base: All respondents n=2142)

The BBC study revealed areas of interest as shown in the figure below:

Table 8: Areas of Interest [40]

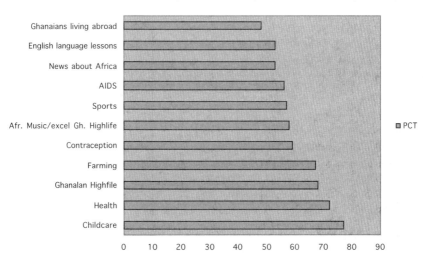

Areas of Interest (Base: All respondents n=2142)

or through the ministry of information. The Ghana sample consisted of 2,142 interviews. Of the respondents, 53 per cent said they understood English, half of these claimed they understood at least a 'reasonable amount'. Over half of the total sample said they had a radio in their home and two-thirds said they had one set only. 'The majority of radios run on batteries (66 per cent), and most respondents say that batteries are usually available when they need to replace them'. (BBCWSS, 1993:9) Ownership of television is significantly 'less common than of radio sets' and 17 per cent of all respondents 'say they have at least one set at home, almost all of which are working'. Of these sets, 62 per cent are black-and-white; colour television and video recorders are both 'less common'. The BBC study concludes, referring to sources of information, that 'the same information sources are relied on for national and international news'. In both cases talking to people is mentioned most frequently.

> The editors and writers have been schooled by the experiences of their predecessors, some of whom were sacked on government orders, or had to leave in order to have their peace of mind ... In Ghana, as in most Third World countries, interference by various officials makes it really difficult for both the private and state-owned media to operate under any appreciable level of freedom and fairness'. (*West Africa*, 1987a:1529)

Of the news items on which the sample were questioned, 'News about Africa' is the most popular (53 per cent are 'very' interested) while 'News about Asia' is the least popular (25 per cent). As shown in the above table, issues of healthcare, childcare, AIDS, and contraception are of the greatest concern, followed by Ghanian 'highlife', agricultural issues, news about Africa and English-language lessons on the same level and, finally, 'Ghanaians living abroad'.

As the study further reveals, television viewing is less common than radio listening.

> One in 10 respondents watch television every or most days, mainly at friends' or relatives' houses. Viewing is highest in the evenings between 19.00-22.30 (GBC News are on at 19.00-19.30 and 21.30-22.00) with a peak between 20.30-21.00. (BBCWSS, 1993:11)

Video watching is less common than television viewing

> ...with only two per cent of all respondents watching every or most days – mainly in public places. Video viewing is highest in the late evenings between 20.00-23.00 hours. The peak viewing time follows immediately after that for television, between 21.00-22.00.

According to the BBC study, audience ratings have increased since the last study was made in 1987. 'While regular listening to the BBC in English is three times higher among men than women (20.8 per cent compared with 9.9 per cent of the sample), it should be noted that the largest increase in the BBC's audience in English has taken place among urban women, aged 35 and above, with secondary education'. The study further reveals that Ghanaians aged 25-44 '...are clearly more likely to listen than any other age group. In terms of education, most listeners are found among those educated to secondary level and above (54 per cent of all respondents)'. (BBCWSS,1993: 15) When the BBC audience was asked about preferred topics, the top interest was in health issues (similar to that of the general audience), but the lower-ranked issues are different. The BBC audience responded, 'News about Africa' and expressed more interest in 'AIDS', 'sports' and 'English Language lessons'. Interest in news is low among women with no formal education and those aged 15 to 19. (BBCWSS, 1993:15) The study also found evidence that the 'BBC audience appears to have a more positive attitude towards foreign stations than the sample as a whole'. (BBCWSS, 1993:16)

Programmes in local languages are necessary

> ...since the six languages used for radio broadcasting is a small fraction considering the fact that there are over 80 different linguistic groups. No provision has been made to cater for minority groups who can understand only their language and cannot also speak or understand the official language, English. (Anepe, 1991:22)

Television in Ghana plays a very limited role because its access is limited to the 'urban elite'. 'The cost of a TV set is beyond the reach of many people. Even though about 80 per cent of programmes of Ghana television are produced locally most of the time, the local productions are inadequate to satisfy local tastes and demands. So people tend to tune to the over-invasive American CNN. Most Ghanaians are looking forward to having a broadcasting system which is structurally and operationally close to the people and above all, a system divested of unnecessary political interference and perceived as truly reflecting the concerns of all sections of the community'. (Anepe, 1992:22) Also until the early 1990's technical transmission problems for television programmes between northern and southern Ghana were quite common.[41] Ghana Television is regarded as 'development education' rather than for the transmission of entertainment programmes. (*West Africa*, 1987a:420)

However, this environment is undergoing some interesting changes. Due to new satellite technology, satellite can be custom-designed for particular market needs. Within this environment, radio and the Internet will increasingly become relevant markets. A new company, WorldSpace, founded by Noa Samara, plans to commercially exploit the radio market in so called 'undeveloped' regions. This company will launch three satellites, AmeriStar (South America), AfriStar (Africa) and AsiaStar (Asia) to provide radio signals to these areas. This company defines its market as developing or undeveloped regions. Revenue sources will be provided by leasing channels, selling premium information services and selling advertisements. Already, various channels have been sold to Bloomberg News; other potential partners are the Voice of America and the BBC.

Besides carrying 'big' signals into the region, this satellite service will also support the inter-regional distribution (essential in this environment) of already existing radio stations, such as a music and information station in Gambia and a music station in Senegal .

State regulated, limited international commercialization environment

This model is defined by the fact that governments own, manage and organise domestic media, and permit domestic commercial broadcasting, especially by foreign owners, but minimally restrict international commercial broadcasting.

Whereas China does not allow foreign ownership or programming in its cable systems, other countries, such as Pakistan, are more open towards the introduction of international programmes. Satellite communication has led to the fact that even within countries with restrictions, various international satellite programmes are available, such as Star TV (owned by Rupert Murdoch) and CNNI, which is the 'only trans-national television news service serving Hong Kong, China, Taiwan and other Southeast Asian countries' (see *Hong Kong and South China Morning Post*, 8, May, 1994). China's policy is to 'protect the fine cultural traditions of the Chinese nation and public order and to give our domestic studios the chance to make better programming' (according to China's Vice-Minister for Radio, Television and Broadcasting. (*South China Morning Post*, 1994)

CNNI was introduced to Bangladesh in 1992. The Bangladeshi Information Minister called for an 'international convenant to define the terms by which satellite television programmers could disseminate information', noting that 'the power of information was something that should be both imposed and resisted'. (*South China Morning Post*, 1994)

It can be argued that these international and global channels have initiated the fragmentation of news on the Asian market.The channel *Asian Business News* was launched in November 1993 in Singapore and intends to serve 'a middle way to chart between Western and Asian news'. (*South China Morning Post*, 1994)

Besides this first 'All-Asian' fragmented news channel, Rupert Murdoch's Star TV is also a player in the increasingly competitive Asian market. Whereas in African countries state regulation does not interfere with international communication, this is not the case in various Asian countries. China, Hong Kong, Taiwan and Korea have forced Star TV to remove the BBC World Service from its menus. News Corporation, which operates Star TV, originally regarded the BBC news service as a 'political liability in Star's quest to develop better relationships with a number of Asian governments, notably the Communist regime in China'. (*Variety*, 1994:35) CNNI will join with ESPN, HBO and Aus TV to launch two other satellite programme systems. It is obvious that Murdoch will expand Star TV's market niche by focussing on local programming. Governments are increasingly trying to regulate the market of international programming and expect international broadcasters to seek relationships with the governments of the regions into which they are broadcasting.

Post-communist transitional environment

Transitional models are characterized by an insecure legal situation (or none at all), a history of socialist media policy and a commercial market in which there are established international and domestic broadcasters as well as various unlicensed local and regional stations. These areas are also targeted by international television channels because they provide a population-dense and economically promising market. The first commercial channel has already been established in Hungary. Nova is a typical model of domestic commercialization in a strong relationship with an international television market. Nova is composed mainly of segments from international channels, such as Disney cartoons, Fox comedies, MTV videoclips and CNN news, since domestic production facilities are still rare and 'domesticated' international products are assumed more likely to attract a large audience share as well as advertisers. 'With its burst of relatively raw, customer-first capitalism, Nova is tapping advertising demand which has been boiling under the lid of the state's private TV moratorium'. (*Business Central Europe*, 1994:28) Nova is still a unique television model on the East European market where the transitional broadcasting phase is defined by limited commercialization, which is officially permitted but unofficially disadvantaged because of transitional government monopolies. Although the commercialization of public service programmes is an ambiguous model, especially in transitional countries, it seems unavoidable because of a decrease in state funds for public service stations. The gradual commercialization of public service programmes, along West-European lines, eg as in Germany, which is being carried out by transitional governments, is confronted with many 'disadvantages such as that programme schedules are not printed in advance, advertisers' maps are not published', 'rates are raised at short notice', 'substitute programmes are aired so that popular programmes are replaced with shows about folk dancing or the national road system'. (*Business Central Europe*, 1994) For this reason the share of advertising on many Eastern European public service transition channels dropped tremendously in the Czech Republic, Poland, Slovakia, Hungary, Romania and Bulgaria. International channels such as CNN, RTL and ABC and media companies such as Bertelsmann and Fininvest are among those who applied for a licence for a commercial channel in Poland. In Slovakia it was recommended by a parliamentary commission that the former second national channel be commercialized by CNN and a domestic broadcaster, between 5 pm. and 5 am.

Russia 'will remain bandit country, shunned by serious western media money and a haven for the country's hundreds of cable TV operators, some no more than a VCR connected through a single apartment block and illicitly showing American movies'. (*Financial Times*, 1992) Although Russia has a media law, it does not, however, regulate broadcasting but print journalism, because television is dominated by Ostankino and

81

Russian TV, both of which continue with governmental journalism. International investors are Turner, with a mix of CNN, children's programmes, geographic documentaries and films. (*Financial Times*, 1992) In Moscow, there is Channel 6, in which Turner holds a 50 per cent interest. Besides Channel 6, TV Moscow, a local city council-funded channel offers a programme with educational content. In addition to Moscow, St Petersburg is an attractive metropolitan market for television, where NTV was established by journalists who formerly worked for the state television companies Russian TV and Ostankino, offering entertainment and news programmes. The share of cable and satellite households is about one per cent which represents 46 million households. (*W&V*, 1993:202) Ostankino is the remaining TV broadcaster for the CIS. Since the parliamentary election, the re-politicisation of broadcast journalism has affected the commercial channel, Channel 6, increasing its audience share because of the re-politicisation process.

Pluralist environment

A new gold rush seems to be transforming Latin American broadcasting into a latter-day El Dorado, in which programmers, cable operators and franchise holders 'are scrambling to stake their claims'. (*Variety*, 1994:37) Whereas CNN is dominant on the overspill market where its only real competitor is BBC World Service, the competition on the pluralist markets has led CNN to tailor its news into appropriate sgements.

Besides CNN and other US news programmes, especially NBC, the Mexican channel Eco is a competitor in the news market niche. The pluralist model, which is one of minimal regulation and thus minimal restrictions on broadcasting, can be found in Latin American countries. The hallmark of this type of broadcasting is that it is state owned but also privately and commercially operated and does not restrict (or restricts minimally) the entry of international channels. The Latin American market is a model for the co-existence of government and commercial broadcasting. This pluralist model refers not only to a diversity of broadcasters in different types of organization but also to a diversity of international broadcasters in this region. This is specifically the case on the Latin American market where the pluralist environment is shaped by satellite televison channels, uplinked from the United States, Venezuela, Mexico, Chile, Peru, Argentine, Canada, Germany, Spain and Italy. The majority of the available 56 satellite channels are transmitted via domestic Latin American satellite systems such as Panamsat and Morelos but also several international and global satellite systems: Intelsat, Spacenet, Galaxy, Hispasat and Brazilsat. Among the 18 satellite channels which have been launched since 1991 are four news channels: namely TodoNoticias, LaRed, CVN, Crónica.

Among the 56 available satellite channels which deliver their programmes in Spanish, Portuguese, English, French, German and Italian there are, besides the Argentinian channels mentioned above, other news channels, such as CNNI, Worldnet, NBC Latino, Telemundo, ECO/Galavisión (news and variety programme *Sur* and *Deutsche Welle'*. [42]

Latin America holds a special place because of its influence on the US and Argentina is the principal market in the region for CNN:

> There are over 8 million TV households in our country, with 30 to 35 per cent who have cable. In addition, there are more than 1.500 cable channels with 3.5 million subscribers ... CNN has a special newscast for the region which airs every two hours beginning at 4:30 pm. (*Noticias*, Argentina, June 1994)

The growing pluralist markets of Argentina and Brazil also influence other regional broadcasting policies in Latin American countries with government restrictions on private broadcasting, such as Colombia, where privatisation of television is currently a political issue:

> Cable systems in Argentina, Mexico, Brazil and even Peru are surging: there's a waiting list for transponders to beam international programming to Latin America, and the privatisation of webs from Chile to Mexico brings the promise of new markets for traditional and DBS suppliers'. (*Variety*, 1994:73)

In this pluralist market transcontinental corporations are shaped by language and cultural links such as those to Spain and Portugal, which jointly operate the Hispasat satellite system. The country with the largest population owning colour television sets is Brazil, the television nation of South America. The second is Mexico (30 million), third Argentina (8.2 million), and the one with the fewest is Uruguay (1.2 million). (*Variety*, 1994,88)

As already mentioned, this pluralist environment forces global channels such as CNNI (as well as TNT Latin America) to tailor a Latin American programme. This consists, for example, of two 30-minute daily newscasts in Spanish, which are delivered via PanAmSat and Morelos 2. Another aspect of this pluralism is that countries of medium income range (so-called transitional countries, in the terminology of development communication), such as Argentina and Brazil, have taken the lead in the broadcasting industry of Latin America, to the point of influencing the programme philosophy of global channels such as CNNI and MTV.

Cable systems operate mostly within metropolitan areas, like Buenos Aires. Argentina has become the prime cable market in Latin America, with about 500 cable systems in operation. Cablevision has about 350,000 cable subscribers; the smaller one, VCC, has about 150,000. Subscribers in Buenos Aires can get CNN, ESPN, HBO Olé, Korean TV, the internationally operating news and entertainment Mexican channel ECO, Televisims in operation. Cablevision has about 350,000 cable subscribers; the smaller one, VCC, has the Brazilian channels Bandeirantes and Manchete, TNT, a Chilean channel, and a local film channel, Space. (*Variety*, 1994:80) In terms of news programming, four local Argentine news services are already on air to compete with the international channels like CNN, ECO and NBC News.

Brazil, the largest country in Latin America and the second largest market in Latin America, is dominated by two megagroups: TV Globo (about 65 per cent share of the Brazilian TV market) and Abril, a publishing company that is involved in vertical integration. Globo launched its operation by setting up the domestic satellite Globosat in 1992. Globo's channels use carrier programmes from ESPN, Tele-Uno, NBC News and Turner Broadcasting. 'Systems being installed have a capacity to deliver 70 channels, 24 of which are already filled with local programming plus an international mix including CNN, Deutsche Welle, TVW from Spain, ESPN'. (*Variety*, 1994:59)

The funding of pluralist markets ranges from total funding through advertising to partial funding, and government and private channels co-exist. The latter include various domestic and regional channels set up by international and global broadcasters, which impedes penetration by globally operating channels such as CNN.

Dualistic environment

This environment is characterized by the co-existence of public service channels and internationally operating commercial channels. The public service broadcasting sector is regulated by the state, and there are distinct restrictions on commercial television operations, national and international. This model is especially found in Western Europe, where diverse public service broadcasters appear on domestic markets in strong competition with various commercial broadcast organizations. Whereas national public service organizations are slowly growing internationally by establishing joint programmes with other European public service organizations (such as 3SAT, and ARTE), commercial broadcasters expand more aggressively internationally. Therefore, the duality of this model applies chiefly to the national and domestic market and less to the international television market in this environment. As in other environments, CNNI, for example, has initiated fragmentation of the news sector in a domestic context (in Germany, NTV) as well as a regional European context (Euronews).

The satellite footprints around the world are increasingly important in defining international communication culture as they regulate the flow of information and communication within a region. The diverse environments and their fragmented diversified programming have to be regarded as specific models of market merging, including that of news and political programming. Whereas the function of CNN on the African market is one of a 'fourth realm' substitute, its function is different in the competitive market of Latin America, where several domestic or regional channels provide 'authentic' news programmes so that the global news channel CNN functions as a supplement. On the post-communist transition market,

CNN's programme competes with governmental broadcasters and national governmental news as well as the local news programmes of NTV in St Petersburg. The dualist environment defines CNN as a commercial 'fact' news broadcaster, and its American-style news presentation competes with traditions of public service in-depth journalism. This merging of markets has direct effects: news has to be distributed in either local, or regional issues (localisation of CNN) in order to be competitive.

The consequences for communication theory are that global communication structures involve new participation models, new political awareness, and the shape of new global political communities as well as new communication spheres. The results for the organizational theory of broadcasting are that because of an increasingly fragmented market and the internationalization of satellite distribution, broadcasting has become more and more a matter of international regulation rather than one of national concern and influence, although in several states where statist broadcast organizations still exist, the statist influence has decreased. Because of the organization of global communication, broadcasting is regulated chiefly either by internationally operating organizations, such as in Europe or by organizations that affect national broadcast laws. This is the endogenous legal model. The exogenous model is influenced by international broadcasting developments (as in India and China).

These models also have consequences for global journalism in the selection of news topics (a new selection process, in view of the expanded global agenda setting) and journalism styles (eg 'fact' journalism), as well as the framing of events in universal or particular news 'language'.

These developments must be taken into consideration when defining the function of a global channel such as CNN in varying circumstances. They are also important in redefining 'foreign' and 'domestic' news, terms which have evolved from the concept of national-oriented terrestrial broadcasting. These categories need to be replaced on the global scale by new dimensions which take account of the concrete political context (differentiating national news) and the wider scope of global news, both human and environmental, and the enlarged background required for contextualising particular news stories. The developments described above lead to new political spheres which supersede national and other traditional social boundaries but lead to a notion of community. (Tönnies, 1963)

The global public sphere is structured by live 24-hour news coverage, by ritual journalism and by broadening and over-emphasizing of news events from earthquakes to press briefings. New types of global political 'interaction' via competing news channels such as BBC, CNBC, CNN and MBC can be observed.

These processes reveal the necessity for a shift of communication theory to issues of global communication as a totality. This does not imply a global homogenisation. It involves meta-theoretical consequences which take into consideration the globally spread intercommunicational flow of media-distributed communication. Seen from this viewpoint media organizations, programming, new audience structures and patterns appear in a new theoretical framework. These developments influence not only communication theory but also journalism, simply through the change from national to international journalism, according to the new definition of national broadcasting in terms of internationality or globalization. In global journalism and the four theories of the press, 'the press' no longer exists. I argue for developing a definition in terms of the topography of communication covered by the relevant media axioms of global communication and comprehension (see also McQuail, 1992:66).

The enlarged definition of nations through their participation in international broadcasting within a framework of internationalization is creating new relations between states, increasingly guided by global norms (see also Robertson, 1990:23).

Notes

1 For the interdependence of universalism and particularism in ancient Judaism, see Long, 1991: pp.21.

2 Which he defines as 'Print- und Bildmedien', 'mündliche, schriftliche oder elektronische Kommunikation', 'modernes Datenwissen', 'klassisches Bildungswissen (Spinner, 1994:34).

3 Wallis and Baran argue that similar developments can be observed in the music and news industries (Wallis and Baran, 1990: pp.247).

4 Those terms and approaches have been brought into the sociological discussion especially by Roland Robertson, whose theoretical implications have influenced to a considerable extent the development of this study; also influential in this area is Mike Featherstone, who contributed a diversified concept of 'global culture' (ie consumer culture).

5 Before the period of Morse's telegraphy, visual signals were distributed via a special code system mounted on top of towers (Höhne, 1977:27).

6 In addition to his list, the Vietnam war was the first televised war and the Gulf War can be regarded as a 'satellite war'.

7 This argument can be illustrated by the television 'spillover' into the regional 'microcosm' of the Caribbean which has always been located within the tracks of US broadcast satellites and has thereby received the international flow of television programs into many small nations. This fact can easily be interpreted by the general and 'old' argument of 'imperialism' which does not contribute much new insight into the diversity of program effects on revitalization of cultural identity or 'third culture' function. Sussman and Lent add an interesting view on this phenomenon, the observation that 'American standards of 'professionalism' and American style formats have gradually begun to take root as important guides to 'quality' and 'professionalism' in broadcasting' (1991:267).

8 The term 'developing country' applies to low- and medium- income countries of the world. These are defined by the World Bank in terms of annual per capita income. Low-income countries are those with an annual per capita income of $ 675 or lower. Medium-income countries have an annual per capita income of more than $ 675, but less than $ 8,356. Accordingly, high-income countries are defined as having an annual per capita income of more

than this amount. These categories are defined on the basis of an economic comparison of all countries of the world, including those with less than one million inhabitants. The World Bank report remarks that these categories do not necessarily imply that all 'developing countries' are undergoing the same or similar process of development and that the term 'countries' does not indicate a legal statement on territorial rights (World Bank, 1994:xiii).

9   This study revealed for the first time the process of information flow within a community. Katz and Lazarsfeld (1969) distinguish between the information reception of an 'opinion leader' and the general public. They observed the specific function of the oral distribution and interpretation of media content by community opinion leaders.

10 According to Lerner, 'development aid to the East ... was initiated in 1949 under President Truman's Point IV Program and rapidly became a fixed feature of American policy. The mood of Point IV - widely hailed as a 'bold new program' and generally understood as a sort of Marshall Plan for the underdeveloped areas- was optimistic and confident' (Lerner 1972:104).

11 An important distinction was made between the terms 'communication' and 'communications', the latter of which can also be understood as the programmatic goal of theoretical approaches. Whereas today communication theory seems more to refer to the communication process itself, the perspective, within the previous decades, of a modernist view was obviously more geared towards another definition, as Davison specifies in his introductory statement of *International Political Communication*: 'Communication' means the 'transfer of ideas by words or other symbols' meaning the whole 'process by which meaning is transferred'. 'Communications' thus indicates the 'messages themselves'. Davison summarizes that 'communication' is 'an almost indispensable word if one wishes to discuss international exchanges of ideas' (Davison, 1965:9).

12 These were Greece, Turkey, Lebanon, Jordan, Egypt, Syria and Iran.

13 This approach was later further developed by Ithiel de Sola Pool.

14 Lerner considers mass media to 'extend the human senses', thus enabling individuals to see and hear things beyond the reach of unaided eyes and ears. 'They do more than this, however. In extending human sensation, they also extend human comprehension. The person who hears or sees a 'media program' is not merely exceeding the reach of his own sense organs; he is being exposed to, and in some way transformed by, a composed and orchestrated version of the new sensory reality. What is more, he is learning how to identify himself by his organs' (Lerner, 1958:60).

15 A somewhat reverse result of neonationalism as a development effect within transitional societies is also observed by Rogers. Neonationalism means the 'process by which individuals change from a modern way of life to a more traditional style of life' (Rogers, 1969:14). Rogers defines Neonationalism as a kind of nostalgia, a symbolic process, an approach to 'be modern' in the traditional way in conjunction with the 'disenchantment with ideas of modernism' (Rogers, 1969:16).

16 Today this concept can be expanded to a citizen of the world and not simply a citizen of a nation.

17 The IPDC consists of 35 member states as an intergovernmental council.

18 Rao, for example, undertook a comparison study of media reception and communication skill development in two Indian villages. (Rao, 1966:50). This study reveals different cultural and aesthetic responses of two Indian villages,

Pathuru and Kothuru, to movies, frequency of newspaper consumption, etc. She shows that Kothuru is more active in terms of newspaper and radio consumption.

19 See below, Chapter 4.

20 This does not so much involve an ideological bias as one which is determined by organizational – ie, commercial – structures and refers to framing of information.

21 In the light of Kivikuru's approach, issues of media imperialism and pop culture can also be discussed. They will reveal that the global dissemination of the same media content, causes different effects which not only refer to developing or developed nations or others but to reception patterns within a synchronized global media culture (Liebes and Katz, 1990).

22 For a psychological discussion of the cultivation approach see Potter, 1991.

23 For further analysis of these new 'imperial' markets, see Sepstrup, 1990.

24 This is the traditional 'persuasion' model, where international broadcasters enter national markets to support political opinion change.

25 See Anderson, 1983; Hannerz, 1990.

26 On the problematic relationship of Intelsat to the US government (see Kavanaugh, 1986).

27 Due to a variety new satellite technology, the conventional licensing requirements can be circumvented (for example by the technical definition of a 'Hybrid' satellite).

28 Intersputnik (see Hudson, 1990:37 and also Mieckiewicz, 1988).

29 Table in Intelsat Annual Report, 1987-88

30 The other global satellite network which has to be mentioned here is Inmarsat, the International Maritime Satellite Organization, founded in 1979 which serves telephone, telex, data and facsimilie transmission as well as for navigation for aircrafts and ships, Inmarsat has 48 member countries.

31 Since the Soviet Union used to lead the world in terms of numbers of satellite launches by annually launching about 'three times as many military and civil satellites as all the rest of the world put together' (Wilhelm, 1990:48/49), Wilhelm argues that the reason for this leadership has to be seen in the fact that Soviet satellites tend not to remain in operation as long as others do and to the 'high priority which the Kremlin gives to space matters both civil and military'.

32 The term 'Hybrid' refers to the technical definition inbetween Broadcasting and Direct Broadcasting satellite technology.

33 Some European Countries established nationwide monopolies, with one institution serving the whole nation and additionally set up regional monopolies within these national contexts in order to serve linguistic requirements such as Belgium and Switzerland.

34 Leo Kirch, a German media entrepreneur and Rupert Murdoch originally planned the adoption of this system in Europe.

35 Today public service broadcasters compete with privately organized television programs for audience shares and seem to move away from their traditional public service programming. 'Ignorance' describes the first years of duality in which public service broadcasters regarded privately organized programming as unequal national market partners. The next phase can be described as 'convergence' which means that public broadcasters are more and more oriented towards the commercial market and seek to compete. The third phase can be described as 'fragmentation' in which the private market segments diversifies its programme by defining new target audiences.

36 Global expansion of CNN not intended in the today's fashion but orginially

implemented as a by-product for CNN in order to benefit from international broadcasters.

37 The only available worldwide data on the reception of news programs which pays attention to the regional specifiation of news broadcasting consists of the BBC Worldwide audience report. This report undertaken by the BBC World Service Audience Research (furtherly abbreviated as BBCWSS), is conducted from a sample of 12 countries and reveals the structure of news broadcasting in these different world areas.

38 Aired Monday through Friday 5:05-11:05 pm. local time, Saturday 10:30 am. - 12:05 am., Sunday 10:30 am. -10:30 pm..

39 Source: Mytton, 1993, p. 10.

40 Source: Mytton 1993, p. 11.

41 'At one period, the transmission station serving the Ashanti region was out of service for two years. In the north, only Tamale had television service, and even then it was not simultaneous transmission with the rest of Ghana. As there was no link facility beween south and north, the films had to be flown from Acra to Tamale for transmission locally the day after they had been transmitted in the south' (*West Africa*, 1988:420).

42 A second segmentation in this environment is shaped by music channels, such as MTV Latin (MTV's Spanish feed), MTV Brazil (MTV's Portuguese feed), Nuestra Música 2, Music 21, Telehits, Cablecito (*Variety*, 1994:44).

2

Global News and the Expansion of Political Communication

Segmentation, or 'individualization', of the former 'mass society' has been defined by Ulrich Beck (1986) in the terminology of political theory as a 'risk society'. This process of individualization is related to a specific change in traditional political and social structures. It is quite surprising that a transfer of this individualization concept to communication theory has not yet been discussed, although the word 'individualization' implies various relationships with communication. The destructuring of traditional patterns of 'togetherness' in a mass society that is becoming ever more 'individualised' is considerably influenced by media. Communication theory has for quite some time criticised the mass audience concept since the increase in channel fragmentation and programme diversity implies a plurality of media content which makes the 'mass media' somewhat outdated even in a national context, let alone internationally or globally. Seen from the viewpoint of globalization, however, these stratification processes can be translated into a hypothesis that we are facing new forms and levels of global standardisation of 'togetherness' in virtual, symbolic or 'real' new collectivities beyond, beneath, or above societal boundaries within a world community or global society. This society is held together by common ethnic and moral norms, ideas of democracy and concern for the global environment, by standardised patterns of childhood and adulthood, social and emotional relations, by collective biographies and individual 'worlds we live in' (*Lebenswelt*) or simply patterns of consumption. Besides this standardisation, we are also facing societal individualization and global stratification processes.

These symbolic communities are established by goods, which Friedman defines as 'blocks of *Lebenswelt*' (Friedman, 1990) selected from the global supermarket of lifestyles offered by the consumer society, (Featherstone, 1991:112) which are 'planned' and 'dreamt about', introducing 'new images and signs'. As Featherstone remarks, this inflation of images brings on an 'overproduction of signs and loss of referents'. (Featherstone, 1991:114) Worldwide ideals of humankind and icons of consumer culture function through the media as globally accepted institutions of political and cultural knowledge. As producers and distributors of symbolic message systems, the media also stratify the general global audience around a specific definition of topics, characters and political crises by creating worldwide news, music and entertainment 'junkies'. Within this context we are also experiencing a new quality of knowledge. In-depth knowledge is replaced by the pace of the demand for 'fast' information on various levels (Spinner, 1994), transmitted via various worldwide media techniques and news systems into the living rooms of the world. These fragments and particles, these keywords and stereotypes, make up a common sphere, and through it take a dominant part in the global 'togetherness' of symbolic communities. Media communication has contributed to the breaking up of traditional collective knowledge, to the shaping of new definitions of the 'good life' and increased demands for political discussion in terms of social movements and extrasocietal, global contexts. The interpenetration of political communication in the media and politics in society is quite obvious, since social movements, or other new political collectivities, are increasingly represented via media-transmitted communication.

Whereas these issues have not yet been discussed in the debate on various aspects of individualization, the phenomenon of a decreasing mass audience has, in a more general sense, been approached from the perspective of communication theory which, regarding the shrinking mass audience as a pendant to the disappearance of mass society, defines various 'counterforces' in the new fragmented ways of communication. These counterforces are most immediately apparent in the new technologies and their implied personalised interaction modes. This force influences the political economy of the communication systems: 'It turns out that the economies of scale in print and broadcast production generate strong counterpressures toward mass-produced, common-denominator, mass-audience media'. (Neumann, 1991:13) It also implies the 'psychology of the mass audience, the semiattentive, entertainment-oriented mind-set of day-to-day media behaviour'. Neumann predicts the elimination of the mass-audience concept especially in political communication (Neumann, 1991:13) and argues that since a 'growing social and political pluralism that corresponds to the diversity of the information environment' (Neumann, 1991:38) exists, new structures of social diversity are shaped. Neumann correctly points out that in the US in particular, the established networks of ABC, CBS, NBC and PBS are decreasing their share in a highly fragmented market. However, this process is no longer unique for the pluralist market of the United States but is also taking place in other broadcast environments (as shown in Chapter 1). The original goal of domestic programming for government-regulated or public service broadcasters is social integration, a political 'unification' through the use of a domestic 'news' framework and explaining the world in a 'domesticated' (Dahlgren, 1991) fashion. These concepts are in decline, as can be observed from public-service-broadcasting market shares anywhere in Western and

Southern European countries. The services are losing their 'cultural' function in many countries, and facing increasing competition with national and international broadcasters, including in the 'news' sector. These networks originally functioned to help the public 'appraise' a country's foreign policy, on the supposition that, as Baran and Wallis argue, 'international news on radio and television could conceivably help us to find out more about how others live and think in the world around us'. (Wallis and Baran, 1990:253) In this sense, a change of information pattern, initiated by new broadcasting organizations, has occurred not only in national contexts but also internationally. Besides these national and domestic developments of audience segmentation, globalization, the trend to worldwide mobility, has increased a tendency for international empathy as opposed to observation. Internationalism and globality has replaced the 'foreignness' of events which happen beyond national borders.

It can also be claimed that not only the stratification of the former mass audience should become a subject of consideration, but also a media-initiated global 'cross-class' communication democracy. As Neumann states,

> Whereas traditionally it had been the economic elite who benefited first from the cutting edge of communication technology, today a professional gold dealer in downtown Manhattan cannot expect to hear about changing prices on the European market any sooner than a hobbyist using a videotex terminal in the Midwest'. (Neumann, 1991:60)

Besides these global cross-class communication patterns, global cross-political communication is increasingly media-related in such a fashion that the same sources of information might be relevant for the global public as well as for political action: 'Today when a news story breaks, such as the disaster of the space shuttle Challenger in 1986, the president and his advisers watch the television reports in the Oval Office along with the rest of the nation'. (Neumann, 1991:62)

Whereas 'modern' political communication used to consist in the distribution of national affairs within the borders of clearly defined nation-states, globalization has led to a more complex 'counter' development – a disappearance of national state interests within a global 'news' community – while at the same time increasing the perspectives of domestic news. It seems as if parallel to (or because of) the global stratification process a new local togetherness has been reshaped which reminds one of the media culture in previous decades, when the media were used to unify the nation.

> Some decades ago, war news, the country's news could be spread among them almost instantaneously. Citizens crowded around President Franklin Roosevelt's fireside to hear him talk, as they crowded around Murrow – their messenger from the battlefield. ... The president's fireside had become more accessible than the mayor's. (Stephens, 1988:279)

The increasing internationalization of news reporting has led to an expanded interest by various segments of the audience in specialised world news content. Besides these new developments, global communication, especially in terms of news, also stratifies the global audience by different modes of communication: 'modern', 'monocultural', 'ethnocentric'. Modernistic communication is characterized by:

(1) A greater degree of 'mindfulness' that is that new 'resources are evaluated as 'better' than 'old' ones, there is a powerful impetus to change, and thus change is celebrated in gleeful mindfulness'.

(2) A 'sense of time', that is that 'earlier' events are seen as 'causing' later ones, and 'new' event/objects are perceived as 'better' than 'older' ones.

(3) Time is perceived as 'finite: a given day or moment will never recur, and all subsequent moments will be affected by what one does 'now'. (Pearce, 1989:145)

Global communication is characterized by fast information, the quality of which is judged by timeliness and not depth, a constant flow of information across time zones, an increasing participation in universal as well as particular events and a redefinition of national-societal context within the news frame of global particularism.

Societal individualization processes which might foster global communication consist in special interest groups, such as political/economic organizations, but also the citizen on the move who appreciates the alien world on the television screen but also – when travelling – wants the familiar environment of sun, sea, sand and wildlife. All these various processes are integrated into a 'global interconnected diversity'. (Hannerz, 1990:237) As diversified global media communication increase, cultures are lifted from an existence within a given society to a broader one with global common bonds. Hannerz contrasts those cultures which are territorial with those 'which are carried as collective structures of meaning by networks more extended in space, transnational or even global'. Hannerz concludes that because of these new structures, cultures are overlapping on a universal and a particular scale.

Whereas the phenomenon of globalization has entered sociological and philosophical discourses in the Anglo-American region, this is not the case in other European countries. Globalization has not been defined within media theory. Although some media theories refer to international issues, these focus more on the transmission process of media programmes originating in America or European countries into international regions. The current discussion on international communication seems to take into account either the technical transmission and its intercultural and intersocietal problems, or new demands for international journalism. The term 'globalization', however, has not entered the academic discourse of media theory in a way that is relevant to current media developments, which are characterized by decentralisation and localisation and which have emerged because of technological, financial, and political and legal developments and are associated with a degree of internationalization (see also Wallis/Baran, 1990:179).

The representation of the 'world' in global particular news programmes: Results of three studies

Unlike global communication itself, the representation of the world within media systems has been the subject of various studies. The following major recent surveys in the field of international communication involve an analysis of 'foreign' programmes in traditional media such as domestic channels or print. The traditional view of conventional networks assumes that a general style of journalism applies to all these news programmes without regard to their organization, new carrier programme journalism or distribution modalities. Another approach attempts a structural analysis of globally distributed media events.

Foreignness in domestic news

One of several large surveys of the representation of foreign news in domestic news programmes was undertaken by Wallis and Baran. They analysed a sample of five American, two British and two Swedish radio and television news programmes in order to specify 'foreign' news reports. In this and other studies, the first problem that arises concerns the question of what exactly is a 'foreign', as opposed to a 'domestic', news story. Wallis and Baran deploy a sliding scale of what is domestic and what is foreign: 'International news reporting tends to reflect the relationships between nations'; for this reason, 'it is quite natural for a foreign news story to glide into domestication. Often journalists will intentionally do this in order to make their stories more understandable and relevant'. (Walllis and Baran, 1990:170) They developed a five-point scale for foreignness, employing conventional distinctions between 'foreign' and 'domestic' in the coverage of these various networks.

(1) 'A train accident in India, for example, where there was no obvious connection with the host (reporting) country would be rated 100 per cent foreign'.

(2) The same story's domestic content would be assigned a zero.

(3) Flooding in the midwestern states of the US 'would be totally domestic in the sample American outlets but totally foreign in Britain'.

(4) If suggestions were made in an American news report 'that these floods were related to the ravaging of the rain forests in the Amazon delta, then a foreign element would have been introduced'. (Wallis and Baran, 1990:172)

Wallis and Baran transfer this differentiated range of 'foreignness' within domestic television news to categories of content analysis so as draw a more detailed picture of the 'Known World of Broadcast News'. They analysed the time devoted to foreign and domestic new stories in American broadcasts on CBS-TV, CNN Headline News,[1] INN News, CH2-KTVU, NPR/ATC, the British news organizations BBC TV, BBC Radio and Swedish TV as well as Swedish Radio.

Table 9: Percentage of Foreign News Items in Various Domestic News Programmes

Source: Wallis and Baran, 1990:172)

The results of the Wallis and Baran study of the percentage of foreign news and the time devoted to it reveal that, despite the fact that Swedish Television and Radio distributed more foreign reports than the other media, it was to the specific amount of domestic and foreign news that one had to look to see the emphasis of a network. After commercials were discounted, *CNN Headline News* produced only 20.8 minutes of general news, of which, according to this study, 3.5 minutes were foreign news. Since this is a headline service, news reports are short and frequent. Comparing the number of stories dealing with national, international, bilateral and multilateral issues, the results indicate 'a general 50/50 rule for the US networks'. However the study also indicates that the amount of time devoted in US television to news about the world 'decreases as one leaves the traditional network half-hours and moves towards the new independents' and the authors conclude that the 'ethnocentricity of the American national suppliers has stayed the same for the last several years (around 50 per cent of foreign stories)'. (Wallis and Baran, 1990:178)

Another type of investigation consisted of a specification of countries involved in the stories. This study reveals that – again – the 'giant continent of Africa is essentially reduced to a few stories from South Africa' and that 'trading nations rarely make the news' (Canada, Japan). The USSR. and

China had a low level of 'newsworthiness' 'except at times of super power summits and ... when disasters and political upheavals occur'. (Wallis and Baran, 1990:183) At the time when the study was undertaken, in 1986, Eastern Europe itself was a whole but hardly existed in 'news' presentation and was thus comparable to South or Central America. The Middle East, on the other hand, did appear regularly in the news on the above-mentioned American, British and Swedish channels. This has been the case for several decades. News of this region consists in a variety of factors 'ranging from Israel and the Palestinians to religious fundamentalism and oil'. (Wallis and Baran, 1990:184) However, as the authors remark, events in South America, Eastern Europe, Africa, and the Soviet Union were more frequently presented in British or Swedish broadcast news than in American.

Table 10: Representation of African News Issues

Stations	Africa									
	CBS TV	CNN HEAD	INN NEWS	CH2 KTVU	NPR/ ATC	BBC TV	BBC RADIO	SWED TV	SWED RADIO	BBC WORLD
%stories										
Africa	2.7	0.8	0	0.6	0.7	1.7	6.4	3.1	4.9	7.0
No of African stories	7	3	0	3	9	5	32	10	18	20
No of South African stories	5	3	0	3	7	5	22	8	14	10

Source: Wallis and Baran, 1990:186

Wallis and Baran noted that when 'Africa' was in the news, it was South Africa that was mentioned. Government conflicts in foreign news were primarily covered by CBS and least on *CNN Headline News*. Reports on international crimes, scandals, and court proceedings 'was a low priority on the CBS *Evening News* but four times higher on BBC TV. ... Neither Swedish radio nor television showed any great interest in international crimes and scandals. For Channel 12, INN, and CNN the percentage figures for foreign scandals and crimes ranged from 7-11 per cent. The equivalent figures for their coverage of this category in domestic stories ranged from 12 to 17 per cent', disasters and accidents were 'not major sources of foreign news'. (Wallis and Baran, 1990:195) Wallis and Baran showed that BBC and *CNN Headline News* presented the majority of stories in the category of 'odd things'.

The New World Information Order revisited

Another study of foreign news was undertaken by Stevenson and Shaw (1984). They approach news communication as 'cultural communication', which includes all forms of communication between nations, such as commercial products, language, and popular culture. In the debate over the north-south and east-west flow of news dissemination, these authors speak of an increasing reverse-flow effect: namely, non-commercial broadcasters in the US broadcasting 'foreign' programmes. The advent of narrowcasting services which seek a narrow slice of the audience provides an increased opportunity for foreign nations to get their programmes on these channels. The authors argue that this opportunity, especially in view of American television, is 'almost unlimited' and that 'the invasion has already begun'. (Stevenson and Cole, 1984:19) This reverse effect is obviously a result of the increased US channel capacity of the early eighties. This process applies today to various global media environments. It can be argued that the reverse effect is a new mode of the era of globalized communication, in which the 'old' imbalance theories (see Chapter 1) cease to be relevant.

Stevenson and Shaw's survey included 17 countries[2] and revealed that in every country 'more attention is given to the local region than to any other part of the world'. This finding applies to Mexican media, which give more attention to Latin America than to anywhere else; to Zambian media, which give more time and space to Africa; to Thai media, which focus on Asia; to Icelandic media, which centre their reports on Western Europe. (Stevenson and Shaw, 1984:37) Besides the vast coverage of issues from the US and Western Europe, with slight slants in different regions, Eastern Europe and other Third World countries were almost 'invisible'. Across the globe – Western Europe, the Middle East, Africa, Asia – 'the nations of Eastern Europe and the Soviet Union are the least visible'. (Stevenson/Shaw, 1984:38). This study also revealed that the cliché of earlier international communication studies, that 'First World' news appears most frequently in Third World countries, had to be redefined.

According to Stevenson and Shaw, it was the Third World, 'that dominates the news of the Third World'. Besides these findings, the authors provided evidence that international news was not dominated by 'social disruption and natural calamity'. They proved that accidents and disasters did not represent 'big news' in any part of the world. 'Across all nations, regions, political, and economic systems, one pattern emerges: news is politics'. (Stevenson and Shaw, 1984:44) 'Between one-quarter and one-half of all foreign news in all of the countries dealt with domestic affairs in other countries or with international relations.' A second cluster of three topics, each averaging about 10 per cent of the total, concerned economics, defence matters (including war), and sports. 'Beyond these five general categories, there is no category of main topic averaging anything like 10 per cent of the total consistently across all countries'. (Stevenson and Shaw, 1984:47)

Stevenson and Shaw also revealed that the big Western news agencies were no longer the major suppliers of international news: 'It can be said that the four Western agencies serve as a major source of international news but surely not the only one and not necessarily even the dominant source'. (Stevenson and Shaw, 19984:53) Other findings of this study were that the Soviet news agency TASS in a country outside of the then Soviet Union was rarely a source for news, and the Non-Aligned News Agencies pool is not mentioned at all. The study revealed that in Latin America a significant use of several of the medium-sized Western European agencies could be noted. In general, the new regional and alternative agencies, which have emerged in recent years in response to the New World Communication and Information order debate, had not as yet become visible in the world's media. Another finding was that media's own correspondents provided 15 to 25 per cent of all foreign news, 'even in some of the smallest and poorest countries'. (Stevenson and Shaw, 1984:56)

The authors conclude that such a striking lack of difference in foreign news is hardly surprising. 'News' is universally defined as politics and foreign affairs and therefore 'newsmakers' are government officials. The activities of ordinary citizens – particularly those who do not act in exceptional ways – are not news in any part of the world. The authors also conclude that 'proximity' and 'timeliness' can be regarded as universal news values and that the amount and variety of information available to editors in various parts of the world was surprising; so, too, was 'the narrow and limited use made of it'. (Stevenson and Shaw, 1984)

The authors confirmed previous studies that the big new agencies provide a great number of news issues. Despite what is generally assumed about Third World news coverage, the study found no evidence that more attention was paid there to natural disasters and accidents than in other parts of the world. Instead, Third World coverage focussed on war and political disruption. It can, however, be argued that this finding may vary from country to country because, due to the increasing participation of Third World countries in global communication, generalising about 'Third World' countries seems to be increasingly inappropriate. Since war and political disruption are 'typical' news items in the Third World, the authors may be justified in claiming that they are typical simply because 'social disruption is greater in the Third World now than in other areas... reporting from the Third World reflects the political situation in that part of the world'. (Stevenson and Shaw, 1984:59)

The authors further argue that the dependence of developing nations on Western news agencies appears to be far less 'pervasive' than had been assumed. 'In most cases, about one-fourth of all foreign news is credited to one of the four Western agencies, although the practice of attribution varies from country to country and much of the news credited to the home country agency or printed without attribution originates with the world agencies'. (Stevenson and Shaw, 1984:59) The authors still found evidence for the genre of 'development news', which consists of 'information about the slow but important progress of developing countries' toward 'social, political, and economic maturity'. Development news is 'not related to specific, fast-moving events, which too often gets left out of the news in the crush of more pressing events'. According to the authors, development news has

> ...the same difficulty competing for scarce time and space as other information not tied to today's events. And Third World editors seem no better than their Western counterparts at finding room for it. Development news, like all news not tied to today's exceptional events, is usually what gets left out'. (Stevenson and Shaw, 1984:60)

Global festive news events

Whereas the studies discussed above analyse 'foreign' news in domestic media channels, Dayan and Katz propose studying news events as such, in order to detect new structures of newsworthiness. In their view, global media events are 'festive' television events, (Dayan and Katz, 1992:5) live 'happenings' which interrupt the news consumption routine. Festive news events are a supertext 'genre.' These supertexts would be the 'funeral of President Kennedy, 'the journeys of Pope John Paul II, 'the Watergate Hearings', 'the revolutionary changes in Eastern Europe'. The authors describe these events as those 'which are organised outside the media' but differ from news events which are initiated by public bodies such as governments, parliaments, or international bodies. (Dayan and Katz, 1992:6) Festive media events can be characterized by interruption of the programme flow, and monopoly of coverage. They are broadcast 'live' from a distant place. 'Festivity' is also characterized by the fact that these events 'put a full stop on everything on air' (Dayan and Katz, 1992:7) and carry semantic meaning. They 'speak of the greatness of the event. And they have a pragmatic aspect as well: the interruption of the sequence of television puts a stop to the normal flow of life'. (Dayan and Katz, 1992:11)

The journalistic style of such live coverage of a remote event dramatically increases the festive quality of the event. It 'takes us back and forth between the studio and some faraway place' and employs 'special rhetorical forms plus the technology required to connect the event and the studio'. (Dayan and Katz, 1992:11) As these authors point out, these events are also embedded in a certain semantic structure which has a 'reconciliation' function. Dayan and Katz also argue that if the event 'features the performance of symbolic acts that have relevance for one or more of the core values of society' this involves 'ceremonial reverence'. Participators and audiences 'unite'; 'almost all of these events have heroic figures around whose initiatives the reintegration of society is proposed'. (Dayan and Katz, 1992:12) Festive events not only 'unify' nations but also unite the world because 'the event enthralls a very large audience. A nation or several nations, sometimes the entire world, may be stirred while watching the superhuman achievement of an Olympic star or an astronaut'. (Dayan and Katz, 1992:11)

Although this concept of festive news events is relevant for global journalism in that it casts light on how a global reconciliation of universal or particular audiences takes place, the authors themselves do not differentiate between the function of festive events for national, international or global audiences. In fact they refer to national audiences which already have a common stock of knowledge so that they attribute a similar value and meaning to a festive event, and are willing to stay tuned despite interruption of their reception routine. It can be argued that festive events reflect universal and particular issues. The increase of global news systems (including the news agency system) which compete for 'festive' events will exploit these commercially attractive types of event in a global, international and national news network. The authors do not examine their different resonance in different cultures. And although they distinguish between diverse patterns of media events (such as celebrating, shamanizing, performing) they do not differentiate between different genres of festive news 'documentation'. Dayan and Katz refer to the general makeup of the audience but not so much to the political, economic or cultural 'reciprocal' effects of these festive news events (where in response events are copied or initiated by competing parties). This might be increasingly the case because media events shape political reality for political leaders as well as for the public.

Although Dayan's and Katz's concept is important for what it reveals about new news journalism, it would be even more valuable if the authors had distinguished between the many different channels that carry festive news, since the character of festivity gradually becomes related to the importance a channel applies to the event. For example, if a full public service channel interrupts its programmme flow for a festive news event, this would indicate a slightly higher societal importance, whereas CNNI's interruption exercises 'festive' breaking news journalism on an almost daily basis.

Besides this, the commercial era has brought to the fore an increasing number of festive programmes and thus decreased and differentiated their importance and unifying effects. The commercial satellite era has also led to interchangeable news events of a festive character. Whereas in previous decades Western news events were broadcast into developing countries via radio (and later television), the increase of global public space due to commercial technology such as satellites and television has increased interest in festive events in developing countries, in diplomatic and crisis journalism.[3]

Dayan and Katz also argue that festive events influence the actor and the action structure (this is commonly called 'television diplomacy').

> Such events associate their principals with sacred values and inspire them in the knowledge that millions, sometimes hundreds of millions, have endowed them with the right to act in the name of those values. Television knows how to dramatise their gestures. Potentially, the actor can do things he could not have dreamed of doing otherwise'. (Dayan and Katz, 1992:75)

On the other hand, participants 'also have something to lose. They are in danger of losing the right to interpret their own gestures. The media make them into symbols, far beyond their power to control'. (Dayan and Katz, 1992:75) Television broadcasters, in the authors' view, also have much to gain and lose because by offering their endorsement to a public event, 'they are catapulted into the centre. They become full-fledged members of the wedding, suddenly welcomed by all'. (Dayan and Katz, 1992:76) A question remains concerning the consequences for new-style journalism, which still attempts to exercise its role as a 'fourth realm of the state', while constantly incurring the risk of a loss of objectivity. When the 'small screen becomes the authorised historian, inviting its vast audience to take part in the chronicling of modernity', these values are modified: they are reinforced in one way, undermined in another, since festive events invite television to compete with the élite's control of the locus of the event and its control of the event's meaning, (Dayan and Katz, 1992:76) which also implies identity-role problems for broadcasters. 'By agreeing to play a role in the representation of public events, broadcasters thereby suspend something of their professional roles as independent critics'. (Dayan and Katz, 1992:76)

Festive news events also have a transforming effect on the perception of history. The process goes something like this:

(1) the festive event addresses a latent conflict;

(2) it reorganizes time and space – that is, history and geography;

(3) thus making formerly unthinkable solutions thinkable.

If the ceremony 'can be viewed as a miniature of the new era, then the events in its wake' demonstrate, that the 'now-thinakable is also feasible'. (Dayan and Katz, 1992:160) The event induces a 'reflexive perception of what came before it. The immediate past is suddenly objectified as an era or a period and given a name. The hours just before the ceremony are now echoes of another era. The past appears as prehistory, and the present is reconnected to an earlier moment when history stopped'. (Dayan and Katz, 1992:164) Society's perception of where it stands has undergone a change.

Effects on journalism are such that media events 'redefine the rules of journalism'; journalists become involved in the events which they report and broadcasters are 'rewarded with status and legitimacy for abandoning their 'adversarial' role, gain status as 'donors' of events'. Media events 'provide media organizations with an opportunity to test new formats and to embark on technical experimentation'. The audience experiences effects such as an interruption of rhythm and focus, transformation of their ordinary role as viewers, a new status for their living rooms, an upsurge of fellow feeling, a connection between centre and periphery. Media events offer moments of technically-induced solidarity. These events have the power to redefine the boundaries of societies and share these media-transmitted events with other nations. (Dayan and Katz, 1992:196-198) These news events are described as festive events because they crystallise latent trends in public opinion and give voice to formerly inarticulate proposals. Other effects on public institutions, in the view of the authors, socialise citizens into the

> ...political structure of society [reinforce] 'the status of the leaders ...displace intermediaries. ...Access to top leaders tends to reduce the operation of selectivity in exposure to political communication ...organizational forms of politics are affected by media events ... lead directly to social and political change ... breed the expectation of openness in politics and diplomacy. (Dayan and Katz, 1992:201-204)

Live broadcasting of media events 'can integrate nations. (Dayan and Katz, 1992:204) Diplomacy is affected by the 'personalisation of power', so that ambassadors 'are made redundant and their role trivialised'.

In this era of global news communication, the terms 'foreign' or 'foreignness' are inappropriate for describing links between an event and its domestic context. The term 'foreign' does not sufficiently reveal the ethnic, cultural or other 'gap' which is implied. In the scope of global communication, the use of the modern terminology 'foreign' and even of 'international' news issues does not reveal the specific exchange pattern of global information. Instead of 'foreign' and 'domestic', the categories 'universal' and 'particular' seem to apply to the global profile of news within an interconnected world and its stratification processes. They also imply a deletion of other international journalism terms such as 'development journalism'. If we employ just the two terms: 'universal' and 'particular' in relation to news, other categories have to be subsumed under these two, but the relationship between the global and the local in world communications, between what is universal and what specific becomes clearer, and the specifics of journalism in a number of media environments are not excluded.

This model disentangles media from society while repositioning both in a global universe where new participation models are coming into being. The question remains of how the assumed reconciliation initiated by festive media events, such as contest, conquest and coronation, is exercised globally. I argue that global festive events can be regarded as 'universal' events. Since in terms of global news communication 'universalism' is decreasing (and can be regarded as the first phase of globalization; see Chapter 1), 'particularism' is increasing because of new participation models in the global news network. I claim further that these two parallel flows involve not only a specific event – the event 'as such' – but also an underlying common ideology, a 'religion' and the idea of a larger level. This is more abstract within the category of universal events than within particular issues. Universal festive events imply concepts of 'humankind', of 'environment', of 'mankind', of 'civilization', of 'democracy', and of 'justice and injustice', whereas particular events more precisely imply a less abstract underlying concept.[4]

Although Wallis and Baran as well as Stevenson and Shaw use a concept of foreignness as presented in the news programmes of domestic broadcasting organizations and print media, their studies reveal some new findings which seem to contradict their underlying concept of 'modernity'. The theoretical discussion referred to in Chapter 1 introduced the concept of 'relativistic modernity', and, within the real world, this relativism had already occurred as Stevenson and Shaw showed (1984). Both tendencies – the empirical practice and the changing theoretical debate – focus on an increased participation by developing countries in global news communication. Another way to approach this idea is to identify universal and particular news issues, which would reveal that universal issues are decreasing whereas the particular are increasing globally. However, these suggested terms do not so much involve the topic (such as social, political, economic or cultural affairs) but its specific framing and mode of presentation.

Although the role of communication in political growth is not new, the quality of it has changed. Whereas in previous centuries the movement of information over distances expanded human societies by extending bonds of identity and interests, the advent of radio accelerated that process by weakening smaller communities, and television opened the world 'without losing contact with accustomed leaders, accustomed subjects of gossip, accustomed newsmongers'. (Stephens, 1988:279) These media implemented a world view of exclusion in which different cultures and societies are defined as 'foreign' and 'alien.' The modern world view gave order to world communication and its effectiveness by employing terms like 'First World' or 'Third World' in designating communication structures. The global view is one in which 'expansion' translates into 'inclusion', where the centre of the world can be anywhere. Moreover, parallel new world centres exist, depending on the particularity of programme content, frame, audience interest and orientation. Not only does this inclusion bring into the 'macroframe' domestic news organizations which become elements of the global whole through new systems of news exchange, co-operation agreements and coorientation practices, it also reveals, in the microframe, a diversified content which includes the globe by appealing to a world 'ideology'. This development is obvious in pop culture, where 'teenagers, for example, may now be more likely to share an interest in personalities, issues and events with their fellows on the other side of town, or even on the other side of the country, than they are with a middle-aged neighbour. In the electronic age, community increasingly is based on commonality of wave length, not locale'. (Stephens, 1988:280) In terms of political communication, this 'satellite footprint communication culture' is less obvious.

The debate on international communication must not only consider global media developments and their effects on international market developments, it must also take in worldwide socio-cultural and political developments tending towards a global society, beyond modern or postmodern viewpoints but in terms of globalization processes.

Globalization, the 'human condition' or 'humankind': Problems of the extrasocietal

The modern view of news communication reveals a strong orientation towards the societal structure of state and nation. Although modern states are increasingly oriented towards norms of international society, in order to redefine a sovereignty that is already being lost, the concept of state and nation is in a process of deconstruction. This is an effect of globalization processes which do not simply expand modern statist political consciousness into one of international or global concern but which shape extrasocietal political communities, values and areas of interest. Although 'the national society in the twentieth century is an aspect of globalization', (Robertson, 1990:26) accelerated globalization began to occur just over one hundred years ago with political, economic and technical advances. Robertson (1990) assumes that within this context other major components of globalization can be seen in relation to concepts of the individual and of humankind. 'It is in terms of the shifting relationships and the 'upgrading' of these reference points that globalization has occurred in recent centuries'.[5] (Robertson, 1990:26)

The process of globalization involves, as already indicated, two parallel developments: it homogenizes and it differentiates. Both processes also involve extra-societal orientations, since global 'polarising tendencies' lift this parallelism beyond state or national boundaries. This shift involves precisely 'the ways in which the world "moved" from being merely "in-itself" to the problem of the possibility of its being "for-itself"'. (Robertson, 1990:23) This model involves a macrostructuralisation of the world order which 'is essential to the viability of any form of contemporary theory'. This comprehension must involve 'analytical separation of the factors which have facilitated the shift towards a single world'. (Robertson, 1992:22) Whereas Cooley's view of the modern enlargement of global consciousness was one simply of human comprehension, of a new comprehension of remote political affairs and events in the twentieth century, the extrasocietal political enlargement due to globalization involves not 'only' comprehension but also action. Examples of this development in extrasocietal political concern can be seen in the increasing popularity of global and international political organizations, such as Greenpeace and Amnesty International (with their 'local' – that is, national – subsidiaries).

Like Robertson, I argue that this extrasocietal global action field is primarily an element of a global notion of the 'human condition' which in today's terminology involves a moral sphere of humanity. 'The human condition' refers not to the concept of 'mankind' as such. It involves an abstract ideological concept of global relativism, but it also refers to precise fields of action (such as policy, humanity, environment, health, population) and concrete concern for geographical areas (such world-crisis regions like

Somalia, Bosnia and China). Robertson defines the collective dimension of the human condition as a common global concern, to be viewed in relation to the concept of cultural community. (Tönnies, 1887, 1963) This term represents a 'sandwich' category in between a liberal globalization approach and the demand (or search) for a connecting element around the globe. The question is whether the human condition can be defined from a global standpoint outside Western philosophy and how it is transferred (or communicated) around the globe. This concept of the human condition is already embedded in 'social action' of any kind. Social action, in Parsons's (1978) view is a concept which is strongly related to societies, and thus even within a world society is an element of national concern. When this concern relates to extrasocietal global matters, it has a symbolic character. This implies also that political 'reality' is more symbolic than social (in Parsons's view) and affects political action insofar as it becomes increasingly symbolic-participatory (for example, is transmitted via 'icons', 'personalities', 'experts', 'representatives' and press 'briefings') and is mediated (for example, in the framework of national, international or global 'relevance') by global information institutions such as CNN and the BBC.

In this respect globalization can be regarded as a new framework for social and political theory as well as communication theory and is able to yield a new metatheory covering the various new structures of global communication. Besides embodying a general shift of international communication theory from the modern point of view to the global, and thus redefining a variety of existing concepts, it also provides a structure for understanding the implications of the new organization of the media, and its effects on various world cultures, and also helps one to see global political communication from an appropriate perspective. The increase in the extrasocietal political spheres corresponds to an expansion of global political media communication. This 'trans-societal' and 'trans-national' level implies, in regard to global culture, a 'third culture' (as initiated by global channels such as MTV, see Featherstone, 1990:1). Seen as an extrasocietal expansion of political information, this third culture easily translates into a third global society (as initiated by CNN, which expressly exercises 'global' journalism and intentionally refers to extrasocietal political information). This process implies new modes of comprehension and new symbolic hierarchies as well as a context without frontiers.

Globalization and modernity

Globalization is a concept which opposes neither modernity, nor postmodernity but includes elements of both. Therefore globalization can be regarded as an enlargement of modernity in a redefined form. It does not imply any intended processes of uni-linear communication (such as those from modernized nations to those which are involved in the process of development) but integrates all different societal stages as well as specific modes of communication.

Opponents of this globalization idea say that it is just another term for the expansion of modern states in areas of economic policy and (pop) culture. Anthony Giddens, who proposes a 'modern' globalization approach, simply transfers the four characteristic stages of modern societal development into a global frame to produce globalization: 'societal surveillance becomes the nation-state system; societal capitalism becomes the world capitalistic economy, societal military power becomes the world military order; and the societal industrialism becomes the international division of labour'. (Robertson, 1992:157)

Traditionally the concept of globalization was part of the debate on 'extrasocietal' affairs: that is, international relations or international studies, where the effect of internationalism was clearly to be seen in national law and politics. (see Robertson, 1990:18)

Globalization and differentiation

As already indicated, Robertson's globalization approach explicitly involves global differentiation, its problems and counterforces. Luhmann (1982) argues that the increasing societal differentiation is directly geared towards a world society and thus ignores sociological differentiation.

In Luhmann's terms, modern society 'has become a completely new type of system, building up an unprecedented degree of complexity' and the boundaries of 'its subsystems can no longer be integrated by common territorial frontiers'. The only remaining system which continues to use such frontiers is the political sub-system, because the segmentation into 'states' appears to be the best way to optimise its own function. Subsystems like science or economics, however, spread over the globe. In Luhmann's view, it has therefore become impossible to limit society as a whole by territorial boundaries. 'The only meaningful boundary is the boundary of communicative behaviour ie the difference between meaningful communication and other communicative behaviour and functional differentiation.' Since all societies communicate 'within the horizon of everything' about which they can communicate, Luhmann assumes that all societies are world societies.

> The total of all the implied meanings for them is the world. Under modern conditions ... and as a consequence of functional differentiation, only one societal system can exist. Its communicative network spreads over the globe. It includes all human (ie meaningful) communication. Modern society is therefore a world society in a double sense: it provides one world for one system, and it integrates all world horizons as horizons of one communicative system. ... A plurality of possible worlds becomes inconceivable. The world wide communicative system constitutes one world which includes all possibilities. (Luhmann, 1982:132)

Whereas Giddens overlooks differentiation in other than modern viewpoints, Robertson argues that the '...whole idea that one can sensibly interpret the contemporary world without addressing the issues which arise from current debates about cultural capital, cultural difference, cultural hegemony and heterogeneity, ethnicity, nationalism ... is implausible'. (Robertson, 1992:161) Robertson opposes Giddens's concept of globalization in which '...the overall argument boils down to an updated version of the convergence thesis – homogenized 'modern man' injected with a special dose of generalized reflexivity'. (Robertson, 1992:161)

In dealing with global processes Luhmann's viewpoint does not sufficiently solve the 'reverse' problem: globalized differentiation. The question remains as to which subsystems are developed by the global system in order to differentiate internally. Robertson's approach raises the question of how global political information affects global differentiation and the deconstruction of nations/states.

Globalization and relativism

Whereas concepts of modernization argue in terms of a 'world order' which is accordingly applied to the global communication context, globalization reduces global interconnectedness from 'order' to 'relativism'. Globalization is thus a matter of a 'conceptual entry to the problem of world order in the most general sense' and requires an 'interdisciplinary' viewpoint. (Robertson, 1990:18) Global relativism is defined in terms of the 'global-human' condition: 'attempting to indicate the structure of any viable discourse about the shape and 'meaning' of the world-as-a-whole paying attention to the issue of global complexity and structural contingency'. (Robertson, 1990:17) This global relativism is difficult to define while avoiding traditional sociological terms which imply different metatheoretical viewpoints. Terms which also refer to an international co-existence are 'international life' and 'cosmopolitanism' and as well as Max Weber's concept of 'modernity spreading across the world'. (Robertson, 1992:158) The concept of globalization itself can be regarded as strongly connected to a critism of conventional sociological approaches towards a global 'whole'.

> Thus we must recognize that globalization was one of the circumstances which produced the particular interests of sociology in its most crucial phase of institutionalisation, but that the interest in globalization was quite slender. (Robertson, 1992)

Globalization is thus embedded in a 'relativistic sociology' approach as well as being involved in its conceptualisation. The relativistic viewpoint implies a 'pattern' of global cultural diversity. It involves global or universal elements of the human condition and concern for it. Globalization also implies a global spread of morality as a basic element for the notion of humankind or the human condition. This refers to the 'concrete structuration of the world as a whole', (Robertson, 1990:20) which reveals a 'global interdependence' and a degree of 'global consciousness'. (Robertson, 1990:22)

Robertson criticizes the term 'internationalism' as being incorrect and inadequate for today's relationships between states. (Robertson, 1990:23) I, too, argue that internationalism is inadequate to describe the differences in social structures throughout the world, and the pattern of global relativism implied by the presence of new political 'quasi-societal' groups. This discussion relates to the debate on the role of the state in a global community. Giddens argues that the development of the modern state has been guided by increasingly global norms concerning its sovereignty. (Robertson, 1990:23) Robertson argues that 'sovereignty resides in the nation to Jeremy Bentham's declaration in the same year of 1789 that there was a need for a new word – namely, 'international' – which would 'express, in a more significant way, the branch of law which goes commonly under the name of the law of nation' as Robertson notes in reference to Bentham (1948:326). (Robertson, 1990:23/24)

Robertson's criticises the false assumption that 'globalism' is already theoretically defined in the construction of 'world systems' and 'world politics'. These concepts refer too much to the modern concept of sociology 'which still represents more an Eurocentric view than a 'real' globalism'. (Robertson, 1990:16) Current sociology as well as 'business, media and other circles' tend to define 'globalization', (Robertson, 1990:19) in a 'modern' fashion without noticing the flaw in the argument.

Robertson pays particular attention to the cultural aspects of globalization. He summarises his arguments in the demand for a multicultural globalization approach which is held together by the human condition. Robertson defines the term 'human condition' in relationship to cultural 'community'. (Tönnies) This latter term represents a 'connecting' globalization approach and the demand for an element that will connect. The question is how the 'human condition' can be defined from a global viewpoint, beyond Western philosophy and on which abstract level (or levels) the definition can be regarded as globally accepted.

The theoretical approach described above casts a whole new light on the phenomenon of global communication, permitting an overview within which global media-network structures can be discovered. This view modifies the earlier approach of 'international' communication insofar as that term is used only for communication between nations. Global communication, however, implies a viewpoint on various transnational (that is, continental, without reference to nations) and global channels (that is, globally operating, like CNN and MTV).

In order to define these new global communication structures, I suggest the following model for analysing the macroframe structure of political news programmes.

109

Macroframe programming and the extrasocietal

International political news programming can be interpreted along the lines of the above concepts. In relation to existing internationally and globally operating channels, the following organizational models can be distinguished.

Model I: Internationalization of national broadcasters

The first phase of globalization was when national broadcasters began distributing programmes internationally. Traditionally, the United States began quite early simply selling its network programmes overseas by marketing US telefilms, and the US was regarded as market leader in the sixties, when the 'truly' international television era began, with other broadcasters modelling their international programme sales on those of the US. Large Hollywood film companies (MGM, 20th Century Fox, Disney and others) had begun to produce television films for their largest markets in Canada, Great Britain, Japan, Australia, West Germany, Italy, Mexico, France, Brazil and Argentina. (Dizard, 1966:160)

> The CBS 1964 year-end report claims that the network is operating abroad in 107 countries and that it is the world's largest exporter in telefilms. NBC, in a 1965 report, tells of sales in 300 markets in 80 countries'. (Dizard, 1966:164)

The networks launched separate divisions for their operations on the international markets and concentrated their sales in those early days on 'light serial programs'. (Dizard, 1966:165)

> One area of telefilm exports where the networks have a virtual monopoly involves news and public affairs documentaries. Although these productions are a distinct minority of the networks' telefilm exports, US public affairs shows are highly popular abroad. From a political viewpoint, they are a prime example to overseas television audiences of American democratic inquiry – and, in particular, Americans' ability to examine their own problems and those of the rest of the world objectively.[6] (Dizard, 1966:165)

Next to entertainment, sport was a lucrative sector in this era for international sales, whereas in the field of news, the networks' export activities were largely limited to providing news film coverage to foreign stations. An aggressive operator in this field in the late sixties was ABC, which invested heavily in strengthening its worldwide newsgathering facilities to serve both its domestic and foreign affiliates. 'However, CBS and NBC both have a strong lead in this field, particularly in the British, Canadian and Japanese markets'. (Dizard, 1966:167) In this era of media expansion, sales were targeted at an assumed worldwide middle class.

After these early stages, national and international broadcasting was still an element on the international television market but was exercised by various countries. The second stage of national and international television broadcasting was the broadcasting of full channels into an international market. For example news programmes originating in Germany started being broadcast internationally as well as at home.

Television was viewed in 1965 as one of the luxury goods of Western countries.

> Only a handful of the more than 90 countries with television operations in 1965 had state-controlled, non-commercial television. Of the rest, about half had a television system controlled directly by the state but permitting some form of commercial participation. In the remaining countries, television operated either as a wholly commercial operation or as a combination of state and commercial operations'. (Dizard, 1966:26)

The reason for the upsurge of commercial television was 'the harsh economic facts of developing and maintaining television operations.... Most governments quickly found out that they could not afford televison as a budgetary item'. (Dizard, 1966:26) Whereas radio operations were financed by licence fees, the 'economics of television would not, however, permit such a simple solution unless licence fees were raised to the point where television would be permanently restricted to an upper-income audience'. (Dizard, 1966:26) Complete commercialization (with merely nominal government supervision) was exercised in Iran, Luxemburg, pre-Castro Cuba, and the Philippines. Limited commercialization with some with state control took place in Italy, Finland and Spain. (Dizard, 1966:27)

Dizard argues that, although admiring the American commercial television market, most

> ...governments took their cue from the European countries whose experience in state monopoly broadcasting was closer to their own. It has been the European rather than the American example which has set the specific pattern of television administrative development throughout the world. (Dizard, 1966: 28)

Among the US broadcasting networks, NBC is the one that has expanded into international markets through joint ventures with Microsoft and Dow Jones. NBC Europe and NBC Asia, the major international NBC outlets, primarily focus on entertainment and documentaries, and also include carrier slots filled by MSNBC, CNBC and NBC Super Sports. In December 1997, NBC and Dow Jones & Company formed a partnership to provide global audiences with fragmented business news programmes. This channel, 'CNBC: A Service of NBC and Dow Jones' will be distributed as a dedicated business channel worldwide.

Model II: National subsidiaries form transnational channels

It is not just the national broadcasters of the US who formed international channels, but also the conventional public service channels of the dualistic media environment in Europe, who began, with the advent of cable and satellite technology in the early eighties, to establish international programmes of a very specific kind. Whereas NBC, as shown above, aims for the worldwide market, European national programmers target primarily an intra-continental one, supporting European cross-cultural communication and understanding. On this basis, the consortium 3 Sat was formed by German, Swiss and Austrian national television to increase the exchange of high quality programming in this German speaking region. Another example is Arte, a French-German cooperative venture, which airs bilingual television programmes, again based on a high standard of programme. The Turkish channel TRT international consists of a mixture of the two Turkish state owned channels and provides entertainment and political information for Turkish audiences throughout Europe. This second stage of television internationalization has become possible through satellite technology and the increasing number of homes equipped with cable and satellite-dishes. At first, broadcasting stations were used as technical rebroadcast facilities for a secondary market supplying programmes from the original channel. This was the case for commercial as well public broadcasters. In the next stage, some of these rerun programs were replaced by authentic productions, until finally a whole channel was formed.

This category also applies to the international channels run by national broadcasters such as BBC World Service Television, currently expanding in conjunction with the cable system operator TCI in the US and Deutsche Welle, the international German television station, based in Cologne with the goal of promoting Germany worldwide.

Model III: National channels broadcast internationally

This model applies especially to commercial channels which distribute their programmes into a transnational region simply because of the technical conditions of satellite distribution or transborder broadcasting. Among these channels are for example German channels such as N-TV, RTL, Sat 1 but also public service broadcasters such as ARD, Südwest 3, N3.

Model IV: Special-interest channels

These special-interest channels are intended for an international and transcontinental audience and are run on commercial lines. They segment the audience according to interests such as news (Euronews, and in Latin America, CVN, Croónica), sport (Eurosport, Sky sport, ESPN), music (MTV, VH-1, Viva), education and documentaries (Discovery), films and other entertainment (Bravo, Sky Movies, Sky Soap, Filmnet), and lifestyle (Travel, QVC). Another development within the last few years is that audiences are segmented by age, especially children (Nickelodeon, Children's Channel, Cartoon Network) and by geographical region (Asianet, TV Asia).

Model V: Global channels

Commercial channels such as CNN and MTV distribute their programs globally. Whereas in the other models, broadcasters gradually expanded their international scope, these channels began by broadcasting globally and developed an additional level of programming 'tailored' for definite geographical regions. These regions are those with high internal competition such as Latin America and Asia (see Chapter 1 for environmental models). These 'tailored' programs are broadcast in local languages and consist of regular and daily slots within the originally globally distributed channel.[7]

Model VI: Carrier programmes

This model consists of a programme slot which is leased to external media organizations which are responsible for the program content and the sale of commercial airtime. This model can be regarded as the 'entry slot' for various media companies, enabling them to reach the international, transnational or even global market. Carrier-programme content is currently dominated by political and economic programming as well as entertainment (Disney Club). Whereas the 'traditional' model of a carrier programme is the one in which a media organization (conventionally a newspaper publisher) produces a programme for a regular slot, these models have developed further to the point where the external producers are not only 'vertically integrated' newspaper publishers but also other television companies (such as CNN, MTV and BBC), which sell a whole programme slot to another such channel (for example, the Hungarian channel Nova). Another model is exercised by CNN, which offers a daily programme, *World Report*, as an 'access' channel for the reports of worldwide broadcasters.

As Negrine and Papathanassopoulos (1990) point out, satellite channels in particular have an extensive need for low-price programmes in order to fill various time slots, outside primetime (and even to fill primetime attractively). As these satellite channels in many cases also need news programming (in order for their offerings to be defined as full programmes) carrier programmes allow publishing companies in particular to access this television niche. For satellite television companies, this cooperation provides the opportunity to fill schedules cost-effectively. As satellite television in many cases broadcasts internationally, the expression 'primetime transmission' no longer refers to the European definition of primetime. The expansion of international narrowcasting as well as the increasing special-audience programmes of these television channels that function as carriers for other channels' programmes also permits the hypothesis that the special audiences are independent from the primetime definition of previous decades. The development from the national 'mass' audience into the internationally homogeneous audience segments leads one to assume a fundamental change in the of diversification of programming.

These macroframe models focus on international, transnational and global broadcasting organizations which have been developed in recent years; a microframe analysis of programme content is also required This analysis would help to identify global information (and the flow of knowledge) about universal and particular issues. As has been argued above, the replacement of the concept of foreign news by a more differentiated terminology reveals to what extent various world regions as well as 'the world' feature in the worldwide programme flow. Universal issues are those of universal concern appealing to a wide audience because of a general topic and or the general relevance of the event in question. Universal events are, for example, war and peace issues, technological and medical advances, fashion, and economic and political issues of an international kind. Particular issues are those involving events which are specific to a restricted community. In terms of global communication, these issues are equally part of the worldwide information flow.

As I have claimed before, the arrival of particular journalism on the global scene is an indicator of a truly media-oriented globalization (in Robertson's definition). The relativism described above consists, in this model, not in a world information order but in equal access to a variety of particular issues within worldwide communication. Various countries which participate increasingly in global communication, such as the so-called 'developing' nations do not seek to participate in order to sell or distribute programs worldwide (unlike those in macroframe Models I-VI). These broadcasters use small programme segments (like macroframe model VII) in order to communicate a particular content to an assumed global community. The worldwide dissemination of universal news issues applies more in this context to broadcasters who have already gained experience in worldwide communication and are located in the countries where these events of universal (political) relevance take place (such as G7 or OPEC countries). Universal issues consist, for example, in world Summits or United Nations conferences.

Because of the increase of international communication along the lines described above, the media and news content disseminated have not only a political and ethnic impact on people's consciousness of a universal humankind, but increasingly on their concepts of particularities. Political media content thus reflects various universal as well as particular elements which may influence state politics as well as international and global politics and thus will shape a redefinition, or at least a differentiated view, of foreign news. This now has to be addressed not only to the target domestic audience but also the international audience or other national audience to which the news film might be sold. On this basis it has to refer to a particular-particular rather than a universal market.

Parameters of a global audience

The stratification of the global news audience is related to the programme flow as well as to the opening of national and regional environments to international and transnational program inflow. The 'individualization' of a mass society in conjunction with a transformation of the former mass audience discussed at the beginning of this chapter applies equally to all worldwide media environments. Because of the decrease of state sovereignty even in restricted media environments, the audience stratification processes are not now confined to Western broadcast markets. The formerly 'transitional' and even 'traditional' societies that used to be unable to participate in the global community because of national broadcast restrictions are increasingly becoming equal members. Transitional societies today are those that are able to transfer themselves into the global community while developing countries find their identity in being 'nations', and the Western world merges to a global community.

I argue that the global media audience is increasingly stratified by globally distributed particular media content. A somewhat similiar approach is developed by Appadurai (1990). Appadurai, too, attempts to destructure the idea of an assumed global mass society which is trapped between 'cultural homogenisation and cultural heterogenisation.' In order to structure this mass society in terms of different dimensions of global culture flow which 'disjoin' the assumed homogenised mass society in a global configuration, he proposes five dimensions:

(a) Ethnoscapes: by this category, Appaduari refers to 'a landscape of persons who constitute the shifting world in which we live: tourists, immigrants, refugees, exiles, guestworkers and other moving groups and persons [which] constitute an essential feature of the world, and appear to affect the politics of and between nations to a hitherto unprecedented degree'. This group also conists of the persons 'with realities of having to move, or the fantasies of wanting to move.' Appadurai remarks that these 'realities' can be found anywhere in the world: for example, 'men and women from villages in India think not just of moving to Poona or Madras, but of moving to Dubai and Houston'.

(b) Technoscapes: this category refers to technology as a mobilizing force. It implies the dimension of distribution of technology as well as the 'export of software engineers'.

(c) Finanscapes: by this category, Appadurai refers to the transnational dimension of economics and finance.

(d) Mediascapes: this dimension refers to 'the distribution of the electronic capabilities to produce and disseminate information ... which are now available to a growing number of private and public interests throughout the world'. This dimension also relates to the 'images of the world created by these media'. Appadurai argues that mediascapes provide large and complex repertoires of images, 'in which the world of commodities and the world of 'news' and politics are profoundly mixed.'

(e) Ideoscapes: this category applies to the ideologies of state as well as to 'counter-ideologies' such as those of movements. (Appadurai, 1990:298/299)

Appadurai also argues that these disjunctive dimensions may replace the conventional centre-periphery models (even those that might account for multiple centres and peripheries). (Appadurai, 1990:296)

The increasing need to view issues of media-related sociology as tied to communication theory becomes most important within the interdisciplinary concepts of 'information' or 'media' society (and societies). The analysis of media-influenced social patterns or of media-shaped social stuctures, described as 'virtual' or 'symbolic' communities, reveals the influence of communication theory on sociology.

A multidisciplinary approach has occasionally appeared in communication theory, but by and large Murdock's and Golding's critique, citing the lack of interrelationship between the theoretical findings of these two disciplines is still profound. Murdock and Golding state that 'media sociologists have generally failed to relate their work to ongoing debates on stratification; theorists of stratification have equally failed to develop an analysis of mass communications'. (Murdock and Golding, 1977:14) They blame both disciplines for ignoring each other's findings given 'the central role of mass communication in relaying social knowledge and social imagery'. Although Murdoch and Golding are especially concerned with the 'collective silence' in terms of social stratification processes in national contexts, their critique may also have validity as regards the growing specialisation of academic discipines, and their increasing complexity, leading to a widening gap between disciplines. Their critique appears to be that stratification theory does not take sufficient account of the findings of communication theory. The general paradigm of communication research, however, is influenced by sociological thinking (and not vice versa). In order to be clearer about communication theory and its view on globalization, it is important to discuss fundamental elements of the current sociological debate on the global human condition.

Notes

1   *CNN Headline News* is the second domestic CNN channel in the United States, devoted to the presentation of short, headline-styled news.

2   Stevenson's method was to take three to four daily papers in each country, main broadcast news, whether radio or television or both. In 1979, his unit is a news item. The countries he examined were the US, in major papers and CBS evening news, and Argentina, Brazil, Mexico, Algeria, the Ivory Coast, Kenya, Tunisia, Zambia, Zaire, Egypt, Indonesia, and Thailand (Stevenson and Shaw, 1984:30).

3   For example, CNN's coverage of Namibia's independence in the *Birth of a Nation* series.

4   It can further be argued that 'festive' events shape the collective knowledge of world generations, and, even more, shape generations according to their 'world' knowledge. See Volkmer, 1992.

5   In this context, Robertson criticises the false assumption that 'globalism' is theoretically defined in the construction of 'world systems', and 'world politics'. 'These concepts refer too much to the modern concept of sociology which still represents more an Eurocentric view than a "real" globalism' (Robertson, 1990:pp.16).

6   Murrow's show, *See It Now* covered the 'indictment of the McCarthy hearings [which] created almost as much as stir in Britain as it did in this country'). 'In the following years all of the well-known US Television public affairs series such as *CBS Reports* and NBC's *Project 20* have been televised in the major television countries throughout the world' (Dizard, 1966:166/167).

7   It is only a matter of time until these slots of a carrier-program type (see Model IV) will be filled by broadcasters from the regional area to which the programme is tailored.

3

Global News for the World Community - Parameters of the Public Sphere between Universalism and Particularism

Although the idea of 'the public' and 'public communication' is a substantial element of communication theory, globalization has brought to the fore a 'public sphere' which demands a modification of conventional public sphere concepts, relating to a new worldwide political community as well to diverse media environments.

The results of the extended global media market and distribution system for news have, been a change in the concept of broadcasting, a modification of programme content and a reshaping of global media environments. Another result, however, has been a slight change in the meaning of the 'public', as related to the media, and the meaning of 'publicity' on a global scale. This process has also initiated a gradual modification of the relation of 'the public' to the communication structure of society, as well as to society itself. It can be argued that because of global communication, the public and its opinion is no longer a substantial element of the political system of a society but has turned into a more or less autonomous global public sphere which can be considered not as a space between the 'public' and the state but between the state and an extra-societal, global community.

Public Sphere concepts

The historical development of the concepts of 'public', of 'public opinion' and 'publicity' must be viewed in relation to the philosophical concepts of the Enlightenment as well as to social developments in the eighteenth and nineteenth centuries, when modern societies were coming into being, with a 'public sphere' which was located between the private and state sphere. It was within this sphere that 'civil' life entered a new phase of modernization. The following three concepts cover the main stages of conceptualisation of the public dimension as it developed from a matter of reasoning and of participation to one of proxy representation.

Kant assumed a strong relationship between individual and 'public' reasoning which was such that reasoning was shaped by the 'public'. The public sphere evolved as a communication sphere insofar as it implied an exchange of political ideas which were formulated in arguments in the language of a 'common comprehension'. It was this comprehension which shaped public reasoning and argumentation as well as the merging of policy and morality, since public agreement limited the principle of individual freedom of reasoning. This public discourse thus had the function of determining a public consensus. The latter was related in Kant's theory to two spheres: the so-called private or unofficial sphere of 'civil' reasoning and the 'public' sphere of academic reasoning within the community of scholars. Kant's use of the term 'public sphere' incorporated the modern notion of the public as a regulatory function of politics in a democratic state, and thus his concept of a public sphere contributed to the social function of journalism as a 'fourth realm' in the sense not so much of a public sphere but as the 'making public' of state affairs.

Kant's concept of the function of 'public' reasoning refers primarily to an agreement arrived at through public discourse and is obvious in the following distinction: 'All actions that impinge on the rights of other people, and whose fundamental principles are incompatible with being made public are unjust'. Kant also states that 'all principles that require to be made public are compatible with justice in politics' (1923) and further,

> I understand by 'making public use of one's reason' what one does as an academic with the regard to the generality of the reading public. By 'private use' I mean what use a man may make of his reason in carrying out a civic office or position, that has been entrusted to him. (Kant, 1923)

Habermas (1992) concludes that Hegel transformed the term 'public comprehension' into 'public opinion'. This, however has different implications for the 'public sphere', as well as the individual citizen, who has to be competent to reach a political conclusion and form an opinion – competent, not in the sense of being a bourgeois property owner but one who is educated in civic matters: a modern 'citoyen'. Hegel's concept of a 'public sphere' was not so much a sphere of reasoning as an 'integrative' sphere within the emerging national civil society of the nineteenth century.

The concept of a public sphere involves an increasing dialectical relationship between the spheres of privacy within society and of public life. It also implies the privatisation of public affairs. The dialectic consists first of all in the slow transformation of public matters into the private sphere and second, in the growing interdependence between private and public issues which began to shape new subspheres in seats of bourgeois culture such as salons but which also modified the former public sphere.

This upcoming culture of bourgeois political reasoning continued to modify the space, the meaning and the content of the former public sphere. Habermas describes the dialectical transformation of the public sphere by the middle of the nineteenth century as follows:

> The private people, gathered to constitute a public, turned the political sanctioning of society as a private sphere into a public topic. Yet by about the middle of the nineteenth century it was possible to foresee how, as a consequence of its inherent dialectic, this public sphere would become under the control of groups that, because they lacked control over property and therefore a basis of private autonomy, could have no interest in maintaining society as a private sphere. (Habermas, 1992:127)

The widening of participatory access interestingly modified the former political public sphere into a new phase of 'public resolution' of any reproductive process in society. (Habermas, 1992:127)

The model of representative publicity relates to a change in the meaning of 'public' in the context of a decrease of public reasoning among the new social groups occuping the public spaces of national communication and the developing media. As Habermas remarks: 'The critical process that private people engaged in rational critical public debate brought to bear on absolutist rule, interpreted itself as unpolitical: public opinion aimed at rationalising politics in the name of morality'. (Habermas, 1992:102) The law of practical reason, political legislation, was subordinated to its control: '...private people had in the meantime formed themselves into a public and had endowed the sphere of its critical use of reason, that is, the public sphere, with the political functions of articulating the state with society'. (Habermas, 1992:104) However what was needed, as Habermas argues, was a 'restricted arrangement to secure for a public opinion' that found itself in the minority, an influence against the prevailing opinions that it was incapable per se of developing. 'In order to save the principle of publicity even against the tyranny of an unenlightened public opinion itself, it was to be augmented with elements of representative publicity ... to such an extent that an esoteric public of representatives could emerge'. (Habermas, 1992:137)

The dialectic relationship of a private and public sphere reversed itself in the twentieth century, when these spheres separated. The public sphere has widened in this century, in terms of discourse, participation and modes of communication. Public discussion has turned into sociability and has taken on additional attributes that

> ...have one tendency in common despite their regional and national diversity: abstinence from literary and political debate. On the new model the convivial discussion among individuals gave way to more or less noncommittal group activities. (Habermas, 1992:163)

Public-sphere sociability has become increasingly informal and lost social and political power, dwindling to informal 'group activities' connected –

and this may imply a new type of public sphere – by public communication. (Habermas, 1992:127)

Habermas describes the public sphere in his view on new mass media: 'The characteristic relationship of a privacy oriented toward an audience was also no longer present when people went to the movies together, listened to the radio, or watched TV'. (Habermas, 1992:163)

The Public Sphere and global mediation

Because of the globalization processes described earlier, the meaning of 'public', no longer exists in the sense that we have just been discussing. As the part played by the media in public debates has increased, the function of a space between the state and the citizens has changed, because the participation of the public audience is channelled through new modes of 'information' and 'consensus'.

Whereas former public service 'spaces' required citizens forming rational political opinions, this 'representative' public fashioned by the media requires information systems and databases. It can be argued that in these circumstances, social consensus – agreement through discourse – is reached via the consumption of the same media products, the same channels and so on. It goes without saying that such a public sphere, especially since national media networks lose more and more authenticity in reporting (because of their international expansion strategies; see Chapter 2), does not relate to political events within society and society's decision about them, but to media-presented political 'festive' (Dayan and Katz, 1993) sensationalism. Political participation in this public sphere is reduced to the reception of representational 'public' issues which are media-transmitted. This public sphere is a public space '...between government and society in which private individuals exercise formal and informal control over the state ... the media are central to this process'. (Curran, 1991:29) The media

> ...facilitate the formation of public opinion by providing an independent forum of debate; and they enable the people to shape the conduct of government by articulating their views. The media are thus the principal institutions of the public sphere or, in the rhetoric of nineteenth-century liberalism, 'the fourth estate of the realm'. (Curran, 1991:29)

The construction of public sphere space has been tremendously widened within the national social context, expanding out onto a global level. Whereas on the national and societal level the participation modalities have been changed to a passive acknowledgment of a daily variety of conflicts, crises, disasters and the debates of the 'representative public' of political leaders, the global level is rich in new cross-cultural, cross-societal and cross-national implications. The global space of an assumed 'public sphere' can be considered as a multi-discursive political space. This has happened because suddenly different concepts of political participation and influence, different modes of political communication became obvious. Just as in international communication global mainstreaming processes of cultural synchronisation have been discerned, a specific synchronisation of a global public audience can also be observed. This term, however, applies not so much to synchronisation of communication within this sphere as to a global synchronisation of the public sphere. This synchronisation has to a large extent been brought about by the internationalization of media and also by the phenomena noted by Appaduari (1990) and described in Chapter 2. This globally acknowledged homogeneous sphere has wiped different modes of political participation and articulation.[1] This sphere can be considered as a new 'representative public zone' whose common bond is not societal traditions of free speech, press freedom or censorship, but a common heritage and cultural forums of rational discourse. The media have become extremely influential since they provide a network among these different global actors and participants, players and consumers. The 'public' thus shaped does not have recourse to rational opinions, to reasoning and discursive agreement.

Communication within this global sphere is related to stereotypes, fiction, and, in Lippmann's term, 'constructed personalities' (Lippmann, 1922:13) and event aesthetics: 'The only feeling that one can have about an event he does not experience is the feeling aroused by his mental image of that event'. (Lippmann, 1922:95) Stereotypes are, in Lippmann's concept, 'a picture of the world': however, a picture of a possible world to which we are adopted.' As Lippmann argues further:

> In that world people and things have their well-known places, and do certain expected things. We feel at home there. We fit in. We are members. (Lippmann, 1922:95)

Interestingly, Lippmann developed his concept of an imaginary public opinion as early as 1922. Although this concept applies to national socio-political contexts, it reveals unexpected structures of global public communication. It can be assumed that the information and communication content within this global public sphere consists of political imagination and fiction. However, this does not imply that all these elements are universally alike. The existence of such a global public sphere has initiated an exchange not of universal but rather of particular elements. It is because of this communication exchange that issues concrning minorities are raised, that Kurdish inhabitants of a German city demonstrate publicly for human rights in Turkey. These demonstrations show how political action and communication are able to back each other up on an increasing scale. The macroframe organization of the media, with its strategies of of fragmentation, diversification and segmentation (see Chapter 1) especially favours particularism (see for example, the increase in ethnic and minority media). (Riggins, 1992)

The political agenda of this global public sphere is shaped by cross-media environmental communication modes: for example by current headlines, programmes like CNN and *World Report* but also by a nightly satellite-delivered news channel broadcast into England by Chinese Television. But the agenda also involves collective cultural issues.

It can also be argued that this global public sphere is not 'public', but is an open extra-societal space which increasingly shapes political opinions. I suggest therefore replacing the term 'global public sphere' by 'mediation sphere' because this latter term suggests a media-related distribution and exchange of knowledge.

The term 'mediation', in regards to international communication, has its roots in the theory of international development communication. It was developed by Daniel Lerner (1962), who used it to describe the introduction of international communication-related modification processes in developing countries: 'people speaking to people'. The term 'mediation', as embedded in Lerner's theory, indicates that 'the idea that international communication is a major agency of social change in the contemporary world is familiar to all of us (but has become a cliché).... . An instance is the notion that international communication consists of "peoples speaking to peoples" (1962:103). In this view, such a sphere of mediation implies a structure in which a transformation takes place. Even these early approaches to development communication had something of the character of 'public communication'.

The context for this change, in my view, is that the roots of universal and individual values, morals and so on, increasingly lie outside society. It can further be assumed that within such a sphere of mediation, political communication is no longer a subject of ideologies or cosmological world views. Ideologies are replaced by substitutes in the same way that the debate within bourgeois culture was replaced by social communities in the nineteenth century. These subsitutes are institutions of information such as CNN (which consists not only of a news organization, but also implies a supertext as the global news channel that presents news and also shapes events).

Especially in the global context of this sphere of mediation, media themselves participate because they not only 'mediate' between global citizens and governments but also 'mediate' exclusively between governments. This is the case when media content, like the live coverage of a world crisis, connects both the global audience to a certain extent and also diverse societal representative institutions which gather information from the same source as the general audience.[2] Media-'mediated' political issues do not consist only in 'pure' information or in the slow dialectic of a rational discourse. Information within the sphere of mediation sphere has a 'dramatic' dimension, too, which is shaped by a picture-driven medium that values news events aesthetically.

The mediation sphere inversely influences media programming, since media, as Gurevitch, Levy and Roeh argue,

...maintain both global and culturally specific orientations ... such as by casting far-away events in frameworks that render thse events comprehensible, appealing and 'relevant' to domestic audiences; and second, by constructing the meanings of these events in ways that are compatible with the culture and the 'dominant ideology' of societies they serve. (Gurevitch, Levy and Roeh, 1991:207)

The authors also remark that in order to be judged newsworthy, an event has to be anchored 'in a narrative framework that is already familiar to and recognizable by newsmen as well as by audiences situated in particular cultures'. (Gurevitch, Levy and Roeh, 1991:207) This relates in sociological terms to Anderson's concept of 'imagined communities' which implies that 'the smallest nations will never know most of their fellow-members, meet them, or even hear of them, yet in the minds of each lives the image of their communion' and 'Communities are to be distinguished, not by their falsity/genuineness, but by the style in which they are imagined'. (Anderson, 1983:15)

Because of the erosion of the socio/political framework and the decrease in the modern global world order, this sphere of mediation is decentralised and unbalanced in its political orientation. Of course, this is the case also because '...the institutional arrangements for transmitting and exchanging television news materials, spawned by the availablity of satellite technology, have transformed the global structure of news dissemination around the world, toward a greater decentralisation of the system'. (Gurevitch, Levy and Roeh, 1991:197) The sphere of mediation does not involve order of any kind, since it is an open extra-societal communication space, but it does, however, affect the particular structures of nations, cultures and so on. For this reason a consensus can never be accomplished, and issues like 'information-rich' and 'information-poor' societies or other terminologies of the Information Age do not apply.

Under this new structuring of global and international extra-societal media, the public sphere, as originally defined (in relation to a nationalist concept of society) as a sphere of societal reasoning, has been replaced by a sphere of mediation. This involves the co-existence of societal and extra-societal 'reality', of a universality deriving from the presence of 'independent' communication – and of particularity defined by national or other forms of 'collectivity' such as peace movements and environment-protection groups operating beyond societal levels. Media internationalization and globalization parallels these growing movements. Whereas Hegel described a dialectic of the private and public spheres, this current development involves a dialectic of national and global, or particular and universal, spheres which operate independently but in specific relation to each other. Whereas some of these new political movements and political non-party activities are of minor national importance, they act on the basis of a global collectivity.[3] In these cases, greater access to globally distributed media increases their global reach and reconstitutes their global collectivity. They gain increased attention in a global, extra-societal context.

Ferguson (1990) describes the new balance of globalization and localisation as 'layering':

> What seems more probable is that increased internationalism in all forms of communication overlays both the current, local ideas about time and space, and the earlier, sensory-based epistemologies where what was directly experienced (seen, heard, touched, tasted or smelled) defined the world with alternative definitions and meanings. This layering of the new upon the old, the novel upon the customary, conveys a temporal elasticity and locational indeterminacy which is, I suggest, more problematic for organizations and individuals than is generally conceded. If this is the case the new media are not providing a boundless media-land of common understanding. Rather, formerly finite absolutes take on a notably relativist character where the temporal consequences may include a trans-historical eliding of past, present and future which replaces old certainties with new ambiguities. (Ferguson, 1990:155)

In relation to a diversified media market and in the context of these new information structures, the idea of citizenry as embedded in the liberal concept has changed. The participation of an active citizenry within a global community is diversified in the same way as common, national and international and global knowledge.

Notes

1   See, for example, Mowlana, 1990.
2   It would be interesting to analyse the global media communication structure within this mediation sphere in view of vertical, horizontal and diagonal global communication.
3   This can consist in a common concern or an actual organization or group.

4

CNN - The Global News Leader

CNNI (Cable News Network International) and the 24-hour news service BBC World Television News of BBC's World Service Television (BBC WST) are increasingly in competition in the global market. Although BBC's World Service Television is not yet available globally – it currently broadcasts into Europe, Asia, Africa, the Middle East, Canada and the USA. – an increase in its technical availability is planned for the immediate future. Competition with CNNI entails several levels. First BBC WST must gain a large global audience share in order to receive credibility as a 'global' network. Second, it needs to gain a large audience in competitive and attractive regional markets, such as Europe, Southeast Asia and the USA. Third, it also needs to make as many cooperative agreements as possible with regional broadcasters for the rebroadcasting of carrier programmes and to have access to satellite transponders in highly competitive markets such as Europe, the US and southern and southeast Asia. Fourth, global expansion can be gained only by co-operation with 'vertical' integrators such as Reuters, who ensure a market expansion in a multilevel news service without further investment (CNNI cooperates with Reuters in order to provide a Videotext news service). The BBC World Service has reached a co-operation agreement with Pearson, the media group which owns the *Financial Times*.

Despite the fact that CNNI and the BBC World Service can be considered the most internationalized news broadcasters, each exercises a specific underlying scheme of 'internationalization' which can be identified in terms of (1) the organizational structure and funding, (2) a specific reputation for global news journalism, (3) market competition, (4) new market opportunities as a news source and (5) out-of-home programmes.

Organizational structure

One of the differences between BBC and CNN is that CNNI is an entirely privately owned, commercially operating station. It has to compete for domestic as well as international audiences by broadcasting an 'attractive' programme in order to be able to compete for air time and to receive subscription fees from international broadcasters who acquire the right to broadcast segments of its output. CNN is also dependent on fees from domestic and international cable operators. Whereas BBC's World Service is a subsidiary of BBC, the public broadcaster, it operates globally as a commercial broadcaster in conjunction with BBC World Televison News. While the BBC is commercial-free and entirely state funded on the domestic market, its global branch operates from the sale of commercial air time. Though the international service does not receive any revenue from the television licence fee levied by the British government, it is not a commercial operation in the same way as CNN. It presents a unique model of the 'commercialization' of a fragmented international public-service channel, taking advantage of BBC news sources, an already existing worldwide network of correspondents, a high global journalistic reputation and the operational facilities of the BBC's news division. It is almost self-explanatory that these different organizational structures involve different programming goals as well as a different requirement in terms of co-operation with other channels in order to have access to news sources.

Global reputation

BBC's international shortwave radio service has had a worldwide reputation for about 60 years. When the BBC began its international broadcasting in 1932, it functioned as the Empire Service, in order to serve the Commonwealth nations. The shortwave radio service was intended to counter fascist propaganda and to launch foreign-language programmes in Arabic and in Portuguese and Spanish for Latin America. Currently the radio service broadcasts in 39 languages (Mytton, 1993). The television service was launched in March 1991.

Whereas the BBC has gained a reputation for objective rather than mass-market-appeal news presentation and gathering, CNN has earned a reputation for airing globally attractive 'mass' news events, such as the *Challenger* explosion, the Tianamnen Square uprising, and others. Because its organizational structure is as a news channel and news source in one, on a commercial basis, it must cover events of this type in order to sell programmes to broadcasters as well as to a large audience.

Competition in regional markets

Regional and local markets gain attraction because they guarantee the technical facilities to tap into a specific market via cable or terrestrial transmission and give access to that market for advertising. Besides these advantages, the need to regionalise a news channel became most obvious when India blamed the BBC for incorrectly representing Indian policy on Murdoch's Star TV in order to tailor news for a political market. The fact that this became an issue reveals the difference on the global market between a primarily national broadcaster such as the BBC WST and a primarily commercial broadcaster such as CNNI. From its inauguration, CNNI has exercised a global participatory model of journalism which most readily avoids regional political problems and, furthermore, opens otherwise closed television markets.

BBC World Service planned to collaborate with the ABC US network in order to pool its international news-gathering resources (*International Herald Tribune*, March, 31, 1993) and cooperate with the South African entertainment pay TV channel M-Net (Botswana), which re-broadcasts BBC programme segments on its pay TV channel M-Net.[1]

In-house news service

Both broadcasters secure their own news resources so as to have exclusive access to news material. CNNI's news-source service has become a model for the launch of similar services for commercial broadcasters who increasingly rely on news agency journalism. CNN has gained an international reputation for live coverage, instantenously transmitted to cooperating broadcasters. Especially in the pluralist environment of the United States, this model has led to the launch of several commercial news services. Whereas in Europe the majority of commercial television organizations subscribe to a variety of major news agencies such as Reuters, Agence France Presse, DPA, WTN and Eurovision, US networks began, on the model of CNN, to provide their affiliates with their own 24-hour news service.[2] The presence of an attractive news channel for the general audience which also functions as a news source for broadcasters has led to new strategies, especially in pluralist environments.

In addition to the above, the United States networks compete increasingly with CNN by expanding their daily news programmes – the number of primetime news magazines has doubled since 1991 – and inventing new technologies, such as online information services or 'news-on-demand.'[3] News-on-demand is a technological development that will enable viewers to watch a news programme at 10 pm instead of 6:30 pm, an idea that is regarded as very appealing. Besides the 'vertical integration' into news agency services or international affiliation, networks have also begun to produce local news programmes in attractive markets. The networks are experimenting too with 'family friendly' news as well as news for a young audience, featuring 'heavy use of graphics, quick cuts between stories, young reporters and in-your-face promotion'. (Tobenkin, 1994:68)

Competition in new market niches

CNN and BBC WST have launched fragmented 'out-of-home' services, such as in-flight programmes.[4] CNN has invented an international hotel subscription in order to increase its dissemination in regions of the world where satellite and cable technology rarely exists. This strategy has led to an increase of CNN's worldwide availability. Still today, CNN is available via hotel dissemination in 25 countries.[5] Additionally, CNN produces a programme package for educational purposes, *CNN Newsroom*, which is satellite-delivered to subscribing schools within the United States and also internationally.

Despite this global and regional competition, CNNI is still *the* world-renowned icon of the new era of commercial news programming, since CNNI invented the market niches for news programming mentioned above and inspired the global news market. The following innovations bear witness to this role.

(1) CNN has earned a reputation among broadcasters for its 'live' coverage of world events. The term 'world events' refers to those political events which are assumed to be of world interest, such as the *Challenger* explosion, the Tiananmen Square riots, Superpower meetings, and exclusive interviews with Saddam Hussein. This coverage of world events has obtained new subscribers for its news source.

(2) CNNI is frequently quoted by news organizations and television stations as well as print media and is used as a co-orientation model.

(3) CNN invented a new technology, satellite newsgathering (SNG), when other news operations were still relying on conventional transmission systems.

(4) CNN has shaped the news format of international broadcasters in the use of graphics, camera angles, and the background monitor screen. It has invented new formats for news, such as the 'newsflash'. Other news operations have followed CNN's lead, such as EBU-Eurovision, which rescheduled its news transmission from five times daily to a permanent service.[6] Its global influence is particularly strong in overspill environments.

The presence of CNN has led to news figuring increasingly as a commodity. CNN has thus encouraged broadcasters, primarily in pluralist environments, to establish various news channels. Examples are local news channels, such as NY1, a news channel for Manhattan. NY1 gained local, national and international attention by being the first news organization to report on the bomb attack on the World Trade Centre on 26 February, 1993. The news operation of NY1 is maintained by video journalism, invented by CNN in its early years, in competitive metropolitan television markets. Regional news channels in the United States are the Orange County News in Florida, News Channel 8 in Washington/DC, New England Cable News, Chicagoland (owned by the *Chicago Tribune*), and News 12 Long Island (*Le Monde*, 1992). CNN has also encouraged the launch of national news channels, such as NTV Germany (of which a 27.9 per cent share is owned by CNN) and Sky News in Great Britain (which is owned by British Sky Broadcasting) as well as the establishment of an international news channel Euronews, belonging to the European Association of Public Broadcasters, Eurovision in Europe and MBC, the Middle East Broadcasting Centre for a transnational Arab community, broadcasting out of London. Other outlets which compete with CNN are, in terms of live coverage of Congress debates and other public-affairs-issues are C-Span and, covering legal and Court hearings, Court TV .

Bloomberg TV, headquartered in London/UK, can be regarded as the fastest growing news service and global competitor of CNN in terms of financial news. Bloomberg news channels broadcast in eleven languages and are therefore successful in attracting regional advertisers. Bloomberg TV provides an interestingly formatted, multi-informational screen, which this service invented. Bloomberg TV currently covers the US (distributed via USA Network and DirecTV), Central and South America, Europe, Africa and the Middle East as well as the Pacific Rim and Asia. This is a unique service, which has been established on a global scale to compete not only with news television and interactive channels (CNN Interactive as CNN's Internet service) but also with regional news programmes (see above) and Reuters and other news services, and is moving into the fragmented global mass-market.

Because of CNN's unique situation in its first years as a cable operation supplying political programming for a national audience, it had to deal with various problems that emerged from the established news organizations. These consisted in restricted access to political events in the White House.[7] The networks also excluded CNN from access to pooled White House material. In a lawsuit, CNN gained recognition as a member of the White House news organization pool on the argument that CNN was 'earnest'. (Whittemore, 1990:196) CNN was also banned by the networks' unions, which refused to accept video pictures from CNN's non-union crews (Whittemore, 1990:261) and from access to the transmission lines of the large telephone companies, AT&T, which had special cooperation agreements with the other networks (Volkmer, 1993). These circumstances laid the foundation for international (and national) cooperation agreements with single broadcasters and were the only solution to providing access to national and international news-event video footage.[8]

International cooperation agreements had also been formed with cable operators in order to convince them to carry CNN in their local cable systems. These early cooperations and privately organised news exchange systems have led to the foundation of CNN's international feed as well as its agency function as the international news source which it operates today.

CNN – The history of a 'news machine'

During its first 10 years CNN has invented new modes of journalism. The fact that news and information were available 24 hours a day has brought about a new understanding of journalism in terms of immediacy, breaking news and fact journalism. CNN also invented the role of the anchor ('newscaster' in British terminology), a role that was downplayed at CNN in its early days in order to emphasise the news itself. (Whittemore, 1990 283)

On 1 June 1980, Lois Hart announced, 'The news will continue from now on and forever', when the Cable News Network began its regular broadcast. CNN was the third available channel in the US cable system. The movie channel HBO (Home Box Office) had been launched in 1972 (McNeil, 1991); Nickelodeon, as a nonprofit must-carry children's channel had already been established; the sport network ESPN was already operating; and USA Entertainment was founded in May 1980, (originating in the Madison Square Garden Sports Network); the music channel MTV followed in 1981.

In a context where most channels were devoted to entertainment, showing films and sport, the setting up of a news channel was regarded by the cable industry as quite peculiar. News and political programming appeared of no or little value to broadcasters. The networks had reduced their airtime in these areas, and news was commercialized in terms of issues, featuring soft news and commercially sponsored anchor presentations. It was assumed that the television audience would not be very interested in political issues. News was presented in a personalised, emotional, dramatic style, magnifying political figures, who were judged by the audience the way they judged actors. (Bush, 1987:331) Politicians were presented in such a way as to evoke emotional responses rather than in political debates and arguments in the context of issues.[9]

Ted Turner, who owned Superstation WTBS, broadcasting from Atlanta, Georgia, into Alabama and Florida, envisioned a 24-hour channel solely devoted to news and information. His idea was to establish a variety of thematic programmes which would be broadcast in magazine-style cycles, such as thirty minutes of politics as in *Time Magazine*, 30 minutes of economic news, like that presented in the magazine *Fortune*, thirty minutes of sport, like that in *Sports Illustrated*, thirty minutes of entertainment, on the model of *People* magazine. These basic thematic structures can still be regarded today as the backbone of the information channel. As opposed to the primetime network news, which was presented by anchors who had already established a celebrity status – people like Peter Jennings and Walter Cronkite – CNN intended to avoid news stardom and reduce news to facts. The role of the anchor or anchor team was defined as simply presenting news in such a way as to focus the viewer's interest on the themes being presented.

In 1980 CNN's audience consisted of one million out of the thirteen million households equipped with cable, and reached 8 per cent of all television households. Besides co-operation agreements with national broadcasters in regions where newsworthy events took place, CNN had to establish a working relationship with the various US cable operators. Turner offered the cable companies a fee of one dollar per subscriber, if the companies in turn fed CNN into their systems. Today CNN is part of the 'must-carry' programme package of basic cable service.[10]

Despite all predictions of the US cable industry, CNN established a promising niche in cable programming, and the networks decided to take a piece of this market by establishing their own news channel. ABC Westinghouse did this in June 1981 by setting up a satellite news channel (SNC), airing short headline-type news sequences. In response to this competing project, Turner initiated his own headline news service, *CNN 2 Headline News*, on 1, January, 1982, which had a head start due to CNN already being well known. This second CNN channel succeeded almost instantaneously on the major markets and drove ABC's channel out of business. Turner took ABC's Headline Service subscribers to CNN 2, and closed the earlier channel. The takeover of ABC's news channel was successful because CNN proposed to cable operators a deal which consisted of signing up for CNN's two news networks by Christmas 1982. If they did so, CNN promised to pay one dollar per subscriber for the next three years: a proposal cable operators could not resist and which led to a disproportionate expansion of CNN within the domestic market of the United States during that period of time.

In 1985 NBC developed plans to inaugurate an all-news channel, but this project failed because of Turner's successful negotiations with the large cable operators. These people had already gained an important gatekeeper function for new cable channel projects. Their increasing power and their ability to select the majority of channels for their systems have made them an important partner in US media industry.

Besides these two television projects, an international news radio station was founded. In 1984, CNN was available in 22 nations of Central America and the Caribbean. This international expansion continued to Europe and Africa and is still increasing, whereas domestic US market shares appear to be shrinking. Recent developments reveal that CNN's reputation in the US is suffering and ratings are in decline because of an increased coverage of soft news stories. (*The Independent*, 7 September, 1994)

CNN sent its satellite signal overseas in the early 1980s in order to gain the right to use news footage from international broadcasters. Although CNN claimed to be an international broadcaster, its programme consisted in those early years of a merger of CNN and *CNN Headline News* both of which originated in the US market and focussed on the US audience. This weakness in international news made the BBC a strong international competitor, since the BBC claimed that 60 per cent of its features were generated for international services. (IHT, 20, 1993)

CNN has become more authetically international within the last few years. It began by anchoring a news programme *The International Hour* (co-anchored from London and Washington DC), live from London in 1990, as well as *World News*. It continued by presenting more international news, even in the US market, by increasing regional language programmes, by setting up a Spanish news channel and a Japanese one (*International Herald Tribune*, 20 January 1993) as well as a

Russian service. CNNI International was launched in the USA in 1995. In Moscow, on Channel 6, which airs a variety of programming and two hours per day of CNNI, CNN's programme is translated into Russian. CNN has been available in Moscow since 1990 on Channel 24. A cooperation agreement with Sputnik/Intervision was already in place. CNN contributes regular carrier programmes to a Russian channel in Moscow as well as to the Spanish Telemundo Group, a New York based Hispanic broadcasting company. International expansion is necessary for CNN as it has already reached all cabled households in the US.[11]

The international American audience can be divided into the following categories: former US citizens, international tourists and travelling professionals. But CNNI's international profile extends far beyond serving these. The per centage of international news exported has reached around 80 per cent. 'News shows such as *Business Asia* and *International Hour* have replaced entries like *Sonya Live* and many of the news programmes depend on a small but growing group of non-American reporters and anchors'. (*Newsweek*, 25, January 1993)

CNN collaborated with a national partner for the first time in Germany. This deal[12] with NTV provided CNN immediate access to the Astra satellite system and gave access to ten million German households (*Frankfurter Allgemeine Zeitung*, 18 December, 1992). To sum up: CNN keeps expanding internationally, and collaborating locally in order to gain local advertisers and explore new market niches, such as out-of-home markets, and customise news markets by using the local languages. CNN is interested in getting international news first and for this purpose has hired anchors from other countries.

Table 11: CNN's International Revenue/CNN's Domestic Revenue:

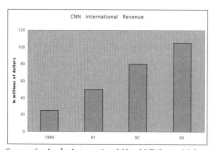
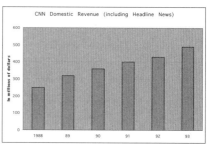

Source for both: *International Herald Tribune*, 20 January 1993

International advertising revenues are slow and subscriptions from cable operators and news sources are important financial backbones. Advertising markets are still regional rather than continental.

Table 12: TBS

Turner Broadcasting System, Inc.

1. Broadcasting
TBS (Superstation), family entertainment
TNT, classis moview, sport events
Sport South Network
CNN
Cartoon Network

2. Video/Film Library
Hanna-Barbera/Ruby Speras Productions (1)
MGM (2)

3. Turner Private Networks, Inc. (TPN)
Airport Channel, Checkout Channel etc

4. Sport Teams/Events
Atlanta Braves (Baseball)
Atlanta Hawks (Basketball)
'Goodwill Games'

(1) eg *Tom & Jerry, Flintstones, The Jetsons*
(2) eg *Citizen Kane, Casablanca, Gone with the Wind*

International expansion strategies also involve programme specials about various regions of the world, such as Asia. Today CNN reaches more than 59 million households in over 140 countries. CNN and CNNI combined reached over 119 million households in 1992. Carrier programmes are, for example, distributed on Channel 6, Bahrain TV, the Volgograd cable channel in the South of Russia. Bangladesh Television (BTV) airs CNNI for six and a half hours daily, and it is seen on three Australian networks.

CNN - The news system

From its beginning CNN was urged to innovate news journalism in order to gain a market segment and to be able to compete with the networks in a small area of programming. The expansion of the news sector into a twenty-four-hour channel required new methods of news journalism and political reporting, a new organization of news-gathering, and a definition of the term 'information'. The driving force was to cut down bureaucracy and keep the organization simple.

CNN – The diversification of a news system

The Turner policy of owning the broadcasting subsidiaries and the technological capacity to transport and sell product without having resourse to any externally-owned medium is also applied to news. News, once gathered, is distributed via various television news channels, as shown in Table 12. Besides the development of a variety of fragmented television news products (for example the sports programme CNNSI as a joint venture of CNN and *Sports Illustrated*, and the financial network, CNNfn), CNN has launched the Internet service CNN Interactive. In recent years, CNNI has increasingly focussed special programme segments for different world markets.

CNN news source

CNN developed as a news source from the need to obtain material from external channels for use in national news operations. These, in turn, could use CNN material in their programmes. Today this scheme has altered traditional local news programmes since they have to compete with CNN. Increasingly they pick up CNN's footage rather than produce local programming. A survey among 12 EBU members in April 1991 which focussed on CNN news sources revealed these results: besides CNN, the members use up to eight news agencies. Among the 12 there were seven public-service stations, two state-owned (former Eastern Europe) stations, and one commercial broadcaster. Two stations were organised as public-service and commercial and public-service and state broadcasters. The tally of use of the CNNI news source, which was established in 1985 with 22 countries participating, reveals that CNN's speed in providing instant news coverage is viewed as unique among news agencies. The quality of reports on events in the US and internationally are regarded as such good quality that they can be used directly for participants' own newscasts. So, apart from its advantage of speed, CNN's live coverage was described by the journalists interviewed as being of great use in their everyday work. Another advantage for broadcasters is that they can use CNN's coverage as an index of daily world events, to see what is happening in the world. Eurovision material, however, is preferred on a 'normal' day. Some of the broadcasters criticise CNN's voice-over technique, which is difficult to dub, and original audio material is sometimes needed. (Volkmer, 1991)

Besides the network competition and local and regional news channels, CNN also has to compete on the US market with a new All News Channel, inaugurated by Viacom Satellite News, Inc, and Conus Communication as a news agency for local broadcasters. The news source consisted at first of a hard news service exclusive to one outlet in each market. A station could pick up up to 45 minutes of hard news per day for use in its regular newscast. It would be notified additionally if a breaking event had occurred which the subscribing station could also use for its programmes.

Table 13: CNN Channel Diversity /

Broadcasting:
'CNN'
'CNN Headline News'
'CNNI'
'Notoiero Telemundo CNN' (CP)
CNN Radio Network
(N-tv: 27.5% share)

Agency:
CNN News source

'Out-of-Home: Markets:
CNN Inflight
CNN Airport Channel
CNN Newsroom
Checkout Channel
CNN Reel News
CNN Teletext (in coop. with Reuters)

The reciprocal agreement with the cable stations consisted in the simple rule that the latter would give their news material to CNN if requested and receive CNN's material if they required it. This agreement was a CNN-specific way of syndication.

The CNN newsroom

The Newsroom is a television project which competes with the schools channel Channel One, operated by Whittle Inc. Whereas Whittle sells airtime even on what it broadcasts to schools, CNN just gathers subscription fees from participating schools. CNN Newsroom consists of a fifteen-minute programme, highlighting events and issues in current affairs, and topics of general interest, supplemented by on-line background material for the schools. This programme is also sold internationally in order to provide up-to-date news programmes for English-language classes in various international schools.

The inflight channel and airport network

The Inflight channel caters to various agencies such as Spafax, who buy programme segments from CNN, MTV, and others in order to provide an in-flight entertainment programme for long-haul flights. The Airport Network was tried out in large US airports such as Miami, and consisted of various thematic cycles. The programme consists of a two hour repeating sequence 'for people on the move', containing the latest news, sports results, business reports, information on travel destinations, human-interest stories, movie previews, a health section, lifeline and People and

Places, and concludes with a weather report and a "fast fact' insert. The programme includes commercials (advertising for luggage [Samsonite], magazines [*Time Magazine* and *New Yorker*], a credit card [Plus Bank Card], or new communication technology [Airphone Service]).

CNN Radio/Sports Radio

A secondary market for CNN's news programme consists of a domestic and international news source for radio broadcasters and a fragmented sports programme for various markets in the United States.

Breaking news and the CNN factor: Issues of commercial journalism

CNN has invented new journalistic styles which were necessary due to the continuous demands of a 24-hour news channel. It had to provide an attractive service in order to survive commercially as a news channel, and, especially in the first years, get access to newsgathering sources outside regular agencies. With its reduced staff of reporters, CNN was finding the going difficult, and was obliged to set up several direct cooperation agreements with other national and international broadcasters. It also invented a new market-attractive journalistic style. This style answered two problems: the channel had to rely on what was, compared to the networks, a limited staff, and as a 24-hour news channel, it was obliged, in order to survive in the news market sector, to present news almost instantaneously: to be first in presenting issues and to present them in a market-attractive fashion. This was needed both to keep up the ratings and if possible increase them, by supplying relatively well-informed people with further information.

CNN invented three journalistic styles and types of news-presentation on this basis: breaking news, unlimited live coverage, and fact journalism.

Breaking news

Whittemore quotes a CNN professional as saying 'Never... have the networks travelled so far and spent so much to cover a story no one is sure will ever happen'. (Whittemore, 1990:182) The idea was to discover a small story that would grow bigger over time. While the story was unfolding, CNN journalists would already be sending back live reports. (Whittemore, 1990:174) This newsgathering and CNN's fact reports have contributed to the image of 'trustworthiness' which was revealed in a poll conducted for *Times Mirror*. It revealed that CNN was regarded as 'the most believable' among the networks, second only to the *Wall Street Journal*. (Whittemore, 1990:299) Viewers were able to sift through the news and separate what was important for them. This news-surfing audience was upmarket, better educated than the average population, and more active as consumers.

Live coverage

'Go "live" as much as possible' was a rule for the early years, very likely prompted by the invention of SNG and further satellite technology. 'Go live ... stay live' applied to coverage of the Haiti crises in 1994. When CNN arrived on the scene, other broadcasters such as the networks were alerted. This live coverage of universal events has contributed to CNN's reputation for instant news coverage and on-the-spot visuals. As one of CNN's presidents, Robert Ross, remarks: 'With only a limited amount of programme time, typically 15 minutes or one half-hour' for news, the 'general network must restrict the number of events covered, tends to edit stories to fill the time'. So, he says, it has 'to add its own comment to put the edited material in context for the viewer'. It may also refuse to report an important speech or, alternatively, may edit the speech to a 30 second sound bite. On the other hand, the full-time news network has an incredible amount of time to fill. It is inspired accordingly, and because it has no general programme schedule to return to, it can cover secondary matters, perhaps ignored by the time-constrained general network, and cover the important matters in full.

In consequence, Ross says that 'live' coverage is necessary,

> ...because timeliness of dissemination is important, but second because taping for subsequent broadcast increases work and handling costs with no corresponding benefit. Live coverage, however, eliminates the opportunity for editing and reduces the inclination for insertion of interpretative material. The viewer receives timely, first hand 'primary source', rather than delayed, secondary, edited information. (Ross, 1991)

The term 'Airwave diplomacy' has been applied to this live-coverage practice. It speeds up political action and responses. This term refers to remarks by politicians such as Fidel Castro, who said 'when there is trouble in the world, I turn to CNN' or Marlin Fitzwater, who stated 'CNN has opened up a whole new communication system between governments in terms of immediacy and directness. In many cases, it's the first communication we have'. (Whittemore, 302) It is assumed that the White House, the Kremlin and other governments issued their official reactions to the events in China's Tiananmen Square on the basis of CNN's coverage.

Fact journalism

The role of the anchor as well as the element of personality in the news itself is downplayed by CNN in order to focus on the presentation of facts. Instead of hiring experienced and well known journalists, CNN invented, in its early years, 'video journalism'. Because of a tight financial budget in the first years, the goal was to recruit young people for a minimium wage and 'give them the opportunity to do everything'. (Kitchell quoted by Whittemore, 1990:122)

With these new styles, the role of journalists has been altered. The concept of 'élites' within the key systems of societal function and reproduction was discussed by C. Wright Mills. (1956, see Lichter/Rothman, 1990) In his view these people make the 'key decisions' within a society. How substantial and closed these 'decision making circuits' are was easy to see during the time of the Gulf War. Lippmann's theory of a social decision-making process which defined the 'class of citizens' as the 'specialized class', and the 'bewildered herd', as the 'spectators' (Lippmann, 1922) who 'serve the people with real power' can be redefined in terms of 'élite', as they not only make decisions but they are also not as well informed today as they were in Lippmann's time in the 20s. Today, when CNN becomes a news source for politicians, for economic leaders and the general 'bewildered herd' alike, the function of Lippmann's categories, which in Chomsky's view continued to act during the Gulf War, obviously have to be described in a new way. (Chomsky, 1991) The media take one of the leading parts within these societal power systems. Besides journalistic studies of the so called 'media élite' (Lichter and Rothman, 1981), which concentrated more on representative audiovisual and print media in the United States, the Media Institute at Washington, DC undertook a thorough survey of CNN in the autumn of 1982 after CNN had been on the air for two years. This study involved a content analysis of the primetime newscasts of the other networks and CNN's *Primenews* newscast, aired during the same period, in order to compare the 'flagship' news programmes of these four channels.[13] The content analysis was intended to search for 'balance', 'sensationalism', 'depth' and 'priority'.

This first study of CNN revealed that CNN gave more time to a:

> ...wider variety of sources, but it also presented a more balanced mix of opposing viewpoints. It relied less on government sources than the broadcast networks and on comments from the 'man in the street' than the other networks. The researchers argue that the more time devoted to the average citizen's reaction (used as illustration for a dramatic news event), means less reliance on information sources. The study reveals that CNN relied more on economists and representatives of business and industry. On CNN, four per cent of business and economic news time could be attributed to a source, compared to 25 per cent of that time on the networks. In practice, this meant that CNN devoted less time to an anchor or reporter discussing the statements of unidentified sources, or editorialising, or simply describing the day's events. (The Media Institute, 1983:10.)

The study also indicated that CNN contained less sensationalism compared to the networks. In terms of the depth of a story, the networks surpassed CNN; CNN was also surpassed by the networks in explaining economic terms. (The Media Insitute, 1983:17) An additional study was undertaken to survey the attitudes of CNN personnel. Of 109 CNN anchors, correspondents, writers, editors, executives and producers to whom the survey was sent, 38 responded. The result of this survey revealed that:

...like the media élite, the CNN respondents were well educated; almost all ... had a college degree, and slightly over a third ... had completed some graduate work or received graduate degrees. ... The average CNN respondent had over 10 years of experience in the news media. (The Media Institute, 1983:32)

The study indicated further that CNN personnel in that early period '...generally possess social values that are markedly more conservative than their media-élite counterparts – values that are, in fact, very much in tune with those of corporate America', since CNN personnel had a stronger preference for 'free-market policies' and a 'stronger opposition to government-intervention policies than did the media élite'. The study concluded that CNN personnel in those days were closer in attitudes 'to business leaders, than to their counterparts in America's most prestigious print and broadcast news outlets'. (The Media Institute, 1983:37) These findings revealed a change of journalistic attitudes in news journalism and hence a change in the media élite, implemented by a new news era in which journalism as a fourth estate with a watchdog role had become differentiated. (see Table 14)

As the study does not refer to the journalistic consequences of being familiar with certain economic theories, this category does not express any theoretical impact on the journalists' work. Interesting, though in a way self-evident, is the conclusion that almost all of the CNN personnel 'either agreed or strongly agreed that people with more ability should earn more'. (The Media Institute, 1983:34) As the Media Institute study compares these results with the Lichter/Rothman survey, the former claims to find a slightly higher degree of economic conservatism among the CNN staff. More interesting is the hierarchy of goals the majority of the 38 CNN employees felt that America should pursue during the next decade. The Inglehart list that was used contains the following items: (1) 'maintaining a stable economy', (2) 'a high rate of economic growth', (3) 'fighting crime', (4) 'making sure this country has strong defence forces', (5) 'progressing toward a less impersonal, more humane society', (6) 'seeing that people have more say in how things get decided at work and in their communities', (7) 'progressing toward a society where ideas are more important than money', and (8) 'trying to make our cities and countryside more beautiful'.

The study is based on Inglehart's category system, which defines goals one to four as representing 'traditional' and goals five to eight more 'liberal' values. The study found that on this basis the CNN staff responded as being more tradition-oriented than the media-élite survey sample of Lichter/Rothman (1981) and concludes,

> This ranking of goals suggests CNN journalists generally possess social values that are markedly more conservative than their media-élite counterparts. ... Based on these responses, it might be said that CNN news personnel are closer in attitudes and outlook to business leaders, than to their counterparts in America's most prestigious print and broadcast news outlets. (The Media Institute, 1983:37)

141

Table 14: Most Important Goals for America in the Next Decade, as chosen by 38 CNN employees and other newspeople

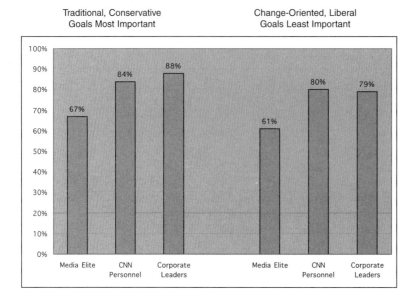

Source: The Media Institute, 1983:36

Table 15: CNNI's International Availability

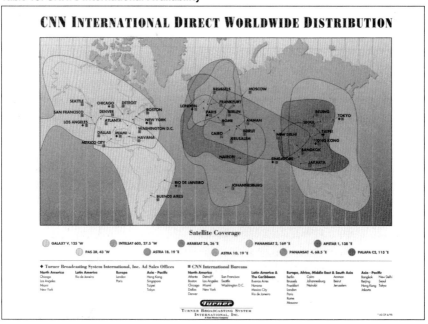

Source: *USA Today*, 15, March 1994

Journalist interviews

In order to evaluate CNN's invention on the journalistic side, five interviews were conducted in March 1991 at CNN's headquarters in Atlanta, Georgia. These qualitative interviews contained 30 questions including the following categories:

(1) Academic education and biographical career,

(2) General views on changes in journalism over recent decades,

(3) Daily news-gathering routines at CNN,

(4) CNN's role in journalistic improvements,

(5) CNN and its relation to the networks,

(6) CNN's responsibilities toward global communication,

Interviewees were selected from different journalistic and professional ranks in order to find variations in approach to global journalism and CNN's role as a globally operating news organization. The interviewees were selected in co-operation with CNN's public relations manager.

The following journalists were interviewed:

(1) the senior producer of CNN's political unit,

(2) a videotape editor of the *Video Journalist's Programme*,

(3) a writer on CNN's *World Report* programme,

(4) the President of CNN's *World Report*, and

(5) an executive producer.

Each interview took between 60 and 90 minutes. After transcription, the interviews were approved by CNN.

Academic education, biographical career: Five case studies

Three of the five interviewees hold bachelors' degrees in some mass communication discipline. Two hold master's degrees, one from Cornell University and one from the University of Warsaw (Poland) and Ohio State University.

Except for the video journalist whose CNN job is her first, the other interviewees had had professional experience before they were employed by CNN.

The senior producer

The senior producer, who is in the age group between 25 and 36, had worked for a radio station in a small town in Nebraska, after which he worked for CNN in Washington, DC, as an associate producer and was in charge of CNN's weekend interview programmes aired from Washington. In 1984 he was transferred to Atlanta and had worked since 1987 for a special series which changed the shape of CNN's news documentary output. He was involved in the production of a series (105 parts) commemorating the 200th anniversary of the American Constitution before he covered the 1989 presidential election, and he was CNN's field producer on Bush's election campaign. In 1989 he worked on a series called *Waging Peace*, which consisted of 30 parts with a two-hour documentary on the efforts at conflict resolution throughout the world.

> I spent six weeks in Africa and interviewed principals in southern Africa about the conflicts that were going on there. Then it was compiled into a two-hour documentary and we did six five-or six-minute stories on the particular region itself; and then I also worked with Special Events at CNN on coverage of the Berlin Wall in November 1989, and then in December the coverage of the Malta summit with Gorbachev and ... Bush ... and then came back to political coverage in 1990 and that's what I do now.

He refused to admit to belonging to any political category and described himself as being politically 'average'. He held a Bachelor of Science degree in communication and journalism.

The videotape editor

She had been employed at CNN ever since leaving college, and was enrolled in CNN's 'Video Journalist Program', which is an entrance-level training scheme.

> And you work the camera and the TelePrompTer, and then you decide where you want to go from there. So I did a little writing, and I decided I wanted to go technical. So I kind of went the route with that, which meant I did some work as assistant director, little bit of technical directing, doing audio for the shows, and then I chose editing, and that's what I have been doing for the past four years.

She considered herself a political conservative, is in the age group between 25 and 34, and holds a Bachelor of Arts degree in radio, television and film.

The **World Report** *writer*

She grew up in Poland and worked there for a weekly newspaper in Warsaw. After she immigrated to the United States she worked as a copy clerk for a newspaper in Florida before becoming an assistant in a news bureau for a Miami station in Fort Lauderdale. After this her journalistic career proceeded as she became associate producer for a national public television business programme. Then she went back to the university and received a mid-career fellowship for a Master's degree in journalism at Ohio State University.

> And after that I did a 10 week fellowship in media management at a place called the Poynter Institute for Media Studies in St Petersburg in Florida. And after that, pretty soon after that, I came to work here.

She was a writer and backup producer for the weekly program *CNN World Report*. She was in the age group between 35-45 and considered herself a political moderate.

The president of World Report

He graduated from Cornell University and holds a Master's degree in journalism with honours. He had worked as a journalist since 1954. He worked for newspapers in various positions such as science writer and Moscow correspondent for the New York *Herald Tribune,* as a science writer for *The New York Times,* a White House correspondent for the *Los Angeles Times* and managing editor of the *Chicago Sun.* He came to CNN in October 1980 as the Washington bureau chief and was one of the journalists of CNN's first period. Later he became CNN's Moscow bureau chief before he 'came back to the United States and started for the CNN *World Report* which was the idea of Ted Turner'. This interviewee was responsible for the setting up of World Report and had been in charge of it since. He was in the 50 and older age group and refused to categorise himself politically as a journalist.

The executive producer

He holds a Bachelor of Arts from Ohio State University in journalism, where he had studied urban affairs, political science, anthropology and economics. He started to work in journalism when he was only fifteen by working for television news at a NBC-affiliated television station in Washington, DC, during the summer when in high school. 'When I graduated from high school I went back to Washington and went to work for WRC and spent my first year at the American University'. At the end of his first year there he went to Columbus, Ohio, as a weekend producer for the ABC station in Columbus. After he had received his college degree, he moved to Denver in order to work as a producer at an independent station. From there he proceeded on his career by working for the NBC station in Denver

> ...as an early morning and later 4:30 pm and then 10 0'Clock producer. Went from there to Cleveland, Ohio, as the executive producer for the ABC station in Cleveland and then to Minneapolis. ... Spent a year there as a supervisor and producer ... and came to CNN in 1984.

At CNN he worked first as a line producer and then as an executive producer for the 4, 5 and 6 0'Clock broadcasts. His age group was 25-34 and he considered himself a political moderate.

General views on changes in journalism in recent decades

Faster pace due to new technology and the advent of a news organization such as CNN are regarded as one general cause of a change in journalism. The growth of electronic journalism has 'far eclipsed print journalism as an important news source'. (Interview No.4) The most experienced interviewee describes in his biography the change of television journalism which he has witnessed:

> When I was new in this business in the 1950's television journalism was a curiosity, radio journalism was important but still not as important as print. You could measure it by all kinds of different things: a White House press conference in the 1950's, television cameras were in the back and the print people in the front. Now that is the absolute reverse. (Interview No.4)

He and others illustrate the pace of the new electronic journalism by using the example of the Gulf War.

> We used to think that television's coverage of the Vietnam War was so immediate. Actually 36 hours for a story to get out of the battlefield into the American home. During this last war people all over the world got news sources live like big destroyers exploding or whatever. That is the whole new dimension. (Interview No.4)

For others, too, the increasing pace of the news being presented plus the extended time scheme within a news channel, is the most important change, perfectly illustrated by the Gulf War coverage.

> People in the United States, people in the world knew what happened in the Persian Gulf pretty quickly because of CNN, and I remember being down in the newsroom when we first heard that Baghdad was being bombed and, you know, this group of people in Atlanta knew it maybe two minutes before the world knew it. And the world knew it because of CNN; the world did know because of ABC, NBC, CBS, Associated Press. The world knew it because of CNN, and I think that's the journalistic accomplishment that's probably the most striking. (Interview No.1)

Alterations in journalism entail not only the way news is presented but also a changing journalistic mentality which was remarked on by one interviewee. To her it becomes apparent that:

> ...a lot of young people go into journalism for the wrong reasons, especially TV journalism: ... a lot of them go for on-air jobs that pay well and give them a lot of exposure but don't have a sense of commitment to knowledge and hard work that comes with a lot of serious journalism that has to be done. (Interview No. 3)

Audience expectations are also considered to be changing.

> It used to be that you would go out and cover a story and then you would come back and look at all of the pictures you had brought back and listen to all of the sound and then [you] wrote up a nice, neat report on the day's event. That does not happen anymore.

Today, he claims, the audience sees the news as it is happening, the audience sees the 'raw news', 'not necessarily uncensored, uncut', which gives the audience much more information to select from and build their own image of the event. By presenting news in this fashion, the role of journalists has altered. They are no longer interpreters of a given situation but, as one interviewee describes it, they act as 'intermediaries', which means that the viewer 'now goes with the journalist to the scene of the story'. (Interview No.4)

Journalistic change is especially apparent in TV, as opposed to print journalism, because of the 'electronic newsroom', which affects techniques of newsgathering as well as presentation. Besides this, CNN's 24-hour news operation requires new techniques. They mean that journalists have to be prepared to present 'the immediacy of what the news is', (Interview No.1) as opposed to other news organizations 'that have a particular slot where they broadcast their news – so they gear up all their news coverage to be presented in this particular hour or two-hour block'. Journalists at a round-the-clock news operation have to be more alert, 'making sure that the facts are correct and making sure that the information that [they] are going to present is clear', because television and radio journalism 'goes by and you don't get it back'. The interviewee claims that journalists have to be careful that technology does 'not take away what your aim should be, and that is to present facts accurately and correctly'. (Interview No.1) The 'facts' of a given event have become the focus of this new journalism. Traditional journalistic practises have had to be redefined to fit the organizational modes of the new-style investigative journalism. A body such as CNN, which is involved in audiovisual as well as in audio news programming, requires on-the-spot, 'breaking'-news fact journalism. The networks or public-service stations in Europe have different approaches. Increasing competition with commercial stations causes them to concentrate on getting their share of the market, rather than thinking in terms of programme philosophies or programme values and public demand.

One interviewee remarked that unlike the previous balance of picture and text, the current relation between pictures and news language is unbalanced. This, in his view, is the case even in television reporting.

> The words in many cases in television news are the facts, are what you report, what you're presenting. And I think you can't get away from that, even though there's a greater dependence on presenting the pictures, particularly in television, and sending the pictures quickly. (Interview No.1)

This procedure entails a journalistic virtue characterized in the statement that the technology should not detract from the fact that journalists have a responsibility not only to present events to the public as fast as they can but to 'step back every now and then and say, 'Is it all that important to get it on first or quickest', when you're not quite sure that it is exactly 100 per cent correct'. (Interview No.1) This resistance to the allure of presenting news without waiting patiently to get the facts right, and the pressure of a 24-hour commercial news operation, can be considered as a virtue of this new journalism. Precision is regarded as the most important attribute by the entry-level video journalist, who states that the news market – and she refers to both televison and the print media – has become more aggressive. (Interview No.2)

The remaining old values in news journalism: the public service function of journalists, their role as a fourth estate in confronting government, and the carrying out of in-depth research, are regarded by the *World Report* writer as being in decline. Preoccupation with market and commercial aspects has undermined these traditional roles of journalists within a society, although, as one interviewee points out, there still exists a dedication to objectivity, 'to the truth, to be as complete as we can possibly be and to being as fair as we can possibly be to everybody'. (Interview No.4)

When asked to define the terms 'news' and 'information', all of the interviewees responded that the difference is just a slight one.

> I think that 'news' is the hard edge, 'news' is what happened in the world today with a strong look at the events of the day. 'Information' is more the lifestyle line, at least the way it is used on television. (Interview No.5)

The *World Report* writer defines information as the 'background pieces that explain the news'.

> News' is hard to define. I never thought about it. I guess [it is] ... delivering ... informing the public about developments in politics and economics and the social fabric of the country. (Interview No.3)

The video journalist and the senior producer define news and information as being the same, both being a 'presentation of the "facts". A presentation of "what we know to be true", "what we know are the possibilities", and "news" is what is new'.

The daily newsgathering routine at CNN

News-gathering is not regarded as part of a specific personal routine. Because of advances in technology, the process of news-gathering has become impersonal through the use of the telephone or SNG. It has become increasingly anonymous.

> It should be a reporter going out, gathering the facts and presenting them. Unfortunately, we live in a society and a world where there is such significance to what may have, one day at one point, been a very narrowly focussed news story [but] now has ... such larger regional, national or international ramifications. (Interview No.1)

He is referring to the 'ripple effects' of news presented in Europe, Asia, Africa. These dynamics, which change over a period of time even as the same news event develops, have to be considered in every newsgathering process. For this reason, there is, in the view of this senior producer, no 'typical' newsgathering process. For each newscast the executive producer selects the news that has already been gathered by the assignment desks. The material is selected in terms of the greatest 'importance ... to our audience', which varies depending on the news show and its spin.

> Our five o'clock broadcast is a very quick look at the headlines and then an informational chip. It is a show aimed at viewers 55 and above. So we spend a lot of time on medical issues, on financial issues, on personalities...the six o'Clock show is a one-hour very hard look at today's top stories. ... So we have to find the 10 or 15 most important stories of the day. And that's a process that is multilayered. (Interview No.5)

All interviewees felt that they were working collectively in a team. One distinguishes between television and print journalism. In his view, television has to be a collective operation: 'You must have a good cameraman, a good producer, a good editor, a good sound technician, good lighting. A good reporter just goes with a pen and a piece of paper'. (Interview No.4) This teamwork requires a common set of journalistic values as well as similar professional outlooks. These basic values are that journalism be accurate, unbiased, 'that there is no slant in the story'; (Interview No.5) further, 'objectivity, completeness, fairness'. (Interview No.4) Especially in response to the frequent live reports the question of avoiding a slant becomes important. One interviewee referred to of 'family atmosphere': 'We all feel like one big happy family'. (Interview No.1) He also remarked that with so many resources to draw on, it is important to work collectively as a team.

This family atmosphere, for all of the interviewed journalists, is most obvious in the newsroom, especially when a story 'breaks' and it shifts into 'overdrive' and 'you can feel the energy level all raised, probably on the level of one hundred per cent, and there is just a hum or an electric charge in the air until the crisis is over and it kind of winds back down'. (Interview No 5)

The newsroom as the heart, the centre of CNN, appears to one interviewee as a 'well-organised, well-orchestrated, smoothly operating news machine, news processing machine'. (Interview No.3)

> They are chaotic when there's a breaking, major story, but more often they're not, major stories are the stuff that CNN is made of, and has been doing for 10 years. ... My other impression is that there are generally, on the upper levels of the newsroom management, very competent journalists ... directing the flow of news. And that there are younger, much less experienced people doing a lot of the standard, basic kind of footwork in the newsroom'. (Interview No.3)

The newsroom is described as follows: 'There is a lot of movement, there is a lot of action, but it is not wasted energy and it is not wasted action.

People know their tasks, people know what they need to do and they do it'. (Interview No.1) The video journalist views the newsroom more in general terms as 'People run around when there is a big story going on. Always full of activity. It's exciting and challenging, too'. (Interview No 2)

International news agencies are used all the time as sources for introductions. They are utilized 'when we can't get somebody there ourselves and sometimes ... even when we are there, the international agencies would turn up with something better than we have'. (Interview No.5)

Quality in journalism and journalistic styles

Although general collective journalistic values were expressed in the interviews, the issue of quality is more of an individual one. One interviewee remarked that it can be measured only '...by your own standards of professionality and not necessarily by the standards of either your viewers or your sources. You measure it by how often you are proven wrong, not how often you are criticised for being wrong'. (Interview No.4)

'Quality' in journalism involves several levels. On the first level, quality is taken from an audience point of view: are the presented reports or images comprehensible and do they answer questions?

> Does it give me a full presentation of the subject that it's trying to present to me, or the news that it is trying to present to me? And if not, why not? Am I told that?. (Interview No.1)

Another one states:

> My feeling is that a newscast has to be interesting as well as informative. Because you can have the most important news of the day and nobody is watching. You haven't done your job because you have to deliver it to the audience. ... You have to involve the audience. (Interview No.5)

Besides these aspects of quality, television journalism requires a matching of pictures and words. In addition, 'quality' means that issues are presented in an interesting, but not dramatic fashion. The video journalist strives for high quality in the presenting of information 'so that the public can get the most out of what you are presenting to them'. (Interview No.2)

When asked for their preferences in the traditional journalistic styles, such as interpretative, precision, 'new' journalism, or investigative journalism, some of the respondents said they liked them all, others that they prefer their own individual style.

One journalist answered: 'The type of journalism that I like is the type of journalism that answers the questions that I want to know, and I can't tell you how many times I sit and watch television, and I see a story on television and I say, 'Boy, that's fine but I want to know more'''. He prefers 'complete, compelling' journalism. (Interview No.1) Another respondent admitted to preferring an individual interpretation of 'precision' journalism: 'I think that journalism is best when it ... gives you the facts that you can use to make up your mind. That includes the precise journalistic facts. ... It then gives an amount of interpretation'. (Interview No.4) He said that at CNN different journalistic styles have to be considered for different presentations of the same issue in various stages of development and taking account of the style of different programmes.

> First of all, we take you as the viewer with us to the story, and that's live coverage, and you can collect your notes in the same way that we collect our notes. Then when the story is over, we tell you what took place in a little summary of what happened. Then later in the day our correspondents can sit back and think about it, analyze it and do an interpretative report. So that when we do our job well, we have done the live coverage, the straight objective report and the interpretive report. (Interview No.4)

Getting the audience involved through interesting and informative news journalism was put thus by another respondent:

> My goal is to make sure that the audience is well informed, is to some extent entertained a little bit, and comes away from my broadcast knowing a little bit more than they did going into it. [The audience understands] a little bit more of what makes the world go around and maybe even has a topic or two for conversation throughout the day. (Interview No 5)

To be biased, whether in terms of CNN's total programming or single reports or programmes is considered negative by all respondents. 'I don't perceive there is a slant to CNN in terms of the network. I don't see as there's a slant by CNN by any particular individuals in terms of our news coverage. And I hope there is not. Because there shouldn't be'. (Interview No.1) The odds on the network's having a slant in news reporting are viewed as low since CNN presents such a diversity of news and political programming thoughout the day that it is difficult to accuse CNN of being biased or prejudiced. However, it was remarked that networks with less news air time and more interpretive reporting might be more likely to have slanted news programming. The video journalist admits that there might be some slant in interpretative reporting but 'everybody is guilty of it'. (Interview No.2)

Another respondent saw news sources as already biased: 'I mean, within the constraints that we work with, in other words, within the constraints of what, let's say, the newsmakers, the people who make the news, make available to us, ... to a degree they manipulate us'. (Interview No.3)

The role of CNN in journalistic improvements

One of the journalistic achievements was seen in the fact that CNN presents news 24 hours a day, thereby 'freeing television news in this country and probably ultimately in the world from the constraints of a half-hour newscast. That's what we had to deal with before CNN came along, with maybe one one-hour show on Public Television'. (Interview No.3) Another achievement was felt to be that CNN is more committed than others to journalism without too many show-business frills:

> ...that you find in a lot of other commercial television. ... Our anchors are less personalities than they are news readers; our reporters are often not necessarily given jobs because they are pretty and they have a good camera face, but because they are intelligent and they write well and they do a good job of putting together a package. (Interview No.3)

Another journalist considers being on the air first as CNN's main journalistic achievement. Besides this, the fact that CNN has forced other news divisions to expand is seen as a major coup.

> We take people to the event live and let them see exactly what is happening and let them make up their own minds. ... I think that we have proved that there is an interest in hard news. For a long time soft television news was headed more into an information format than a news format. ... We have changed the deadlines of news-gathering because we are always on deadline. There is always the next show. (Interview No.5)

One of CNN's accomplishments is giving news added depth as well as more time. Besides these achievements, CNN's global scope is also considered an important invention.

> For the first time you can watch a newscast in Atlanta and see the same newscast in Tokyo or in Bonn or in Moscow. So that there is not a filtering of the news through different government agencies. There is a chance for it to be seen in an unbiased presentation around the world. (Interview No.5)

CNN's relation to the other networks

CNN was regarded as doing fewer in-depth pieces (as compared to *The McNeil-Lehrer Newshour* on PBS) but was about to change that (Interviews were compiled in March 1991). Since then, CNN has started *Special Assignment* and other programmes. Unlike the networks, CNN presents a lot of news that is geared towards a global audience: 'I think the main focus at CNN ... over the broadcast news ... is the fact that we can bring live news to an audience, a world audience where the others can't in many instances; and we do it'. (Interview No.1)

As the *World Report* writer remarked: 'We present "the news" and we present "the headlines" and then we present some analysis to it. We do not do commentary. The other networks tend to do commentary... .We may not be as polished as the other networks'. (Interview No.5) Time was also mentioned as a significant difference between CCNB and the news presentation of the networks. It was remarked that the network's journalists can do a more 'polished' job because they work all day for 'that one half-hour show'. (Interview No. 5)

CNN's international context

It was acknowledged that CNN's relation to international governments is that 'leaders around the world watch CNN and know what CNN is and turn to CNN looking for news presentation'. (Interview No.1)

It was admitted that CNN had been accused of being used by international governments 'to get a message out'. (Interview No.1) This process was judged as not necessarily being incompatible with journalistic objectivity.

> If they are presenting something to other reporters, to the rest of the world, there is nothing wrong with CNN being part of that. I don't think CNN gets anything exclusively because we are, in terms from world leaders, because we are CNN to send out the message. CNN gets its access because people know who we are outside the United States, and I think that people are aware of who else sees CNN – and in that, I mean CNN has influence, not because it tries to have influence but it is accessible and people see it and thus it can be perceived as being a conduit between news or between world leaders and national leaders. (Interview No.1)

The programme *World Report* especially was judged to have relationships with international governments, even those who controlled their country's media. The *World Report* interviewee remarked: 'We get contributions from media around the world, so sometimes we negotiate with people who are either directly involved in government or are employees of the government because they work for the media'. (Interview No.3) Governments were regarded as information sources for CNN's general output:

> That is, that Governments are our sources and we deal with them on the editorial side, on the journalists' side as news sources. We deal with the Kremlin in the same way we deal with the White House, or we deal with Fidel Castro in the same way we deal with John Major, and nothing more than that. (Interview No.4)

Another interviewee denied that there existed anything like a 'relationship' between CNN and international governments:

> I know that we have been used by governments in the past to get their point of view across because, my God, we are watched everywhere. We are watched in Cuba, we are watched in Moscow, we are watched in Libya. When Muammar Gaddafi wants to get his point of view across, he picks up the phone and he calls CNN and says, 'Hey, I have got an interview. Would you like to interview me? I have got something I want to tell you. I have a peace plan.' Yasser Arafat does the same type of thing. It was done with Saddam Hussein during the war. We had an interview ... with him

when nobody else [did]. So in that sense we are used to purvey a point of view but I don't think there is any official relationship with them. (Interview No.5)

The working relationship of CNN with international networks was judged as being effective. The journalists were unable to compare their programme quality with those of other international networks.

The only access we have to any overseas broadcasting is any of the Spanish, Univisif CNN with international networks was judged as being effective. The journalists were unable to compare their programme quality with those of other international networks. The only access we have to any overseas broadcasting is arative. Whereas a co-operative relationship exists with ITN/London and WTN/London, the relation to the EBU was viewed as competitive.[14] (Interview No.4 and Interview No.1)

It was argued that additional news sources such as ITN and WTN are needed because '...we can't staff bureaus in every country around the world. We need to have that relationship to bring the truly global newscast to the air each day. (Interview No.5) In terms of presence around the world, name recognition and reach, CNN was judged ahead of other international news organizations. (Interview No.3)

Television power and responsibility in national and international politics

In American politics, television was regarded by the interviewees as the most powerful medium, since campaigns '...are run through television appearances, through campaign commercials on television and whereas there may have been a lot more personal appearances, one on one, a candidate to the people, the population'. (Interview No.1) It was further argued that candidates in the United States manipulate the news '...by the timing of events, by what speeches are delivered, when ... by the lack of access to candidates throughout the day. They use us as free commercial time'. (Interview No.5)

Internationally, television was felt to have speeded up political news events and influenced developments which effected '...changes in climate, changes in public opinion because of television. I think it speeds up the process of expectation by the population or if there's an expectation by the world, the answer will come through television'. (Interview No.1) CNN's global approach was reckoned highly in terms of letting the audience judge for themselves on the basis of the information supplied by the news.

It was also remarked that the relationship between television and the public is changing, nationally as well as internationally: 'Yes, it is becoming more and more of a tool for resolving conflicts and disputes, and making people, letting people use it to air their grievances'. (Interview No.3) The fact that television is becoming more powerful was attributed especially to

CNN's worldwide political influence: 'Certainly, this network is becoming more powerful, and it is sometimes very scary to see how powerful we are and how easily we could get used and contribute to world events'. (Interview No.3)

Another respondent remarked that CNN is less powerful than 'people give us credit to be'. (Interview No. 4) He felt that the news sources control the agenda of television:

> We can help to set the agenda a little bit. But generally if the politicians don't want go along with us, we can't do a thing. Sometimes we exert a lot of power. It is always hard to tell when. (Interview No.4)

CNN's responsibilities towards global communication

The view was expressed that the American population had not had the chance to receive sufficient information on developing countries.

> I think the world because they now have access to seeing and learning and hearing about developing nations, places around the globe that they have never heard of or knew nothing about, are taking a greater interest and I think that is part of the responsibility of television news and a news network and a global operation. (Interview No.1)

But the interviewees did not think that journalists need feel any responsibility towards developing nations or bringing about change in the world: 'I see my responsibilities as a journalist to be informing and explaining, not influencing events'. (Interview No.3) It was further argued that 'breaking' news covers those events which take place in Western countries or have a bilateral relation. But in general,

> ...there is not a whole lot of interest in developing nations until there is a problem with a developing nation. And then once there is a problem, it is probably too late. So to some extent, I guess producers and editors are to blame for not getting stories out and talking about problems before they happen. (Interview No.5)

CNN was viewed as being in the forefront in coverage of developing nations, as opposed to other US networks, since CNN has a bureau in Nairobi and one in Santiago.

> But a lot of that stuff does not get on the air until there is a problem. You run into a vicious cycle. ... So you have to pick and choose very carefully and find the real strong nuggets of information in a developing country ... but it may be one story a month rather one story a day or one story a week that really deserves to be told. (Interview, No.5)

Journalists took account of the global audience in their daily work. 'In the work that I have done', said one interviewee, 'I think probably the global approach of CNN is to be aware that there is an international news audience so that we can't take for granted that the viewing audience knows of political ins and outs'. (Interview, No.1) *World Report* is regarded as being the most global programme. 'We have a multicultural, multilingual staff with different expertises, different strengths, different backgrounds and that is to me the key to providing a global network and a global information service ... not to have it dominated by American staff'. (Interview No.3) The general impression of the respondents was that the global approach of CNN would be improved in the future. In order to globalise CNN, one journalist favours targeting domestic audiences with domestic issues.

> Because any domestic audience, be it in the United States or in the Soviet Union or in Europe, is primarily interested in the events in their neighbourhood and in and around their backyard. They want to be talked to in certain terms. If you start forcing other terms and other stories, I think you run the risk of alienating them. (Interview No.5)

Journalists felt no responsibility to propagate globalism since 'CNN has no responsibilities to anything except gathering and presenting news. That's very important for us to keep in mind and very important for our viewers to keep in mind in thinking about us'. (Interview No.4)

The CNN journalists interviewed consider themselves part of a free news organization which does not operate under any political influence. One journalist contrasted CNN with other broadcasters who work under varying degrees of political propagandist influence, such as the news organization of what was then the Soviet Union, SABC in South Africa, or ZDF in Germany. 'They have less of it [propaganda] than the others ... But as a government broadcaster they are still beholden'. (Interview No.4) It was argued further that CNN has to cover 'all the news' because, due to the increasing dynamic on the global news market, 'the news that had a lesser significance to us five years ago has a greater significance to us now and has a greater significance to our worldwide audience as opposed to just the US national audience'. (Interview No.1) The *World Report* writer expressed responsibility because the global newscast contained highly biased pieces. Her responsibilty consisted in 'balancing' these reports for a world audience:

> We strive on this show to stay away from value-laden terms; we try to present the dry facts. It is always very challenging to a writer to try and stay away from words that could potentially have some values injected into them. This classic debate about 'guerrilla' versus 'freedom fighter' versus 'terrorist'. (Interview No.3)

Responsibility was also expressed by others: 'I think it is still in the back of our mind ... that there is news to be covered throughout the world and that people are watching us throughout the world'. (Interview No.1)

Global news also consists of local news which is regarded as 'disaster-oriented.' Supplementing non-disaster-oriented news stories from local stations was viewed as a task for CNN. (Interview No.1)

Table 16: Satellite Distribution of CNNI

Astra 1B, Intelsat VI F1, Intelsat V F8, Galaxy 1, Pan Am Sat 1, Arabsat 1C, Palapa B-P, Morelos II, Brazilsat, Thor, Superbird B.

(Compare with Table 15)

The domestic audience and the international target group

The typical domestic audience for CNN is regarded as better educated than average, above average income and specifically interested in news: 'They are interested in knowing what goes on, they don't turn on the news because it's habit, but they turn on news because they want to turn on the news and see what is going on'. (Interview No.1)

The *World Report* viewer is considered as being more sophisticated than the average CNN viewer. 'We think that the *World Report* viewer has more education, more knowledge about the world, more understanding and means to learn to understand more, has generally probably a higher income'. (Interview No.3)

The international audience consists of several audiences, according to one respondent.

> One is the transplanted American audience, people just like myself who live in Atlanta, and who, when they get to a hotel in Hamburg, ... want to be able to turn on the news and get it in the same way they get it in Atlanta. ...The next audience is composed of expatriate Americans, people who work for IBM or Lever Brothers or Ford Motor Company or whatever, who live in Hamburg the year round. ... Then beyond that, we want to get to the truly international audience. The most important part of that would be the so-called opinion makers, the government officials, the big businessmen, the leaders of the greatest institutions in society: trade unions, professional institutions or whatever. Beyond that, last, but still important, we want to get to the mass audience. (Interview No.4)

These audiences do not influence any journalistic style, though they are taken into consideration in presenting the news in a comprehensible fashion.

CNN is described as a dynamic news operation, ready to experiment, which operates in accordance with its own values. According to Schmidt and Weischenberg (1994) today's broadcast journalism is comparable to industrial production.

> The production and processing of current themes – the primary function of journalism as a system – is governed by the criteria of commodity – production in modern societies. It must be set up in such a way, both organizationally and technically, that it meets the

> criterian of economic efficiency in particular. (Schmidt and
> Weischenberg, 1994:224)

This seems to be the case in a 24-hour 'news machine' such as CNN which requires instant news 'production' as well as audience appeal.

Apart from individual journalistic approaches, the tendency is to present fact journalism, which is considered as being objective and precise. Slants, prejudices or biases are not regarded as much of a problem of CNN because of its 24-hour news presentation and a natural balance within it and also because of the attempt to present dry facts.

The journalists interviewed revealed a professional mentality which can be described as 'dynamic', 'experienced', 'open to worldwide expansion'. A global approach, in the view of these journalists, was a general, more universal approach, one which, since CNN is a globally operating news channel, is focussed more on world events of general relevance than on detailed particular journalism. Although some interviewees, especially those who were involved in international programs, showed a distinct world view, those who were involved in domestic news programmes showed a more 'Americanized' view on global journalism.

All the interviewees very definitely applied the values of 'objectivity' and 'fact' to journalism. These categories are used as ethical 'rules' of journalism. However, it is surprising that none of the respondents doubted that such entities as 'objectivity' or 'facts' exist. It seems that these terms related, for them, more to certain journalistic 'values' rather than concepts of 'truth.' It can also be argued that objectivity is incompatible with such concepts: because events have to be presented in a general fashion, there are no in-depth insights which would possibly reveal the 'truth'. Schmidt and Weischenberg argue that 'precise' journalism, 'new journalism' and 'investigative journalism' (Schmidt/Weischenberg, 1994:230) can be regarded as critical and thus 'truthful' styles.

These classifications do not take account of the fact that fragmented broadcasting organizations have to develop new styles such as 'fragmented journalism', an overall category covering a variety of journalistic styles. Fragmented journalism has to take into account the special audience sector targeted by a fragmented channel, as well as the variety of news formats.

The *World Report*: An approach to global communication

Whereas the interviews revealed the wide universal angle of CNN in its domestic and international programme, the following analysis of CNN's 'World Report' suggests the unique particular journalism of the channel.

CNN *World Report*: The world's only 'global newscast'

'CNN *World Report* is the world's largest international news exchange and the only global newscast': this statement, appearing in 'CNN World Report''s information brochure, indicates the fact that CNN's *World Report* is far from being an ordinary newscast. Unlike other CNN programme segments and news programming, *World Report* (CNNWR) is a globally unique news programme in many respects.

One of these is that it is made up of reports produced by international broadcasters for this programme segment, which CNN broadcasts unedited and 'uncensored'. Contributors receive the right to broadcast any segment they may need in their own news programmes.

Don Flournoy attributes the success of CNNWR to various factors:

> Timing, politics, economics and advancements in technology all helped set the stage for the *World Report* venture. Technological factors, such as telephones that work, easier access to satellites and hand-held cameras and computers have allowed for more timely and cost effective communication. The emergence of a political climate for freer use of the media and the easing of restrictions on the flow of electronic information across national borders played a role. At the same time there was an apparent rising public demand for unfiltered news, while local broadcasters were themselves anxious to get their stories aired to broader publics. Without these forces at work it is unlikely that the *World Report,* or any such egalitarian news arrangement, would have yet appeared in the international arena. (Flournoy, 1992:49)

The Sunday CNNWR version is equipped with international sound and transmitted on two audio channels. Scripts for the anchor's introduction are available through data transmission service. The daily CNNWR programme was 15 minutes long when it began in 1989; since 1993 it has consisted of a half-hour show on Tuesday, Wednesday, Thursday and Friday. The model is based on the following set of guidelines, which are published in an information brochure for participating broadcasters:

> The producer of the daily CNN *World Report* solicits reports on specific topics for a given day or week. As with all CNN *World Report* reports, the broadcasters themselves may decide whether or not to report on the topic we request. The editorial content of the report is solely that of the contributing organization. We also encourage contributors' suggestions for reports for the daily program. [CNN] ...'will always broadcast reports produced for the weekend programme on the weekend programme. We also plan on broadcasting some material from the weekly programme during the daily broadcasts, because the reports are timely and deserving of even greater exposure'. ...'There is a possibility that reports for the daily programme may not be aired due to the nature of breaking news. In the event the programme is pre-empted for live news coverage, CNN *World Report* will do its best to broadcast all reports but is not obligated to air all of the pieces submitted for the daily programme. (CNNWR, 1993)

159

In Flournoy's view, CNNWR and other CNN journalism styles are created to be cost-effective in a news system operation, a quite logical consequence. However, CNN has creatively designed and invented new types of journalism that are both cost-effective and of a high standard. Flournoy states that CNNWR made 'CNN the clearing house for a diversity of news stories that no other station could have even if it spent a fortune'. (Flournoy, 1992:61) Flournoy regards CNNWR as a model for the future when the local journalist, rather than the American, would cover stories. 'The next generation of foreign correspondents for the US media ... may be foreign.' The local reporter is already in place and will cost a tenth of what is needed to maintain an American in the field. 'What is more important, the native already has a visa, doesn't need a translator and is familiar with the territory'. (Flournoy, 1992:63) As CNN's president, Ted Turner, remarks:

> CNN's desire is to make as much use of the *World Report* contributions in the regular newscast as possible. Part of the job of the staff is to see to it that those materials are not overlooked, that the International Desk is kept appraised of hard news leads, or of events that have changed. (Flournoy, 1992:64)

The programme's audience is not large by television standards – the weekday segment attracts about 458,000 households per day, the one on Sunday about 194,000. The value for viewers consists in the opportunity to see news with a global perspective. CNN *World Report* can be regarded as a model for future global news programmes, where various broadcasters might collaborate on programmes about subjects like the environment. CNNWR is regarded as a marketplace of news and views 'from different countries'.

The history and the programme concept

World Report as a substantial element of the CNN system was established in 1987. Turner's idea was to launch a news programme in which many voices from around the world could be heard, in which multiple news topics, views and angles could be broadcast. The idea was developed after Turner read the complaints of the developing countries in UNESCO's MacBride report.

The programme segment *World Report* provides worldwide broadcasters and news organizations with a forum for their news reports. *World Report* is aired in three different versions: a daily version, consisting of a fifteen-minute programme (as part of the Show *International Hour*, 6:45 GMT), an edition begun in 1993 which is broadcast twice daily, from Tuesday to Friday (6:30 and 9:30 GMT) and a weekly programme airing twice on Sundays on CNN and CNNI in a variable length of at least two, or maximally three hours, aired by CNN at 3:00-5:00 pm ET and midnight, by CNNI (9:00-10:00 GMT) and 7:00-9:00 GMT) (CNN World Report Contributors Conference).

Although censorship is not exercised, CNN occasionally has to exercise some 'editorial work'. This happens in three ways: One is selecting the story sequence, for example, the lead story. Some journalists also submit a story more than 2.5 minutes long so that CNN has to cut it in order to meet the time limit. In the early days of *World Report*, some reports had to be rejected as they 'did not meet minimal standards'.

CNN's contribution to the programme consists mainly in the organization of the programme and the guarantee of a minimum presentation level.

Contributors deliver the reports to CNN. The contributing news organization pays the cost of production as well as that of delivery to Atlanta, preferably by satellite. The participating countries are permitted to use CNNWR in their own news programmes by transmitting either the whole programme or just parts of it. Those countries, however, which cannot receive CNN's satellite signals and thus are unable to make a return use of CNNWR, receive CNNWR at CNN's expense for transmitting to earth stations in their countries. Participating news organizations are asked to contribute any content they wish and cover any topic they wish 'from their perspective'. Though CNNWR encourages participants to contribute daily hard news 'including lots of good video showing the rest of the world what the contributor's country and life in it are like', (CNNWR, 1993) which may also be used in other CNN news programmes, the majority of reports submitted consist of political issues of some kind (see following Table) on general, not specifically current, lines. Participants are asked to contribute regularly each week, but if they don't, they are still permitted to receive and use CNNWR news material even if they contribute only once a month. The official regulation is: 'Contributors receive rights to all material on CNN *World Report* each week to use as they see fit in their country. CNN receives the rights to use all the material on CNN *World Report* in its network programming as well as in CNN *World Report*.'

Although CNN requests reports on current political issues if possible, the value of *World Report* journalism does not consist in meeting the expectations of a Western television station and its national and international news competitors. The value of a programme slot which permits news organizations all over the world to transmit their points of view globally has to be counted in terms of its effect on the political sphere in the country of origin as well as on the international community. The value of *World Report* value for different global regions are the following:

(1) It supports international and global concerns such as population problems, as seen for example in statements by UN representatives such as Nafis Sadik, (who appreciates *World Report* for this reason. (See quotation in Flournoy, 1992:76).

(2) For developing countries, the programme offers the chance to put their points of view on international political and social issues or present those topics which do not appear on the agenda of the big news agencies.

(3) Within crisis regions *World Report* is used not only as a global newscast but also as a communication platform in order to communicate bilaterally with the opposing party.

(4) Besides the former the programme is also used as a propaganda forum for totalitarian nations (Cuba, China).

(5) It functions as a marketing medium for a country to encourage tourism or to delete stereotypes.

(6) It also provides rare news reports which broadcasters would not be able to acquire otherwise because of a lack of their own international staff and because of the 'local' view.

(7) It also functions as a communication tool between expatriates and their home countries (for example, Armenians living in the US).

The agency and news programme

As already indicated, the *World Report* programme also functions as a news agency for participating organizations. This exchange offers unique opportunities in terms of access to news, especially for those countries which do not have access to traditional big agencies. *World Report* has eliminated the centre-periphery model of news exchange since it provides material which allows communication even on the periphery without reference to the centre. Formerly news-dependent nations, as Flournoy argues, now have:

> ...the capability to collect and distribute their own news. This gives them a way to break out of the old order, making possible what has been so difficult to manage until now: horizontal exchanges between neighbouring or new neighbouring states. It gives nations far from one another unprecedented opportunities to tell their own stories in their own way, in some cases by-passing the First World altogether. (Flournoy, 1992:53)

Acting as a *World Report* news source provides additional communication circuits to the stations themselves. In this sense CNNWR is used as a 'peripheral' as well as a 'horizontal' news exchange system.

Although the periphery-and-centre model has been eliminated by *World Report*, the model of information-poor versus information-rich countries does persist. Those countries with poor information sources are more dependent on programmes such as *World Report* than those who enjoy the service of the large news agencies and do not need to go through the complicated process of monitoring the whole *World Report* programme in order to select issues for their own channels. The news exchange system has obvious value for information-poor countries.

According to Flournoy's survey, journalists in information-rich countries claim that the reason for not using stories in their own programme is limited news space in a full television channel, which selects news according to traditional news 'values' which do not include outsider reports. They argue further that their audience expectations are different or that their programme philosophy does not correspond to *World Report* material. On the other hand, Flournoy reports that TSS-Soviet Union had used about 80 per cent of its reports in their newscast 'World in a Week' in 1989. (Flournoy, 1992:80)

Although both information-rich and information-poor countries participate in *World Report,* their use is different. It can be argued that information-rich countries only contribute regular reports, whereas information-poor countries also use reports in their programmes or monitor *World Report* regularly. (see Flournoy, 1992:73) Flournoy found in his survey that 30 per cent of participating stations 'make no use of the programme to which they contribute stories.' Another 52 per cent of those responding 'do use at least a quarter of the material each week'; some 'use individual reports, some use the materials as a source of file or stock video'. (Flournoy, 1992:79) He further concludes that 'only 25 per cent use CNN *World Report* as a separate programme. Twenty six per cent of those using *World Report* aired the show immediately, 37 per cent aired the show at a later date. Thirty seven per cent of those using the CNN-distributed news indicated the material is translated and subtitled or translated and dubbed'. (Flournoy, 1992:79)

The CNNWR professional programme

CNNWR offers contributors and other CNN clients a training programme, the 'CNN International Professional Program' (IPP). This consists of practical journalistic experiences at CNN's headquarter in Atlanta, Georgia. This training programme consists of a six-week session in which the participants become familiar with CNN and its operation and technical facilities. They are also involved in CNN's news production within the field of their own speciality. They 'may observe CNN's National and International Assignment Desks in action ... as well as the Satellites Desk and Graphics department'. But 'assignments may also be with particular units such as CNN Medical or CNN's Central Booking and individual programmes such as CNN *World Report,* Future Watch or *Week in Review'.* (CNNIPP Information Material, October, 1993)

Besides gathering experiences in a different news organization to their home station, the participating journalists, who must be fluent in English and have at least three years' experience, have the opportunity for professional exchange with others participating in the programme. Since the programme was set up in 1989, correspondents, assignment editors, producers, anchors and managers from 47 countries have already participated. This training programme involves a 'TV correspondence course' and communication with contributors.

Table 17: *World Report* Participants

Middle East

Countries	News Organizations	Sample	Frequency
Abu Dhabi	UAETV		
Bahrain	Bahrain TV	X	2
Cyprus	CyBC Cyprus	X	13
	Bayrak TV N. Cyprus	X	3
Dubai	Dubai TV	X	1
Iran	IRIB, Iran	X	2
Iraq	Iraq TV		
Israel	IBA Israel	X	7
Jordan	JTV Jordan	X	6
Kuwait	Kuwait TV	X	5
Lebanon	Future TV Lebanon		
Oman	Oman TV		
Qatar	Qatar TV		
Palestine	Palestine Broadcasting Corp.	X	1
Saudi Arabia	Channel 2, Saudi Arabia	X	1
Syria	Syrian TV		
Yemen	YRTV Yemen		
		TOTAL	**41**

Africa

Countries	News Organizations	Sample	Frequency
Algeria	ENTV Algeria		
Angola	TPA Angloa	X	2
Burundi	RNTB Burundi		
Cameroon	CRTV Cameroon		
Egypt	Egypt	X	3
Ethiopaia	ETV Ethiopia	X	3
Ghana	GBC Ghana	X	5
Mozambique	TVE Mozambique		
Namibia	NBC Namibia	X	3
Nigeria	NTA Nigeria	X	2
Sierra Leone	SLBS Sierra Leone	X	1
South Africa	SABC South Africa	X	9
South Africa (Bophuthatswana)	BOP TV South Africa	X	3
Sudan	SNBC Sudan		
Tunesia	RTT Tunisia	X	1
Uganda	Cable Sat Television Uganda		
Zambia	ZNBC Zambia		
Zimbabwe	ZNC Zimbabwe	X	2
		TOTAL	**34**

Europe

(1) Western and Central

Countries	News Organizations	Sample	Frequency
Austria	ORF Austria	X	1
Belgium	Way Press International	X	6
	RTL TV-1 Belgium		
Germany	Deutsche Welle	X	1
	ZDF Germany	X	6
Ireland	RTE Ireland	X	1
Netherlands	RTNV Netherlands	X	10
Switzerland	SRI Switzerland	X	13
United Kingdom	BBC	X	8
	TOTAL NUMBER		**46**

(2) Southern

Countries	News Organizations	Sample	Frequency
Bosnia-Herzegovina	Bih Bosnia-Herzegovina		
Croatia	HTV Croatia	X	3
Greece	Antenna TV Greece	X	9
Italy	RAI Italy	X	3
Macedonia	Macedonian TV	X	1
Portugal	RTP Portugal	X	4
Slovenia	TV Slovenia	X	8
	Libra TV Slovenia	X	1
Spain	Euskal Telebista, Spain	X	2
	TV Catalunya, Spain	X	6
Turkey	TGRT Turkey	X	1
	TRT Turkey	X	6
Yugoslavia	RTV Belgrade	X	2
	Studio B, Yugoslavia		
	TOTAL NUMBER		**46**

(3) Northern

Countries	News Organizations	Sample	Frequency
Estonia	Estonian TV		
Finland	YLE Finland	X	5
Greenland	KNR-TV Greenland		
Iceland	Channel 2	X	2
Latvia	Latvian TV	X	4
Norway	NRK Norway		
Sweden	SVT 1		
	TOTAL NUMBER		**11**

(4) Eastern

Countries	News Organizations	Sample	Frequency
Armenia	Armenian TV	X	4
Bulgaria	BT Bulgaria	X	1
Czech Republic	CT Czech Republic	X	3
Georia			
Poland	TVP Poland	X	8
Romania	Romanian TV	X	5
Russia	TV Co Nike (Pertrozavodsk)		
	Ostankino	X	3
	Russian TV	X	4
	Seti-NN		
	VA Bank	X	1
	TOTAL NUMBER		**29**

Asia

Countries	News Organizations	Sample	Frequency
China	CCTV China	X	8
Guam	Gia, Cable TV	X	1
	Kuam Island News	X	1
Hong Kong	Cable News	X	2
India	Doordashan, India	X	4
Indonesia	RCTI, Indonesia		
	TVRI Indonesia		
Japan	TV Ashai Japan	X	8
Korea	KOTV Korea (N)		
	KBS Korea (S)	X	1
Malaysia	RTM Maylasia		
Marianas	Mariana Cablevision	X	2
Nepal	Nepal TV		
Pakistan	(PTV) Pakistan	X	3
Philippines	ABS-CBN Philip	X	1
	GMA7-News Philip	X	1
Singapore	SBC Singapore	X	11
Sri Lanka	SLRC Sri Lanka	X	4
Taiwan	TTV Taiwan		
	CTS Taiwan	X	1
Thailand	BBTV-7 Thailand	X	1
	TOTAL NUMBER		**49**

The Americas

(1) North America

Countries	News Organizations	Sample	Frequency
Canada	Global TV	X	5
	ITV	X	7
United States	CNN	X	11
	TOTAL NUMBER		**23**

(2) Central America and the Caribbean

Countries	News Organizations	Sample	Frequency
Bahamas	Bahamas TV		
Barbados	CBC		
Belize	Channel 5		
Cayman Islands	CITV	X	4
Cuba	ICRTV	X	5
	Cubavisió	X	1
Curaçao	Teleçuracao	X	2
Haiti	Téléhaïti	X	2
Honduras	Telesistema Hondureño	X	2
Jamaica	JBC Jamaica		
Mexico	Channel 13	X	1
Panama	RPC-TV4	X	2
Costa Rica	Teletica		
El Salvador	TCS News	X	5
Jamaica	JBC Jamaica	X	1
	TOTAL NUMBER		**24**

(3) South America

Countries	News Organizations	Sample	Frequency
Argentina	America 2	X	2
Brazil	TV Globo	X	3
Bolivia	Canal 111-P.A.T	X	4
Chile	Canal 13	X	1
Colombia	TV Hoy	X	1
Guyana	Guyana TV	X	1
Paraguay	CVC	X	1
	SNT	X	1
Peru	ATV	X	1
Trinidad	TTT		
Uruguay	Teledoce Television Color	X	2
	TOTAL NUMBER		**17**

Australia

Countries	News Organizations	Sample	Frequency
Australia	Channel 7	X	6
	SBS	X	1
	Network 10	X	2
New Zealand	Sky Television	X	1
		TOTAL NUMBER	**10**

Table18: Countries and Regions of CNNWR Professional Program Participants

Eastern Europe	Albania, Armenia, Bulgaria, Czech Republic, Poland, Lithuania, Romania, Russia, Ukraine
Western/Central Europe	Finland, Germany, Ireland, Latvia, Norway, Switzerland
Southern Europe	Greece, Macedonia, Portugal, Spain, Turkey
Latin America	Argentina, Belarus, Brazil, Colombia, Ecuador, Guayana, Trinidad, Uruguay, St. Lucia
Africa	Bophuthatswana, Egypt, Ethiopia, Ghana, Keyna, Namibia, Nigeria, South Africa, Zambia, Zimbabwe
Asia	China, Malaysia, Mongolia, Philippines, Singapore, Taiwan, Thailand
Middle East	Cyprus, Jordan

Source: CNN World Report Information (10/1/1993)

In order to be eligible for the programme, all participants have to be full-time employees of television news organizations which 'are either participants in the CNN *World Report* or international clients of CNN and must participate on a voluntary basis'. (CNNWR, 1993) Four training sessions take place each year.

Content analysis

Method of research

The overall goal of this analysis is to find evidence on which to base a hypothesis about new emerging spheres of global communication. As 'traditional' terrestrial broadcasting as well as satellite transmission distributes programmes internationally, new programme types which refer to these new target audiences are just being developed. My analysis of the content of these follows the three conditions laid down by Kerlinger (1973):

(1) The sample must be systematically chosen and all content must be treated in precisely the same manner. Coding procedures must be uniform.

(2) Content analysis has to be as objective as possible and use clear and precise operational definitions and rules for classification of variables.

168

Middle East

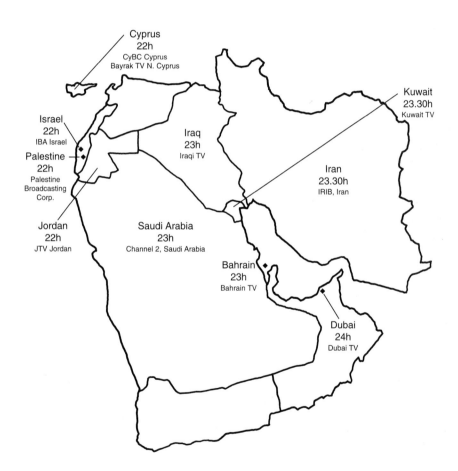

Cyprus
22h
CyBC Cyprus
Bayrak TV N. Cyprus

Kuwait
23.30h
Kuwait TV

Israel
22h
IBA Israel

Palestine
22h
Palestine
Broadcasting
Corp.

Iraq
23h
Iraqi TV

Iran
23.30h
IRIB, Iran

Jordan
22h
JTV Jordan

Saudi Arabia
23h
Channel 2, Saudi Arabia

Bahrain
23h
Bahrain TV

Dubai
24h
Dubai TV

Africa

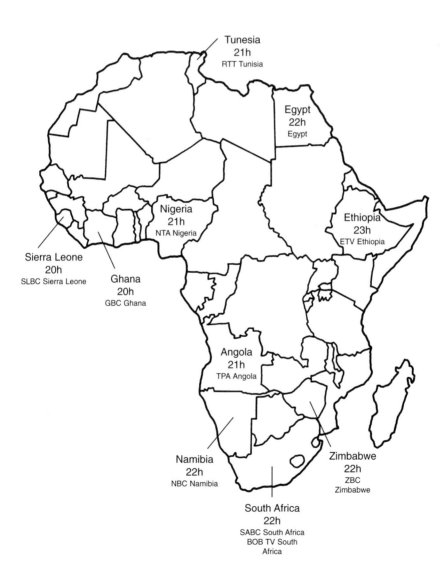

Tunesia
21h
RTT Tunisia

Egypt
22h
Egypt

Nigeria
21h
NTA Nigeria

Ethiopia
23h
ETV Ethiopia

Sierra Leone
20h
SLBC Sierra Leone

Ghana
20h
GBC Ghana

Angola
21h
TPA Angola

Namibia
22h
NBC Namibia

Zimbabwe
22h
ZBC
Zimbabwe

South Africa
22h
SABC South Africa
BOB TV South
Africa

Western /Southern Europe

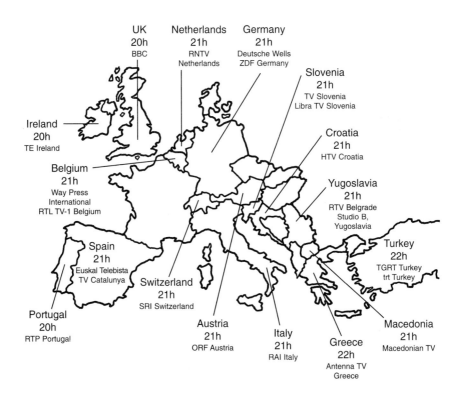

UK
20h
BBC

Netherlands
21h
RNTV
Netherlands

Germany
21h
Deutsche Wells
ZDF Germany

Slovenia
21h
TV Slovenia
Libra TV Slovenia

Ireland
20h
TE Ireland

Croatia
21h
HTV Croatia

Belgium
21h
Way Press
International
RTL TV-1 Belgium

Yugoslavia
21h
RTV Belgrade
Studio B,
Yugoslavia

Spain
21h
Euskal Telebista
TV Catalunya

Turkey
22h
TGRT Turkey
trt Turkey

Switzerland
21h
SRI Switzerland

Portugal
20h
RTP Portugal

Austria
21h
ORF Austria

Italy
21h
RAI Italy

Greece
22h
Antenna TV
Greece

Macedonia
21h
Macedonian TV

Northern/Eastern Europe

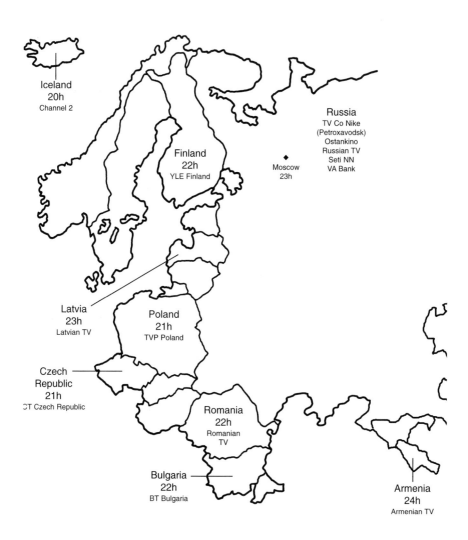

Iceland
20h
Channel 2

Finland
22h
YLE Finland

Russia
TV Co Nike
(Petroxavodsk)
Ostankino
Russian TV
Seti NN
VA Bank

Moscow
23h

Latvia
23h
Latvian TV

Poland
21h
TVP Poland

Czech
Republic
21h
CT Czech Republic

Romania
22h
Romanian
TV

Bulgaria
22h
BT Bulgaria

Armenia
24h
Armenian TV

Asia

Japan
5h
TV Ashai Japan

North Korea
5h
KOTV Korea

South Korea
5h
KBS Korea

China
4h
CCTV China

Taiwan
4h
TTV Taiwan
CTS Taiwan

Pakistan
1h
(PTV) Pakistan

India
1.30h
Doordashan,India

Sri Lanka
1.30h
SRLC Sri Lanka

Mariana
4h
Mariana
Cablevision

Hong Kong
4h
Cable News

Thailand
3h
BBTV-7 Thailand

Singapore
4h
SBC Singapore

Philipines
4h
ABS-CBN Philip.
GMA7-News Philip.

North and Central America

Canada
Global TV
ITV

◆ Vancouver
12h

Montreal
15h ◆

USA

CNN

New York
15h ◆

◆ Los Angeles 12h

Cuba
15h
ICRTV
CubavisiÓn

Haiti
15h
Téléhaiti

Mexico
14h
Channel 13

Jamaica
15h
JBC Jamaica

Cayman Islands
15h
CITV

El Salvador
14h
TCS News

Honduras
14h
Telesístema Hondureño

Panama
15h
RPC-TV

Curaçao
16h
Telecuraçao

South America

Guyana
17h
Guyana TV

Colombia
15h
TV Hoy

Peru
15h
ATV

Brazil
Rio De Janeiro
17h
TV Globo

Bolivia
16h
Canal 111-P.A.T.

Paraguay
16h
CVC SNT

Argentina
17h
Amerika 2

Chile
16h
Canal 13

Uraguay
17h
Teledoce Televisora Color

Australia

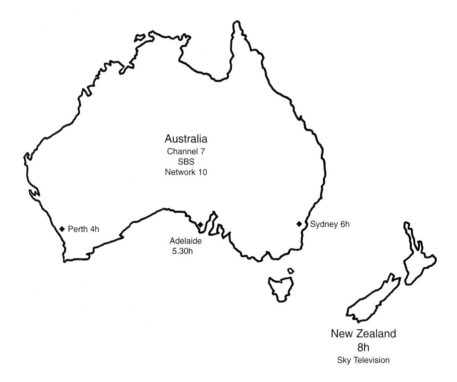

Australia
Channel 7
SBS
Network 10

◆ Perth 4h

Adelaide
5.30h

◆ Sydney 6h

New Zealand
8h
Sky Television

(3) Content analysis is quantitative, since the 'goal of the content analysis is the accurate representation of a body of messages'. (Wimmer and Dominick, 1987:166)

This analysis of the *World Report* involves a three-dimensional approach: it codes 'messages', news organizations, and conceptual parameters of *World Report* journalism as exercised by anchor presentations, updates and packaged thematic programme segments.

In 1990, I undertook a pre-test, consisting of a sample of 192 news units. Following this pre-test, some variables were modified. The questionnaire aims at revealing 'spheres' of mediation in a global public sphere arena in which *World Report* seems to be a substantial element.

The analysis coded only the English-language report on anchor stories. Visual material was not coded because international news journalism and the presentation of multicultural 'signs' and political codes require multicultural coders to interpret visual data correctly. Furthermore, news presentation is dominated by words, and for this reason visual-data analysis seems to be more appropriate for other media genres or issues. (Ball and Smith, 1992)

Hypotheses

This study was undertaken in order to find a pattern of global news communication in terms of particularity and universality. Such a pattern permits one to create various hypotheses which refer:

(1) to the news organization itself;

(2) to the content;

(3) to their relationships.

My intention was to identify those news organizations which already target an international audience and to compare their news reports with those which broadcast to a national or local audience. I argue that use is made of CNNWR by those news organizations which already have an interest in worldwide broadcasting in order to widen the public sphere for specific issues, to be 'present' in the programme, use it for public relations or use it to a rebroadcast stories that have already been broadcast on the 'home' channels.

The above three dimensions are necessary for an analysis of content that will test reveal specific assumptions about the emergence of a global public sphere. *World Report* is regarded as a mini-global public sphere, since it allows general access to worldwide broadcasters, is open in terms of topics submitted and transmits them globally. Although I restricted my analysis to news organizations, this involved not only national television stations but also international agencies and media centres. In this sense it also took in a variety of viewpoints.

Decentralisation of gatekeeping

It is not CNNWR but the editors in the participating news organizations who are the ones who open or close the 'gate' for international news distribution via CNNWR and select programmes for distribution. Legal and organizational regulations interfere with many new opportunities in broadcasting which come with the new broadcasting technology. These restrictions may hinder a news organization to some degree from being on international channels (as is the case with public service organizations).

The participants: New players in the global public sphere

The analysis revealed that national, regional, international and public, state-owned, commercial and private broadcasters all use CNNWR as a channel or medium to deliver their reports and perspectives to interested global audiences. Among these participants are several which can be considered as new players in this field and the existence of which is made possible by channels such as those of CNNWR, which provides a programme-carrying facility. These broadcasters are organized beyond state and nation level, with a universal or particular reach. Examples follow.

(1) News organizations of global political organizations: United Nations Television, UNESCO TV.

(2) News organizations of regional and continental political organizations: the European Parliament.

(3) News organizations of partisan political organizations: PLO TV (in 1990), Afghan Media Centre, South Africa Now.

(4) Publicly-funded national broadcasters who are already involved in international (that is, interregional) broadcasting.

(5) Political and private broadcasters who are nationally involved in the vertical integration of political media, such as TGRT, a Turkish television channel that is owned by *Türkye* a Turkish right-wing fundamentalist newspaper.

(6) News organizations that operate on the agency level, such as 'Way Press International', a Belgian private press agency which is also involved in the production of international carrier news programmes.

(7) Local, especially independent broadcasters which have long been focussed on the 'schizophrenia' of 'localisation' and 'internationalization'. (Wallis and Baran, 1990) Whereas in recent years (not at least because of the advent of CNN and other new news sources), local broadcasters in the US have become involved in the presentation of international news, some have already begun to produce news reports for *World Report* which are aired globally. Wallis and Baran do not refer to the fact that internationalization may also include the international exchange of local news programmes. This approach would require a clear definition of 'international' in terms of local as well as national broadcasters.

Flournoy states,

> Labour unions, religious groups, political organizations, business and industrial organizations are finding ways to by-pass the traditional monopolies of the state to tell their stories and interact with others. The groups have begun to rely on their own resources, trust their own abilities to define problems as they see them, set goals, devise strategies and make decisions independent of those officially in charge. (Flournoy, 1992:66)

A process which Flournoy describes as a 'de-institutionalisation of news', is occurring which he defines as when 'untrained people, equipped with a camera cover or offer events they think are newsworthy' and which avoids the traditional gatekeeping function of news journalism. (Flournoy, 1992:67) Some of the weekly contributors are government broadcasters 'with a public diplomacy mission, such as the mission served abroad by Voice of America and Worldnet of the US State Department. Their mandate is to 'explain the policies of the government and convey to viewers abroad a more complete picture of life in the country from the point of view of that country'. (Flournoy, 1992:68)

CNNWR is also used by 'traditional' broadcasters who see it as an additional opportunity to disseminate their reports worldwide, and by internationally operating broadcasters (such as Deutsche Welle) to gain an additional news medium.

Framing of events

I argue that within the field of global communication the special framing of events becomes important because this implies facilitates comprehension by the target audience. The news frame makes a news event appeal to a specific audience.

New journalism

A new type of journalism can be seen in the decentralised gatekeeping of the *World Report* programme and the variety of different styles of journalism. These may consist in the following.

(1) Interactive journalism

This is defined as a type of journalism which reacts to another news report. It is clearly biased, not objective.

(2) Reciprocal journalism

This consists in the fact that *World Report* segments are transmitted back into the countries where they had originated. (see Volkmer/Melton, 1990)

(3) Showcase journalism

This style shows *World Report* as a global platform. Showcase journalism implies the presentation of unique national or regional features.

The public sphere of 'world report'

Because of the growing CNNWR 'community model' in which journalists are part of and participants in a global community of their peers, reinforced by the CNNWR ideology, by the organization of yearly *World Report* conferences and by the value of the news organizations for CNNWR as providers of news reports, CNNWR regards itself as a 'United Nations of TV broadcasters'. In this respect, CNNWR functions as a public outlet for the worldwide broadcaster to present fresh news stories that would not otherwise appear.

The variables and a definition

The categories of interpretation were chosen so as to reveal any close connection with the idea of global journalism. The programmes were taped between February 1993 to November 1994.

Variables consist of those items that have any connections with an approach to global journalism. I drew the categories from Stevensen's survey on 'foreign news' 1984 and from CNNWR research (*World Report* Kit, January 1990) and completed them with categories which also match the goals of the study.

The unit of analysis

The unit of analysis I used was either a single report, provided by an international broadcaster (either 'traditional' or private) or an anchor story if it did not consist of an introduction to a report. Unlike the situation in the first years of CNNWR and the pilot study, recent programme developments include anchor stories.

World Report Specials consist of programme segments each dedicated to a single overall topic. These specials have increased in recent years. According to Flournoy's analysis, the first ones appeared during the Christmas season in 1987, when contributors were asked to submit stories 'about how Christmas was celebrated in their countries', one on Aids in 1988, in (June) 1989 on abortion, in August on the Non-aligned Movement, in December 1989 on refugees and the homeless, on German reunification in December, 1990, in March, 1991 on the Ramadan celebration, in April 1991 on religion and ethnicity. According to Stevenson's survey, a topic or story can be defined as follows: 'the kind of event or situation that the item is mainly about'. (Stevenson, 1983:26) Although, as Stevenson remarks, subtopics may also become subject of investigation, they were not considered in the content analysis of CNNWR. The subject of concern is the main topic.

Categories

The categories of analysis consist in the following: (1) topic, (2) country or region of news organization, (3) news organization, (4) type of news organization, (5) main programme type of news organization, (6) main programme geography, (7) angle of event, (8) type of event, (9) occurrence of event, (10) quality of event, (11) experts presented in story, (12) actors in story, (13) framing of event, (14) type of story or anchor story, (15) programme segment of *World Report*.

The basic categories refer to the events reported, to the broadcasting organizations submitting stories, to the experts and actors in stories. Each of these categories is defined and further specified in the Definition List of Value Labels. The analysis focusses on the following dimensions.

The event

The event was analysed under 'topic' and 'framing'. It can be argued that it is the framing in particular of globally distributed programmes that points to the audience at which the programme is specifically aimed. 'Event' means in this sense the event which provides the centre of the story. The framing refers either to the context given to the event in international terms, or to an international event itself.

The news organization or contributor

Contributing news organizations were investigated, as it is important to distinguish the different participating organizations in terms of their original programme distribution, programme concept and broadcasting technique. As programmes like *World Report* provide space for carrier programmes it is reasonable to suppose that these are beginning to be produced worldwide, by programmers specialising in this sector.

The experts and actors

Experts presented in a story can be of any kind: from the man or woman in the street to the expert scientist. They are always introduced by name, title or function, and my coding is drawn from these inserts. Experts' functions and identification are drawn from the supers included in reports. The actors presented in a story tend to reveal its particular slant. In many cases they are used to make the story comprehensible.

The category system is considered as being exclusive in variables and allows multiple answers. Each variable consists of many categories which can be combined when there are only a few occurences.[15]

Selection of the sample

The sample was selected by criteria which take into account the programme concept of CNNWR. Although the programme is broadcast daily, the weekly programme slots of CNNWR have to be distinguished from those at the weekends. As described above, the programme concept involves a longer time slot on Sundays than on weekdays, which affects the content. The Sunday edition, being of greater length, reveals a broad variety of topics. For this reason, 'traditional' sampling techniques of content analysis, such as selecting a sample week (which involves a random start and a selection of programmes afterwards) or a composite week (involving no 'more than two days from one week [to] be chosen' in order to guarantee a balanced content) (Wimmer and Dominick, 1987:173) were inappropriate.

Another reason for choosing both Sunday and weekday editions is that the content of the sample has to be investigated in terms of fresh news. As the programme is set up as a global forum, some of the content might cross-refer, or refer to the same topics from different angles. Additionally I investigated whether programmes selected for 'World News' were taped simultaneously for possible re-use, when topics on CNNWR were chosen or picked up by 'World News'.

The composition of the analysed *World Report* editions is shown in the following table:

Table 18: Composition of the Sample[16]

Date of 'World Report'	Frequency of Reports (%)
February 21, 1993 Sun.	30 (7.6%)
February 28, 1993 Sun.	35 (8.8%)
March 4, 1993 Thurs.	27 (6.8%)
March 7, 1993 Sun.	39 (9.8%)
March 14, 1993 Sun.	33 (8.3%)
March 21, 1993 Sun.	35 (8.8%)
March 28, 1993 Sun.	34 (8.6%)
April 12, 1993 Mon.	25 (6.3%)
May 16, 1993 Sun.	32 (8.1%)
June 20, 1993 Sun.	27 (6.8%)
June 27, 1993 Sun.	26 (6.5%)
November 21, 1994 Mon.	25 (6.3%)
November 27, 1994 Sun.	29 (7.3%)

As can be seen in the above table, the majority of reports analysed were Sunday editions. These have a greater length and a 'higher' value, as they cover the week's stories. The Sunday edition provides the contributors with additional 'international sound' because the programme is sent out on two audio channels (CNNWR information kit, August, 1993). The unit of analysis is one report, submitted by a news organization and an anchor story, which consists of a single news item, presented by the anchor without a following report on the same issue.

CNNWR: A new model of global journalism

Each *World Report* programme consists of around 25 reports. After the 'World News' segment, a short 'Headline' newscast and a commercial break are followed by visual lead-ins from three stories from the first half-hour. One of the anchors, Ralph Wenge or Ralitsa Valisseva, speaks the voice-over. After this the anchors welcome the viewers to the programme[17] and introduce themselves. Then one of them presents the first story.

The role of the anchors is to bring the reports up to date, by explaining the broad context of current developments of which the issue to follow is directly or indirectly a part. These contexts are created by reference to the current politics or the overall political situation of the region, similar events, or similarities between countries within a region or having a common culture. It is also necessary to balance reports, especially those which chiefly consist of propaganda (such as reports from Cuba, China and Turkey). The role is also one of explaining events, perhaps giving a short historical overview of the occurrence or similar, related issues and subjects. These are quite often supported by inserts of maps which highlight the region in question. The anchor introduction also updates previously reported issues in order to give them some reality since most of them do not refer to a specific current 'breaking' time frame.

'News value' is the staff answer given to the question of how you decide which stories to package together. Positioning and the order of the line-up is an editorial judgement based on a sense of what pieces will play with one another, either because they have a common theme or because they represent a common geographical area. Increasingly the lead stories are the breaking news stories followed by the feature material. (Flournoy, 1992:36) Some of the stories are also aired on other CNN and CNNI news programmes.

Almost all of the 397 reports in the sample were specifically produced for CNNWR. This fact could be ascertained either from the logo of the originating news organization, or by stylistic features indicating that the English audio was added to the original language package, or by the presence of anchors from the news organization, or else the original program itself is mentioned in the credits, or subtitles in the original language (such as Japanese) are shown. *Earthwatch*, which is an environmental programme aired by CNN, was mentioned in one CNN contribution.

41.3 per cent, or 164 of the 397 reports, are part of a packaged programme. This means that these reports were part of the regular programme segments, such as 'Human Rights' (5.5 per cent), 'Environment' (11.6 per cent), 'People and Places' (15.9 per cent), 'Money and Markets' (15.2 per cent or 25 reports). Increasingly, CNN requests reports on issues thought of as global, such as the environment or women's issues. These general topics are distributed among the various sectors of which the programme is composed.

This packaged-programme type includes all stories related to the overall topic. Stories which cannot be aired within this programme (for technical reasons such as arriving too late in Atlanta) are aired in the subsequent shows. Examples of these overall packages, which are part of the sample, are 'Common Bonds', a special programme focussing on women's issues in Africa and 'Environment', dealing with all aspects and fields of environmental problems and concerns. A small segment, headlined 'Growing Pains', focussed on the transitional problems of Eastern Europe. 'Common Bonds' consisted of 38 reports, 'Environment' of 27.[18] Some reports on women's issues appeared among those held over for a later issue of CNNWR.

Table 19: Number and per centage of topical reports in each package

Topic (F3)	Story Part of Packaged CNNWR Programme	
	Yes	No
Politics	7 (4.3%)	47 (20.2%)
Military/Defense	6 (3.7%)	24 (10.3%)
Economy	21 (12.8%)	19 (8.2%)
Agriculture	6 (3.7%)	1 (0.4%)
Environment	32 (19.5%)	14 (6.0%)
International Aid	1 (0.6%)	7 (3.0%)
Human Rights	5 (3.0%)	15 (6.4%)
Social Services	1 (0.6%)	5 (2.1%)
Crime/Victims	6 (3.7%)	15 (6.4%)
Religion	9 (5.5%)	9 (3.9%)
Science/Technology	8 (4.9%)	2 (0.9%)
Health/Medicine	17 (10.4%)	7 (3.0%)
Sport	2 (1.2%)	1 (0.4%)
Human Interest	13 (7.9%)	14 (6.0%)
Natural Disasters	-	1 (0.4%)
Culture	13 (7.9%)	20 (8.6%)
Education	8 (4.9%)	14 (6.0%)
Tourism	1 (0.6%)	5 (2.1%)
Liberation	4 (2.4%)	7 (3.0%)
Law	4 (2.4%)	6 (2.6%)
TOTAL	**164 (100%)**	**233 (100%)**

The type of event, reported in packaged and requested programmes, can be interpreted as hard and soft news. It can be argued that because of the specific programme package, a report attracts a larger audience, since it can be directly compared to other reports and gains more attention because of this. Hard news stories: events involving conflict, diplomacy, agreement, violation, negotiation and movement, are presented alongside soft news:

accidents, curiosities, discoveries, sports, festivals and celebrations. The analysis revealed that events of the hard news type were represented by 82 cases, whereas soft news was represented by 107 cases.

Of the reports in CNNWR's programmes having an international aspect, this was: in 7.9 per cent of cases, multinational; in 3.7 per cent, international-regional; in 0.6 per cent international-global; in 6.7 per cent supranational. Particular angles such as bilateral interests were present in 6.7 per cent of the reports, and a local aspect in 28.7 per cent. The majority (45.7per cent) had a national slant.

Of the 161 out of 164 packaged or segmented reports in which an event was framed one nation was involved in 50.3 per cent, more than three nations in 14.4 per cent, two nations in 10.6 per cent. Events were framed in terms of an ecological region in 9.3 per cent, a cultural region 4.3 per cent, a capital city 4.3 per cent, a rural area or village in 3.7 per cent.

Twenty-one of the reports analysed consisted of 'anchor stories'. These are defined as any story other than a 'lead-in' story, presented by an anchor but not followed by a report on the same issue. Anchor stories consist of live interviews with international journalists, present in the studio or over the telephone or visual material with voice-over commentary by the anchor. Other anchor-story types consist of updates of an issue which had been presented in a previous programme. Eleven anchor stories consisted of video footage with voice over, seven cases consisted of updates, and one three occasions a journalist was interviewed.

Although the anchor tries to actualise the submitted story, the majority of the sample did consist of reports that covered topics without any on-the-spot footage. In 77.8 per cent or 309 cases, no current event or topic was specified or referred to. Events that had occurred two to seven days before the *World Report* programme was aired, were covered in 15.4 per cent. *World Report* is not seen by the participants as a hard news programme but more as a background, secondary information source which supplements the hard news stories by other 'local' or particular perspectives. It functions as a secondary news source for broadcasters and the interested audience in order to assist in the interpretation of events.

The contributions from worldwide broadcasters that were analysed consisted mainly of reports (78.7 per cent, 306 cases). Documentary reports (on conferences, festivals or political occasions) were ranked second, with 14.9 per cent or 58 cases. The three categories 'Press Conference', 'Official Announcement' and 'Interview' were ranked third.

Events presented in the reports were chiefly upbeat (58.7 per cent). These dealt with positive events in politics, the military, the economy, the environment, and so on, such as diplomacy, agreements, negotiations, and movements.

In the majority of cases (88.5 per cent, or 332 cases) the part of the world where the event took place and the news organization that reported on it correspond. This happens through bilateral agreements in which the country in question is involved, local stations report on occurrences within their geographical region, and national broadcasters report on events within a country or in some parts of it. Other situations include events which can be regarded as multinational (such as religion) but which are specific to the broadcasters' country: the news organization is located in the area where the event takes place. In those 19 cases in which there was no such correspondence, other connections (such as historical ones) exist between the country in which the event takes place and the country of the news organization. An example where the country in which the event occurs and the country where the station is located do not correspond would be Portugal reporting on civil war in Angola. Other situations might involve relationships such as those of neighbouring African countries. It is explicit that a substantial element of *World Report* programme philosphy requires especially 'authentic' reports.

Of contributing news organizations, 86.2 per cent, or 325 cases, offered a full programme service, 8.2 per cent, or 31 cases, were those that produce only carrier programes, such as the two UN television stations in Paris, UNESCO TV and United Nations Television in New York, Way Press International, a Belgian news agency, and EPTV, the television department of the European Parliament. Other carrier programmess that regularly participate in CNNWR, though not appearing in the sample, are UNRWA, as the third United Nations television department, and the television department of the Organization for Economic Co-operation and Development. In the sample 5.6 per cent, or 21 cases, offered a fragmented programme, such as Deutsche Welle, RNTV Netherlands, and CNN. Various of the national broadcasters who generally participate in CNNWR already already broadcast an international version of their domestic output via satellite: some of these are Ostankino, Russia; TV Globo, Brazil; CCTV, China; ZDF, Germany, ORF, Austria and SRI, Switzerland in the '3SAT' satellite channel; RAI, Italy; Middle East Broadcast Centre (with headquarters in Lebanon and London); TRT Turkey; and CNN as well as news organizations such as Way Press International, which also produces a news programme for Hong Kong (*Today's World*).

The main location of these news organizations' programmes is national (81.2 per cent, or 306 cases), multinational (10.1 per cent, or 38 cases), local (7.4 per cent, or 7 cases), international regional, and global (1.4 per cent, or 5 cases). Not only do national broadcasters have an opportunity to be involved in global distribution via CNNWR, so do local news organizations, such as ITN Canada (headquartered in Edmonton) which contribute regularly.

Decentralised Gatekeeping

The goal of the study was to reveal CNNWR's distinct quality in the context of global communication as well as in new models of global journalism. In both contexts, conclusions can be drawn in universal as well as particular terms. CNNWR exercises a model of decentralised gatekeeping, where the decisions about which stories to offer are made by journalists of the participating broadcast stations.

Flournoy asked in his survey of CNNWR contributors how they know what is acceptable to CNN. According to him, they are aware of the fact that CNN will accept 'anything'. In their view, there are 'no constraints other than the libel issues and the length of the story'. As Flournoy remarks, 'Contributing reporters and their agencies or governments are the first and only gatekeepers of content'. Some journalists answered that they forward 'World Report type material' (Flournoy, 1992:32) if they regard it as such. Since the majority of the CNNWR contributors are regular contributors, they have also become part of the CNNWR community, which gathers once a year at CNN's headquarters in Atlanta and quite often exercises a close relationship to the CNNWR staff. The annual meeting contributes a social relationship within this community as well as serving as a platform to discuss issues of global politics and journalism. Since these journalists function as gatekeepers through their understanding of the overall programme philosophy, they might be involved in conflicts of loyalty with their own news organizations, especially when the latter are state-run.

Developing and developed journalism and new particularities (Topics)

The majority of reports (31.2 per cent, 124 cases) of the sample of 397 cover the range of political, economic or military issues. This fact indicates that *World Report* is regarded as a primary political forum. The fact that CNN is involved in this programme as a prestigious American news channel might also indicate that more regional and national issues, as opposed to world politics, are brought to the attention of the world and thus also to American policy-makers. These issues either involve propaganda for political ideologies of a kind rarely picked up by American networks or other Western news organizations, or put a new, though important spin on an issue, or draw attention to problems that are not covered by politics or news agencies. Political issues are defined as those which deal with interior or foreign politics, official and legal representatives, partisan activities, elections, campaigns, the activities of ministries, institutions, espionage, revolution, turmoils, strikes, peace efforts, immigration policies and political crime. Military issues include defence, armed conflicts, threats of conflict, negotiations, settlements, arms deals, and military actions of legal and partisan parties. The economy involves agreements on trade, tariffs, imports, exports, capital investment, stock issues, and monetary questions.

Flournoy quotes a study which analysed the topics presented in other US networks apart from CNNWR. The study concludes that 75 per cent of international network news consisted of military, defence, foreign domestic relations, crime and justice, whereas 35 per cent of the *World Report* refers to these issues. The researcher argues that in 1989 CNNWR also covered such issues as foreign relations, science and ecology and education and ethnic relations. (Ganzert and Flournoy, in Flournoy, 1992:38)

Second (13.9 per cent, 53 of 397 cases) are ranked those issues which deal with culture and education. These are art, music, literature, high culture and folk culture; educational systems, organizations, institutions, projects. These issues are chiefly covered by news organizations.

News organizations presented 114 of the 124 issues having political, military and economical content. The remaining 10 are 'anchor stories.' Of these 42 cases, 36.4 per cent were submitted by state-owned news organizations, 25 cases, or 21.9 per cent by commercial, 24 cases, or 21.1 per cent by public service organizations. Post-communist transitional organizations submitted 18 reports (15.8 per cent), public relations 3 (2.6 per cent) and private organizations (such as a university television station) 2 (1.8 per cent). This finding reveals that politically relevant reports were mainly submitted by state-owned broadcasters which regard *World Report* as a political forum, whereas public service organizations apply a different value to the programme.

The table also indicates the function in which *World Report* is viewed by different types of broadcasters. Whereas public service stations, mainly located in Western Europe, report firstly on events in the 'Curiosity' category, second on 'Conflicts', third on 'Decision and Agreements', state-owned broadcasters report on 'Festivals and Celebrations', 'Curiosity', 'Decision and Agreement.' Public relation Stations such as UN television departments report on 'Curiosity', 'Movements', 'Conflicts', Post-Communist transitional organizations on 'Curiosity', 'Conflict', 'Decision and Agreement.' Since unique occurences are subsumed under 'Curiosity', these reports involve strange or rare events.

According to Aggarwala (1979), development journalism consists of information on local regional progress in social change. Thus development journalism refers less to political issues, and more to social projects, culture, health and human interest issues. This implies that news emphasises agricultural or economic problems, 'educates' the audience in order to enlist their cooperation. As Griswold and Swenson, who transfer development communication issues to media issues in a rural American community, argue:

> This view focuses on improvements in the quality of life as well as in material conditions. It also stresses self-development rather than development imposed from the top down, but sees development

Table 20: Topics covered by CNNWR

Topic (F3)	Number of times	Percentage
Politics, Military/Defense Economy	124	31.2 %
International Aid Human Rights Liberation	39	9.8%
Agriculture Environment	53	13.4%
Culture Education	55	13.9%
Social Services	6	1.5%
Crime/Victims	21	5.3%
Religion	18	4.5%
Science/Technolgy	10	2.5%
Health/Medicine	24	6.0%
Sport	3	0.8%
Human Interest	27	6.8%
Natural Disasters	1	0.3%
Tourism	6	1.5%
Law	10	2.5%
Total	**397**	**100.0%**

as a process of social change in systems, structure, organization or facilities and not just change in the knowledge or participation or status of individuals. (Griswold and Swenson, 1992:583, see also Chapter 1)

It consists of 'protocol news', news on protocol activities of the political leader, dictator or the government which symbolizes the new nation. (Stevenson, 1988:146) Flournoy describes a survey, undertaken by Dilawari of the Ohio research team, which had analysed 167 stories from industrialised countries and 141 stories from developing countries and had found out that news of industrial growth submitted by developing nations and by developed nations were almost in balance. Flournoy also quotes another Ohio study, undertaken by Park *et al*, in which 566 *World Report* contributions were analysed.

In the presentation of domestic news ... both the developed and the developing countries focused more on development news than on non-development news. Yet, both the developed and developing countries oriented their coverage more toward non-development news in what they offered as international news (news involving two or more nations). (Flournoy, 1992:40)

Table 21: Main type of event by category of news organization

Main Type of Event	Public Service	State Owned	Commercial	Public Relation	Post-communist Transition	State owned	Private	Other
Conflict	11	4	10	4	10	4	1	-
Diplomacy	4	8	5	1	3	-	-	
Decision/ Agreement	10	14	8	3	5	5	-	
Violation/ Violence	7	12	16	3	5	1	-	-
Festival/ Celebration	7	23	3	2	2	1	1	-
Accident	-	2	2	-	1	-	-	-
Curiosity	23	19	38	6	21	7	3	2
Discovery	6	3	1	1	-	1	-	-
Sport event	1	1	-	-	-	-	-	-
Negotiation	-	3	1	-	1	1	-	-
Movement	8	10	3	5	5	2	1	-
Investigation	2	-	1	-	-	-	-	-
Undefinable	-	-	1	-	-	-	-	-

The term 'development news' was invented to bring about a change in Western reporting on the Third World, so that its problems and developments were presented from a national point of view and not as Western news events. Since the inauguration of programmes like *World Report* and the emergence of a global public sphere, development issues have to be regarded in a slightly different way. From the global perspective, national, cultural or regional issues are particular issues. Although this term seems to be quite apolitical in its general sense, on a basic level it implies a principle of equal access and equal presentation among other particular issues. The evidence revealed in the studies quoted above indicates that this model no longer holds. Besides, news journalism is not homogeneous within a country. Even in developing countries, such as Ghana and Nigeria, alternative news operations are available for the societal élite, the Western-oriented population. For this reason it is not the country itself that has to be referred to, but the news organizations. It also involves news organizations which operate at a lower level than the state or nation (eg locally) or at a higher (eg the UN). Besides the increase in direct competition in news reports from developing and developed countries, the fact that all reports must present issues in a widely comprehensible style eliminates – at least for the *World Report* community – the old dichotomy between developing and developed news. The term 'the CNN factor', originally implying pace and a certain journalistic style also affects international news reporting in the CNNWR programme, since CNN has high prestige on account of being an American and a global channel, watched by world politicians, and thus invites the presentation of 'proofs' of democracy movements, as well as problems which have to be communicated to a world audience. Of the reports analysed , 203 cases frame the reported event in relation to one nation, 56 cases in relation to more than three nations, 50 cases to two nations. In the fourth rank are issues which are framed in relation to a capital city, or ecological or cultural region.

Politics, Military Affairs, the Economy

The topics presented are dominated by the fields of politics, military matters and the economy. The 54 political, 30 military and 40 economic events were analysed in terms of their timeliness, which was relatively pronounced in the case of 24 political, five military and 13 economic events. The event had occurred usually two to seven days earlier and was coded as 'This week' or 'Recently'. The date of the event to which the report related was mentioned either by the anchor or in the story. In the first categories – 'Politics', 'Military/Defence', and 'Economy', – 82 of the 124 reports were not definable in terms of the time of the event.

Table 22: Politics, Military/Defence, Economy and Timeliness of News

Topic (F3)	Same Day	2-7 days ago	8-14 days ago	15-30 days ago	More than 30 days ago	Undef- inable
Politics Military/Defense Economy	1 (0.8%)	27 (21.8%)	2 (1.6%)	5 (4.0%)	6 (4.8%)	83 (66.9%)

Fifty per cent, or 62 of these 124 reports on politics, military matters and the economy refer to positive events. In 66 of them, expert opinions are represented. These experts belonged in 37 cases to the government, in 13 cases to industry, were in nine cases economics experts, and in five cases experts on general policy experts (such as representatives of non parliamentary parties), and in one case represented the parliamentary opposition. One case referred to an expert in the police, four cases to military people, and one case to an expert who was part of the societal élite, such as a former government member or a former president.

In 65 cases (52.4 per cent) personalities in those 124 stories were members of some institution (the foremost were government, military or political agencies). The special field of the figure was national in 107 of these 124 cases on 'politics', followed by nine cases, international, eight local, and only five multinational and also partisan. Supranational (such as religious representative) applies to only two cases.

The majority of events presented in the 'Politics', 'Military and Defence' and 'Economy' categories were slanted towards a national context. Of the stories, 35 of the 54 political ones, 13 of the military and defence ones and 27 of those on economic matters were represented in this category. Political stories and military and defence stories were secondarily considered 'bilateral' in emphasis. Nine of the political stories, eight of the military and defense stories, and four on economy were international-regional and local. Since political stories also involve interactive journalism (see below), these bilateral stories cover neighbouring conflicts and interests.

The majority of the 54 (29.6 per cent) of the political reports dealt with issues which involve decision and agreements. On the second rank of political issues was 'Diplomacy' (11 reports, 20.4 per cent), on the third, 'conflict' (10, 28.5 per cent). Thirty reports on 'Military and Defence' broke down into six reports in three categories; 'Diplomacy' and 'Conflict' broke down into only two categories, with five reports in the 'Curiosity' category. Economy, 40 reports, is represented in the categories 'Conflict' by 11 reports, 'Curiosity' by 10 reports (25.0 per cent), 'Decision and Agreement' by eight reports (20.0 per cent). The relationship between topics and event types is significant. This result shows, that 'hard' political, economic or military issues, as represented in the categories 'Conflict', 'Diplomacy', 'Decision and Agreement', 'Violation and Violence' are in the majority. The relationship of hard news to 'soft' news stories in politics was 40 to 14, in military or defence 20 to 10, and in the economy 24 to 16.

Culture, education

Fifty-five (13.9 per cent) cases deal with cultural and educational issues. They reported on literature, art, music festivals and celebrations, on folk culture, media and educational systems and projects: against illiteracy, for example.

Types of events in this category, which consisted of 33 stories on culture and 22 on education and culture were predominantly in the 'curiosity' category (16 stories in culture and 10 stories in education). 'Festivals/Celebrations' is ranked second in the 'Culture' category (11 stories) and there were five stories on 'movement' in education.

International Aid, Human Rights

Content analysis here reveals that 13.4 per cent, or 53 cases, focussed on issues which centre around disaster relief, industrial development, military aid (UN Peace Corps), their missions and projects. In terms of type of event, 'International Aid' (eight stories) is represented with four stories in the 'Violation or Violence' category, and 'Human Rights' (20 stories) with five stories coming under 'Movement', four stories in 'Conflict', 'Violation or Violence' and 'Curiosity'.

Agriculture, Environment

39 cases of the 397 reports analysed come under this category (ie 98 per cent). Seven stories were presented in the 'Agriculture', category of which four stories refer to the 'Curiosity' type of event, 14 of the 46 stories on environment are part of the 'curiosity' category, 11 refer to 'Violation and Violence', and six to 'Decision or Agreement'.

Liberation/Movement

Eleven stories fell into this topic category. Five stories were part of 'Movement' in terms of type of event.

New players - The emergence of new news organizations

CNNWR has encourged original kinds of news organizations, which hardly have a chance to broadcast their programmes anywhere else. Among these are those that represent new types of 'privately' organised news services, such as U.N. television, UNESCO television, the Afghan Media Centre, and Middle East Broadcasting Centre.

Table 23: Programme type and number of submitted reports

	Full program	Fragmented program	Carrier program
Main Program Type of News Organizations	325 (81.9%)	21 (5.3%)	31 (7.8%)

Types of full-programme stations

The majority of reports, 325, or 86.2 per cent were submitted by television organizations which offer a full programme service. Full-programme types of television stations are those which offer at least eight hours per day of a mixed programme with entertainment and information. They may be:

(1) Public-service organizations, the programme goal of which is to inform, to entertain and/or to educate and is financed either by audience fees alone (one example is the BBC, United Kingdom) or by a mixed financial budget, consisting of fees, state subsidies and the sale of commercial airtime.

(2) State broadcasters put together and run by a government subsidiary. These channels (such as ICRT Cuba, CCTV China or TPA Angola) are financed by government funds.

(3) Full-programme broadcasters financed by government funds but gaining additional income by the sale of commercial airtime. These are the ones which are classified as 'state-run-commercial'.

(4) Post-Communist transitional types. All are currently from the former socialist East European region and are currently in a process of developing from state-run organization to public-service. Although some of them have already been established, such as MTV, Hungary, others, such as Ostankino, Russia, are still in transition. These latter are confronted with a commercial national and international context in which they have to find their own identity as public-service stations. For this reason, since all of these broadcasters are in the process of reshaping their journalism goals and gathering new experiences of a new 'public', I have classified them as post-Communist transitional in order to identify their profile in the global public sphere of *World Report*.

Whereas historically the public-service organizations were established to provide a national programme for a mass as well as a minority audience, some of them have already begun to expand internationally through satellite distribution. These are the German broadcaster 'ZDF', which has put together a joint programme with SRG Switzerland and ORF Austria. Besides these, state-run stations like CCTV China, which has extended its news service onto such channels as Ostankino, Russia (see above), have internationalized their programmes so as to target the expatriate audience.

Public-service organizations contributed 80 reports (21.4 per cent), state-owned, 99 reports (24.9 per cent), commercial broadcasters 89 reports (23.7 per cent), post-Communist transitional 53 reports (14.1 per cent), state-owned commercial 22 (5.9 per cent). Whereas some of them, like ZDF, operate a full service internationally, others separated off their news departments and produced an international carrier programme with either news which is simultaneously broadcast on an international feed (carrier-programme type) or is produced for international distribution, like TCS News, El Salvador. Others are producing carrier programs for the international channel of a particular region, such as 3 SAT (which includes ZDF) and Chinese News & Entertainment.

Besides those listed, there are other broadcasters who gain unique access to an international or global audience through programmes such as *World Report*, like local broadcasters who serve a community or region. This category involves such organizations as ITV Canada, a commercial local broadcaster which frequently contributes programmes. ITV has produced seven reports within the sample on 'Agricultural and Environmental issues as well as on 'Criminal' issues, 'Human Interest' and 'Culture'. All of these reports have a strong local framework. Another type would be a territorial news organization such Bop TV, Bophuthatswana, besides Ciskei, Transkei and Venda, one of the four South African territories. TV Catalunya and Northern Cyprus, invaded by Turkey, which is admitted only by Turkey itself. Twenty-eight reports (7.4 per cent) were submitted by these local broadcasters.

Broadcasters who offer a full programme have contributed 325 reports out of a definable 377 (20 reports were contributed by anchor stories). Of these 325 reports, 46 (14.2 per cent) focus on issues in the 'Politics' category, 37 stories (11.4 per cent) were on 'Environment', 32 reports (9.8 per cent) on 'Economy', 27 stories (8.3 per cent) on 'Culture', 23 stories (7.1 per cent) on 'Human Interest', 20 (6.2 per cent) on 'Health and Medicine', 15 (4.9 per cent) on 'Religion',15 (4.5 per cent) on 'Education', nine (2.8 per cent) on 'Liberation.' Submitted stories on 'Science and Technology' and 'Law', were seven (2.2 per cent) in 'Agriculture', six reports (1.8 per cent) in the categories of 'Tourism' and 'Social Services', five (1.5 per cent) under 'International Aid', two (0.6 per cent) in 'Sport', and one (0.3 per cent) under 'Natural Disaster.'

Sixty-three of the reports from the 80 public-service organizations were news stories. Twelve were documentaries (that is, a conference, a festival, et cetera), using a great deal of o-tone and on-the-spot video and focus on one situation. Three reports consisted mainly of live interview, one of a press-conference briefing and one of an official announcement.

State-owned broadcasters, who submitted 99 reports, also submitted 72 reports as news stories, 18 as documentary, five as press conference coverage, two of an official announcement and a live interview. There is also no difference between these two types and commercial journalism, except that three reports covered live interviews, one a press conference and none fell into the category 'official announcement'. None of the reports in the sample used a larger portion of a commentary on an event, although CNN World Report does not explicitly request only news stories. All the fragmented and carrier programs included were involved in international broadcasting.

Local broadcasters produced 28 reports, of which five focus on cultural issues, three on 'politics', three on criminal issues. Two reports fell into the categories of 'Agriculture', 'Environment', 'Religion' and 'Law.' Hard-news issues, such as politics and economy, were less well represented by state-owned than by national or international broadcasters. 'Culture', 'Education', 'Science and Technology' were represented by eight reports, 'Religion' and 'Social Services' by three, 'Agriculture and Environment' by four.

Carrier programmes

Besides the stations offering a full range of product, which have their own carrier programmes, new 'players' have appeared in the field of carrier-programme production. These new producers are bound to expand in future, with the increasing availability of internationally operating satellite channels due to the commercialization of satellite organizations (see Chapter 1), the number of privately and commercially operated channels seeking programme material, the sale of time-slots by networks and the multiplication of independent productions.

Among the producers of carrier programmes are the public relations agencies of large organizations, such as the UN, which has currently three departments, (UNTV, UNESCO TV and UNRWA TV), and EPTV, the European Parliament Public Relations Division.

Thirty-one reports, 8.2 per cent of the sample, were submitted as carrier programmes. These consisted in a university programme, a news agency one, and programmes from the UN and the European Parliament public relations departments. Whereas the local carrier programme did not have much political coverage, the carrier program of UNTV, which contributed 13 reports, focussed on issues with a global 'hard news' character. These reports involve military or defence topics (four reports), economics issues (one report), those about the environment (one report), international aid (two reports), human rights (four reports), health and medicine (one report) and education (three reports). Reports on events occurring during UN projects are of the type originally described as development journalism.

The difference between the 'traditional' type of development journalism and the global journalism of these public-relations organizations is that these issues arise from regional or national contexts but are framed in an international or multinational scope. These public-relations organizations contributed nine of the 25 reports in the 'Agriculture and Environment' category, eight in 'Culture, Education' and three in both the 'Politics, Military, Economy' and 'International Aid and Human Rights', categories.

As carrier programmes depend on national or international broadcasters to be aired, their focus could be more international in terms of giving the event a context. It should be noted that *World Report* itself provides a unique forum for the airing of carrier reports from international broadcasters. Whereas the common carrier programme consists for example of a programme slot, *World Report* is an advanced carrier programme model, since single reports by worldwide broadcasters offer this opportunity to all organizations, even those which are involved only in national broadcasting. Producers of carrier programmes submitted 31 reports, from 377 identifiable news organizations. As the following table indicates, the major topics are human rights (five reports) and education (five reports), followed by environment (four reports), the economy and international aid (three reports).

Since the majority of carrier programme producers participating in CNN's *World Report* are public-relations divisions of international and global political organizations, their reports focus on issues which are less frequently covered by full programmes (15 reports – 4.6 per cent of the 325 full programme reports – covered human rights and education), whereas the environment and the economy are popular issues in ful-length programme reports. Only five reports (1.5 per cent) from the 325 full programme participants focussed on issues of international aid.

The public relations news divisions used only the journalistic genres of news stories (23) and documentaries (2). News organizations in the post-communist transitional category submitted 53 news stories, eight documentary reports, one official announcement and one live interview. 25 stories were submitted by a public-relations carrier programme producer and six by a private organization.

Table 24: Topic by carrier programme

Topic	Carrier Program		Other Broadcasting Stations as full Programs or Fragments as Other	
Politics	-		47	(13.6%)
Military/Defense	2	(6.5%)	26	(7.5%)
Economy	3	(9.7%)	36	(10.4%)
Agriculture	-		7	(2.0%)
Environment	4	(12.9%)	38	(11.0%)
International Aid	3	(9.7%)	5	(1.4%)
Human Rights	5	(16.1%)	15	(4.3%)
Social Services	-		6	(1.7%)
Crime/Victims	-		21	(6.1%)
Religion	-		16	(4.6%)
Science/Technology			10	(2.9%)
Health/Medicine	2	(6.5%)	22	(6.4%)
Sport	-		3	(0.9%)
Human interest	3	(9.7%)	23	(6.6%)
Natural disasters	-		1	(0.3%)
Culture	3	(9.7%)	29	(8.4%)
Education	5	(16.1%)	17	(4.9%)
Tourism	-		6	(1.7%9
Liberation	1	(3.2%)	9	(2.6%)
Law	-		9	(2.6%)
Total	**31 (100.1%)**		**346**	**(99.9%)**

Fragmented programmes

Twenty-one of the reports (5.6 per cent) were contributed by fragmented news organizations and consisted of fragmented news programmes such as CNN, or international programmes from individual countries, for example those of Deutsche Welle, Germany and RNTV, Netherlands. Fragmented programme organizations are those which focus on some specialised field, resulting in narrowcasting. In the case of Deutsche Welle and RNTV this means a nationally produced programme for an international audience. Programmes of this type contain entertainment as well as information segments, which narrowcast in as much as their programmes represent a national culture. Another fragmented programme appearing in the sample is CNN, the domestic US programme which focusses on news and information.

Of the 21 reports submitted by fragmented news organizations, 10 fall into the categories of politics, military matters or the economy; one report focusses on international aid and human rights, four on culture and education, two on science and technology, two on health and medicine, one on sport and one on law. As compared to 'full' programmes, fragmented programmes do not cover the whole topic range. Their topic range covers issues of news and information and culture.

Of the fragmented programme submissions, 11 reports came from a commercial fragmented news organization (CNN), nine from public-service organizations (Deutsche Welle and RNTV Netherlands).

Profile of news organizations and topics

Public-service stations submitted 79 reports (21.1 per cent of the sample). They primarily present stories which involve curiosities (23 stories), conflict (11 stories), and decision and agreement (10 stories). State-owned stations submitted 99 (26.4 per cent) stories, focussing on events of the festival or celebration type (23 stories), curiosities (19 stories), and decision and agreement (14 stories). Out of a total of 89 stories submitted by commercial stations, the dominant category was curiosity (38 reports- 23.7 per cent); second came violation or violence (16 stories), third 10 stories in the conflict category. Public-relations organizations, which submitted 25 reports, of which the largest number were of the curiosity type (six stories), followed movement (five stories), and conflict (four stories). Post-Communist transitional organizations submitted 53 reports, of which curiosity dominates as the type of event with 21 stories, secondly, conflict with 10 stories, and decision and agreement with five stories. State-owned commercial news organizations submitted 22 reports, of which curiosity dominates with seven stories, decision and agreement with five stories, and movement with two reports.

News regions

Using the media environments approach (see Chapter 1) content analysis data must be related specifically to such environments. It will be found that those regions defined as 'crisis regions', such as the Middle East and Africa demand particular attention. It can be argued that broadcasting stations in these regions primarily submit reports under the topic categories of politics, military and economy. It can be argued additionally that broadcasters from these crisis regions are among the frequent contributors to *World Report*. On the other hand, it can be claimed that broadcasters from these regions who submit just a few reports carefully select a certain topic and category for their reports for the assumed world audience. For this reason, the analysis focusses both on the frequent participants and their topic profile as well as the less frequent participants and those who rarely participate.

Although CNN does not encourage several news organizations from one country to participate in the programme, this is nevertheless the case in Turkey, Russia, and Germany. CNN tries to avoid an overload from one country in its programme and thus asks for co-operation among a country's broadcasters. This might become a problem because news organizations are increasingly targeting an international audience and are no longer part of a national broadcasting system, especially since carrier programme producers are on the increase and in the commercial sector in particular they are internationally organised (for example, RTL, Germany). In this sense it is not the number of news organizations but the number of topics involving a partiular country that should be restricted. Doing this would also allow a new public sphere: one where journalists of Western countries do not 'parachute in' to deliver a report, where 'locals' do not report, but where the point of view taken is like the one already exercised by UN Television.

Considering the media environment and the 'news region', it appears that crisis regions gain attention to their problems by using the *World Report* public sphere. Where as Western countries do not participate frequently in terms of political programmes or hard news, developing nations, those that are less well represented ('peripheral'), contribute regularly.

The following analysis categorises news regions as follows: the Middle East, Asia, Eastern Europe, Western Europe, Southern Europe, Australia and New Zealand, South America, North America, Central America and the Caribbean, and Africa.

The Middle East

Middle East countries which submitted reports are Bahrain TV, CyBC Cyprus, Bayrak TV Northern Cyprus, Dubai TV, IRIB Iran, IBA Israel, JTV Jordan, Kuwait TV, Channel 2, Saudi Arabia and Palestinian Broadcasting. Of these 10 broadcasting organizations, nine are organized as state-run, one is a public-service organization (IBA Israel). These 10 organizations submitted 41 reports.

The most active participant is CyBC with 13 reports, nine reports of which are in the politics, military and defence and economic categories.

Because of the Cyprus crisis, which began in 1974 with the occupation of Turkish troops in the northern part of the country, Cyprus is involved in permanent political turmoil, which is also proved by the fact that northern Cyprus is acknowledged as a Turkish territory only by Turkey itself. For this reason Cyprus uses the CNN *World Report* to constantly point to its problems that are due to the Turkish invasion. *World Report* thus became a forum for political, military and economic problems in connection with this crisis.

The second active participant is IBA Israel, with seven reports. Israel submitted four reports in the category of politics, military and defence, and economics.

The third active participant is JTV Jordan, with six reports. Four of these can be defined as politics, military, economy.

Bayrak TV submitted three, of which one is part of the category, 'politics', one focussing on 'culture and education', and one in 'crime/victims'. Bahrain TV submitted two, which are part of 'politics'. IRIB Iran submitted two reports in the 'politics' category; one report was submitted by Dubai

Table 25: Numbers and Categories from Each Middle East News Organization

Station / Count / Row Percent / Col. Percent	Politics Mili./Def Economy	Int.Aid H.Rights Liberation	Agricult. Environ	Culture Education	Social Services	Crime/ Victims	Religion	Science/ Tech.	Health/ Medicine	Sport	Human interest	Natural disasters	Tourism	Law	Row total
Bahrain TV	2 / 100.0% / 13.3%														2 / 4.9%
CyBC, Cyprus	3 / 23.1% / 20.0%	3 / 23.1% / 75.0%	3 / 23.1% / 42.9%	1 / 7.7% / 16.7%					1 / 7.7% / 100%		1 / 7.7% / 33.35%		1 / 7.7% / 50%		13 / 31.7%
Bayrak TV, North Cypr.	1 / 33.3% / 6.7%			1 / 33.3% / 16.7%		1 / 33.3% / 100%									3 / 7.3%
Dubai TV			1 / 100% / 14.3%												1 / 2.4%
IRIB, Iran	1 / 50.0% / 6.7%		1 / 50.0% / 14.3%												2 / 4.9%
IBA, Israel	4 / 57.1% / 26.7%			2 / 28.6% / 33.3%									1 / 14.3% / 50.0%		7 / 17.1%
JTV, Jordan	2 / 33.3% / 13.3%	1 / 16.7% / 25.0%	1 / 16.7% / 14.3%	2 / 33.3% / 33.3%											6 / 14.6%
Kuwait TV	2 / 40.0% / 13.3%						1 / 20.0% / 50.0%				2 / 40.0% / 66.7%				5 / 12.2%
Channel 2, Saudi Arabia							1 / 100.0% / 50.0%								1 / 2.4%
Palestinian Broadcasting			1 / 100.0% / 14.3%												1 / 2.4%
Column Total	15 / 36.6%	4 / 9.8%	7 / 17.1%	6 / 14.6%		1 / 2.4%	2 / 4.9%		1 / 2.4%		3 / 7.3%		2 / 4.9%		41 / 100%

TV in 'agriculture', one by Channel 2, Saudi Arabia, in 'religion' and one by the Palestinian Broadcasting Company in 'agriculture.'

Asia

The Asian broadcasters are located mainly in southern Asia and Southeast Asia. Of the 15 Asian broadcasters, two are public-service stations, (SLRC Sri Lanka and PTV Pakistan), three are state-organised (CCTV China, KBS South Korea and SABC Singapore) and eight are commercially organised, which are: CTS Taiwan, Guam, Kuam Island News, Cable News Hong Kong (as part of Wharf Cable Company), TV Ashai, BBTV-7 Thailand, Mariana Cablevision, GMA 7-News Philippines. Doordashan, India, is state-run and commercial.

Of the 49 reports submitted by these 15 broacasters, the highest contributor, with 11 reports, is SABC Singapore. CCTV China and TV Asahi, Japan, submitted eight reports. Four reports were produced by Doordashan, India, and SLRC Sri Lanka, three by PTV Pakistan, two by Cable News Hong Kong, Mariana Cable and one by Guam, Kuam, KBS South Korea, ABS-CBN Philippines, CTS Taiwan, BBTV 7 Thailand, GMA 7-News Philippines.

SBC Singapore submitted two of 11 stories in the categories 'Politics', 'Military', 'Economy'. Cable News Hong Kong submitted one of two stories on 'Politics', Doordashan two of four stories in 'Politics/Military', TV Asahi two of eight in 'Politics', KBS Korea one in 'Politics', SBC Singapore two of 11 in 'Politics', SLRC Sri Lanka, two of 4 in 'Politics', Mariana Cable, one in 'Politics', GMA-7 Philippines, only one in 'Politics'.

Eastern Europe

The former Soviet states and other broadcasters in Eastern Europe are in a process of defining and identifying new roles in broadcasting. Broadcasters in this region contributed 30 reports. The largest number of reports originated from TV Poland, with eight, followed by four from Armenian TV, Romanian TV and Russian TV. Three reports were submitted by Ostankino, Russia, and CT, the Czech Republic. These were two by Georgian TV, one each by VA Bank, Russia and BT Bulgaria.

The largest number in the category 'Politics/Military/Economy' was contributed by Poland, with five reports on 'Politics'. Besides TV Poland, no other post-Communist – transitional news organization contributed more than one report in the 'Politics' category.

Northern Europe

Eleven reports were contributed by this region. YLE Finland, a public-service broadcasting organization, contributed five reports, of which four focus on political issues. Latvian TV, a post-Communist transitional news organization, submitted two in 'Politics', and Channel 2, Iceland, a commercial broadcaster,

Table 26: Number and Categories from Each Asian News Organization

Station — Count / Row Percent / Col. Percent	Politics Mili./Def Economy	Int.Aid H.Rights Liberation	Agricult. Environ	Culture Education	Social Services	Crime/ Victims	Religion	Science/ Tech.	Health/ Medicine	Sport	Human interest	Natural disasters	Tourism	Law	Row total
CCTV, China	6 75.0% 35.3%	1 12.5% 25.0%						1 12.5% 100.0%							8 16.3%
Guam Cable TV													1 100.0% 100.0%		1 2.0%
Kuam Island Guam		1 100.0% 25.0%													1 2.0%
Cable News, Hong Kong	1 50.0% 5.9%								1 50.0% 16.7%						2 4.1%
Doordashan, India	1 25.0% 5.9%		1 25.0% 16.75%	1 25.0% 20.0%					1 50.0% 16.7%						4 8.2%
TV Asahi, Japan	2 25.0% 11.8%	1 12.5% 25.0%	2 25.0% 40.0%						1 12.5% 16.7%		2 25.0% 50.0%				8 16.3%
KBS, South Korea	1 100.00%% 5.9%%														1 2.0%
PTV, Pakistan			2 66.7% 33.3%		1 33.3% 33.3%										3 6.1%
ABS-CBN, Philippines			1 100.0% 16.7%												1 2.0%
SBC, Singapore	2 18.2% 11.8%			2 18.2% 40.0%	1 9.1% 33.3%		1 9.1% 100.0%		3 27.3% 50.0%		2 18.2% 50.0%				11 22.4%
SLRC, Sri Lanka	2 50.0% 11.8%	1 25.0% 25.0%			1 25.0% 33.3%										4 8.25%

Table 26: Number and Categories from Each Asian News Organization (part 2)

Station / Count / Row Percent / Col. Percent	Politics Mili./Def Economy	Int.Aid H.Rights Liberation	Agricult. Environ	Culture Education	Social Services	Crime/ Victims	Religion	Science/ Tech.	Health/ Medicine	Sport	Human interest	Natural disasters	Tourism	Law	Row total
CTS, Taiwan			1 100.0% 16.7%												1 2.0%
BBTV-7, Thailand													1 100.0% 100.0%		1 2.0%
Mariana Cablevision	1 50.0% 5.9%		1 50.0% 16.7%												2 4.1%
GMA 7- News Philippines	1 100.0% 5.9%														1 2.0%
Column Total	17 34.7%	4 8.2%	6 12.2%	5 10.2%	3 6.1%		1 2.0%	1 2.0%	6 12.2%		4 8.2%	1 2.0%		1 2.0%	49 100.0%

Table 27: Number and Categories from Each Eastern European News Organization

Station / Count Row Percent Col. Percent	Politics Mili./Def Economy	Int.Aid H.Rights Liberation	Agricult. Environ	Culture Education	Social Services	Crime/ Victims	Religion	Science/ Tech.	Health/ Medicine	Sport	Human interest	Natural disasters	Tourism	Law	Row total
Armenian TV	1 25.0% 9.1%	2 50.0% 28.6%		1 25.0% 33.3%											4 13.3%
BT, Bulgaria	1 100.0% 9.1%														1 3.3%
CT, Czech Republic	1 33.3% 9.1%	1 33.3% 14.3%	1 33.3% 50.0%												3 10.0%
Georgian TV	1 50.0% 9.1%										1 50.0% 50.0%				2 6.7%
TVP, Poland	5 62.5% 45.5%	1 12.5% 14.3%				1 12.5% 50.0%		1 12.5% 50.0%							8 26.7%
Romanian TV	1 25.0% 9.1%	1 25.0% 14.3%	1 25.0% 50.0%					1 25.0% 50.0%							4 13.3%
Ostankino, Russia				2 66.7% 66.7%	1 33.3% 100.0%										3 10.0%
Russian TV	1 25.0% 9.1%	2 50.0% 28.6									1 25.0% 50.0%				4 13.3%
VA Bank, Russia						1 100.0% 50.0%									1 3.3%
Column Total	11 36.7%	7 23.3%	2 6.7%	3 10.0%	1 3.3%	2 6.7%		2 6.7%			2 6.7%				30 100%

Table 28: Number and Categories from Each Northern European News Organization

Station Count Row Percent Col. Percent	Topics Politics Mili./Def Economy	Int.Aid H.Rights Liberation	Agricult. Environ	Culture Education	Social Services	Crime/ Victims	Religion	Science/ Tech.	Health/ Medicine	Sport	Human interest	Natural disasters	Tourism	Law	Row total
YLE, Finland	4 80.0% 57.1%			1 20.0% 50.0%											5 45.5%
Channel 2, Island	1 50.0% 14.3%							1 50.0% 100.0%							2 18.2%
Latvian TV	2 50.0%			1 25.0% 50.05%					1 25.0% 100.0%						4 36.4%
Column Total	7 63.6%			2 18.2%	3 6.1%			1 9.1%	1 9.1%						11 100.0%

reports in one of two stories on political issues. Within this region, seven reports on 'Politics' were contributed and two on 'Culture/Education'.

Western Europe

Forty reports were contributed by Western European broadcasters. The largest contribution originated from SRI Switzerland, with 13 reports, followed by RNTV Netherlands with 10. The BBC submitted eight, and Way Press International, Belgium, participated with six reports. One report each was contributed by ORF, Deutsche Welle, and RTE Ireland. Six of these seven broadcasters are public-service stations, one (Way Press International) is a private press agency which only produces carrier programmes (such as the news programme *Today's World*, which is available on Hong Kong Cable).

SRI contributed five reports in 'Politics', three in 'Agriculture'. RNTV submitted two reports in the category 'Politics/Military/Economy'.

Southern Europe

Twelve news organizations in this region contributed 46 reports. The heavy contributors were Antenna TV Greece, with nine reports, of which three were part of the category 'Policy/Military/Economy'. TV Slovenia contributed eight reports, of which only one can be regarded as political. Six reports were contributed by TV 3 Catalunya, Spain, of which only one refers to political content of any kind. TRT Turkey reported in four cases on political issues.

HTV Croatia submitted three reports, of which one had a political content, whereas RAI, Italy, did not refer to political issues. One of the two stories submitted by RTV Belgrade focussed on political topics. One contribution was submitted by Macedonian TV in the 'Politics' category. Libra TV, Slovenia, did not refer at all to political issues. TGRT Turkey submitted one report.

Four broadcasters of this region are public service stations. These are RAI Italy, RTP Portugal, TV 3 Catalunya, Spain and TGRT Turkey. Two are state-run: Euskal Telebista, Spain, and TRT Turkey. One us a commercial broadcaster – Antenna TV Greece – and five are post-Communist transitional broadcasters: HTV Croatia, Macedonian TV, TV Slovenia, Libra TV Slovenia and RTV Belgrade.

Australia and New Zealand

Broadcasters in this region contributed 10 reports. These were from Channel 7, SBS, Network 10, Australia, and New Zealand Sky Television. Channel 7 submitted the largest number of reports, namely six, of which one was an element in each of the 'Politics', 'International Aid', 'Health and Medicine', and 'Law' categories and two in 'Human Interest'. One report each was contributed by SBS, Australia, and New Zealand Sky Television (the first report on *World Report*): in the 'Health and Medicine' category by SBS and 'Culture and Education' by the New Zealand news organization.

Table 29: Number and Categories of Each Western and Central European News Organization

Station / Count / Row Percent / Col. Percent	Politics Mili./Def Economy	Int.Aid H.Rights Liberation	Agricult. Environ	Culture Education	Social Services	Crime/ Victims	Religion	Science/ Tech.	Health/ Medicine	Sport	Human interest	Natural disasters	Tourism	Law	Row total
ORF, Austria		1 / 100.0% / 50.0%													1 / 2.5%
Way Press, Belgium	2 / 33.3% / 18.2%		1 / 16.7% / 16.7%						1 / 16.7% / 14.3%		2 / 33.3% / 50.0%				6 / 15.0%
Deutsche Welle, Germany		1 / 100.0% / 25.0%													1 / 2.0%
RTE, Ireland	1 / 50.0% / 5.9%								1 / 50.0% / 16.7%						2 / 4.1%
RNTV, Netherlands	1 / 25.0% / 5.9%		1 / 25.0% / 16.75%	1 / 25.0% / 20.0%					1 / 50.0% / 16.7%						4 / 8.2%
SRI, Switzerland	5 / 25.0% / 11.8%	1 / 12.5% / 25.0%	2 / 25.0% / 40.0%						1 / 12.5% / 16.7%		2 / 25.0% / 50.0%				8 / 16.3%
BBC, United Kingdom	1 / 100.0%% / 5.9%														1 / 2.0%
Column Total			2 / 66.7%		1 / 33.3%										3 / 6.1%

Table 30: Number and Categories of Each Southern European News Organization

Station / Count / Row Percent / Col. Percent	Politics Mili./Def Economy	Int.Aid H.Rights Liberation	Agricult. Environ	Culture Education	Social Services	Crime/ Victims	Religion	Science/ Tech.	Health/ Medicine	Sport	Human interest	Natural disasters	Tourism	Law	Row total
HTV, Croatia	1 33.3% 7.1%	1 33.3% 25.0%		1 33.3% 10.0%											3 6.5%
Antenna TV, Greece	3 33.3%		1 11.1% 33.35%	1 11.1% 10.0%		1 11.1% 20.0%	1 11.1% 33.3%				1 11.1% 33.3%			1 11.1% 50.0%	9 19.6%
RAI, Italy						2 66.7% 40.0%			1 33.3% 100.0%						3 6.5%
Macedonian TV	1 100.0% 7.1%														1 2.2%
RTP, Portugal	1 25.0% 7.1%	1 25.0% 25.0%				1 25.0% 25.0%							1 25.0% 100.0%		4 8.7%
TV Slovenia	1 12.5% 7.1%	1 12.5% 33.3%	4 50.0% 40.0%			1 12.5% 20.0%					1 12.5% 33.3%				8 17.4%
Libra TV, Slovenia				1 100.0% 10.0%											1 2.2%
Euskal Telebista, Spain				2 100.0% 20.0%											2 4.3%
TV3, Spain	1 16.7% 7.1%			1 16.7% 10.0%			2 33.3% 66.7%				1 16.7% 33.3%			1 16.7% 50.0%	6 13.0%
TGRT, Turkey	1 100.0% 7.1%														1 2.2%
TRT, Turkey	4 66.7% 28.6%	1 16.7% 25.0%	1 16.7% 33.3%												6 13.0%
RTV Belgrade, Yugoslavia	1 50.0% 7.1%	1 50.0% 25.0%													2 4.3%
Column Total	14 30.4%	4 8.7%	3 6.5%	10 21.7%		5 10.9%	3 6.5%		1 2.2%		3 6.5%		1 2.2%	2 4.3%	46 100%

Table 31: Number and Categories from Each Australian and New Zealand News Organization

Station / Count / Row Percent / Col. Percent	Topics														
	Politics Mili./Def Economy	Int.Aid H.Rights Liberation	Agricult. Environ	Culture Education	Social Services	Crime/ Victims	Religion	Science/ Tech.	Health/ Medicine	Sport	Human interest	Natural disasters	Tourism	Law	Row total
Channel 7, Australia	1 16.7% 100.0%	1 16.7% 100.0%							1 16.7% 50.0%		2 33.3% 67.7%			1 16.7% 100.0%	6 60.0%
SBS, Australia									1 100.0% 50.0%						1 100.0%
Network 10, Australia				1 50.0% 50.0%							1 50.0% 33.3%				2 20.0%
New Zealand Sky TV				1 100.0% 50.0%											1 10.0%
Column Total	1 10.0%	1 10.0%		2 20.0%							3 30.0%			1 10.0%	10 100%

Network 10 submitted two reports, one under 'Culture and Education' and one in 'Human Interest'.

Three of the participants are commercial broadcasters; only SBS, Australia, is a public-service organization.

South America

This region is represented by 17 reports from 10 news organizations. Canal 11 P.A.T. Bolivia, a commercial broadcaster, contributed the largest number of reports from this region. These 4 reports consist of 'Politics' (2), 'Agriculture (1) and 'Crime and Victims' (1). TV Globo, the large, internationally operating commercial station of Brazil, submitted three reports, of which two fall into the 'Crime and Victims' category and one in 'Science and Technology'. America two, Argentina, submitted two reports under 'Agriculture', and 'Crime and Victims', and Teledoce Televisora Color, Uruguay, also contributed two, in the categories of 'Agriculture' and 'Culture and Education'. One report was contributed by Canal 13, Chile, a private university broadcaster, in the category of 'Science and Technology'. TV Hoy, Colombia, submitted one on agriculture; CNC, Paraguay, one on international aid; SNT, Paraguay one on human interest; ATV, Peru, one on crime and victims and Guyana TV one in the 'Politics' category.

Of these 10 broadcasters, one, Guyana TV, is a state-owned broadcaster, whereas eight are commercial: America 2, Argentina, Canal 11-P.A.T, Bolivia, TV Globo, Brazil, TV Hoy, Colombia, CNC Paraguay, ATV Peru, and Teledoce Televisora Color, Uruguay. One news organization, Canal 13, Chile, is a private broadcaster, managed by a Catholic university in Chile.

The topic profile of the reports submitted from South America is 'Crime and Victims', five reports, 'Agriculture', four reports, 'Politics', three reports, 'Science and Technology', two, and 'International Aid', 'Culture' and 'Human Interest' one report.

North America

Twenty-two reports were submitted by only three broadcasters in this region. The largest number were contributed by CNN (domestic US channel), with 10 reports; seven by a local Canadian broadcaster from Edmonton, Alberta, and five by Global TV, Canada. CNN submitted eight reports under 'Politics', one each in 'Agriculture', in 'Culture', in 'Health and Medicine' and in 'Law'. The local broadcaster contributed two in 'Agriculture' and 'Culture', one in 'Crime and Victims', and two in 'Human Interest.' Global TV's five reports fell under the categories 'Politics' (2), 'Agriculture' (1), 'Crime and Victims' (1), and Tourism (1). All three participants are commercially organised.

Central America

Broadcasters in this region contributed 22 reports, which were submitted by 12 broadcasters. Two broadcasters submitted five reports each. These were

Table 32: Number and Categories of Each South American News Organization

Station Count Row Percent Col. Percent	Topics Politics Mili./Def Economy	Int.Aid H.Rights Liberation	Agricult. Environ	Culture Education	Social Services	Crime/ Victims	Religion	Science/ Tech.	Health/ Medicine	Sport	Human interest	Natural disasters	Tourism	Law	Row total
America 2, Argentina			1 50.0% 25.0%			1 50.0% 20.0%									2 11.8%
Canal 11-PAT Bolivia	2 50.0% 66.7%		1 25.0%			1 25.0% 20.0%									4 23.5%
TV Globo Brazil						2 66.7% 40.0%		1 33.3% 50.0%							3 17.6%
Canal 13, Chile								1 100.0% 50.0%							1 5.9%
TV Hoy, Colombia			1 100.0% 25.0%												1 5.9%
Guyana TV	1 100.0% 33.3%														1 5.9%
CVC, Paraguay		1 100.0% 100.0%													1 5.9%
ATV, Peru						1 100.0% 20.0%									1 5.9%
Teledoce, Uruguay			1 50.0% 25.0%	1 50.0% 100.0%											2 11.8%
SNT, Paraguay											1 100.0% 100.0%				1 5.9%
Column Total	3 17.6%	1 5.9%	4 23.5%	1 5.9%		5 29.4%		2 11.8%			1 5.9%				17 100%

Table 33: Number and Categories of Each North American News Organization

Station Count Row Percent Col. Percent	Topics Politics Mili./Def Economy	Int.Aid H.Rights Liberation	Agricult. Environ	Culture Education	Social Services	Crime/ Victims	Religion	Science/ Tech.	Health/ Medicine	Sport	Human interest	Natural disasters	Tourism	Law	Row total
Global TV, Canada	2 40.0% 25.0%		1 20.0% 25.0%			1 20.0% 50.0%							1 20.0% 100.0%		5 22.7%
ITV, Canada			2 28.6% 50.05%	2 28.6% 66.7%		1 14.3% 50.0%					2 28.6% 100.0%				7 31.8%
CNN, USA	6 60.0% 75.0%		1 10.0% 25.0%	1 10.0% 33.3%					1 10.0% 100.0%					1 10.0% 100.0%	10 45.5%
Column Total	8 36.4%		4 18.2%	3 13.6%	3 6.1%	2 9.1%			1 4.5%		2 9.1%	1 2.0%	1 4.5%	1 4.5%	22 100.0%

Table 34: Number and Categories of Each Central American News Organization

Station / Count / Row Percent / Col. Percent	Topics Politics Mili./Def Economy	Int.Aid H.Rights Liberation	Agricult. Environ	Culture Education	Social Services	Crime/ Victims	Religion	Science/ Tech.	Health/ Medicine	Sport	Human interest	Natural disasters	Tourism	Law	Row total
CITV Cayman Isl.		1 25.0% 25.0%	1 25.0% 25.0%	1 25.0% 33.3%									1 25.0% 100.0%		4 18.2%
ICTR Cuba	3 60.0% 50.0%	1 20.0% 50.0%										1 20.0% 100.0%			5 22.7%
TeleCuraçao														1 100.0% 100.0%	1 4.5%
TCS News, El Salvador	1 20.0% 16.7%					2 40.0% 100.0%			1 20.0% 100.0%		1 20.0% 100.0%				5 22.7%
TéléHaïti							1 100.0% 50.0%								1 4.5%
Telesistema Hondurena, Honduras	1 50.0% 16.7%		1 50.0% 50.0%												2 9.1%
JBC, Jamaica	1 100.0% 16.7%														1 4.5%
Channel 13, Mexico				1 100.0% 33.3%											1 4.5%
RPC –TV 4, Panama				1 50.0% 33.3%			1 50.0% 50.05%								2 9.1%
Column Total	6 27.3%	2 9.1%	2 9.1%	3 13.6%		2 9.1%	2 9.1%		1 4.5%		1 4.5%	1 4.5%	1 4.5%	1 4.5%	22 100%

213

ICRT Cuba and TCS News El Salvador. ICRT Cuba, the only state-owned news organization in this region submitted three reports in the 'Politics' category, one in 'International Aid' and one focussed on one issue in the 'Natural Disasters' category. TCS News El Savador submitted one under 'Politics', two on 'Crime and Victims', one on 'Health and Medicine', and one on 'Human Interest.' Four reports were produced by CITV Cayman Islands, one each in 'International Aid', 'Agriculture', 'Culture', and 'Tourism', two by Telesístema Hondurene under 'Politics', two on 'Crime and Victims', one on 'Health and Medicine', and one on 'Hucultural issue and one on religion. JBC Jamaica produced one report on politics. Channel 13, Mexico, contributed one report on culture, and TéléHaïti submitted one story in the area of religion.

Except for Cuba, which is the only state-run broadcaster in this region in the sample, TCS News El Salvador, TéléHaïti, Telesístema Hondureño, JBC Jamaica, and RPC TV4 Panama are commercially organized, and the state owned-commercial ones are CITV Cayman Island and Tele Curaço. Channel 13, Mexico is a private broadcaster.

Within this region, six reports were produced in the 'Politics', category, three in 'Culture', two in each of the following categories: 'International Aid', 'Agriculture', 'Crime and Victims', and 'Religion'. One report focussed on issues which are part of the categories of 'Tourism', 'Health and Medicine', and 'Law'.

Africa

The 11 broadcasters of this region contributed 34 reports. The most frequent participant in *World Report* is SABC South Africa, with nine reports. This state-owned commercial broadcaster produced one political, four agricultural, two cultural reports and one under 'Crime and Victims' as well as in 'Science and Technology'. Five reports were submitted by GBC Ghana, the only public-service broadcaster in the African region. GBC produced three reports on culture and one each on political and agricultural issues. Three reports were contributed by ETV Egypt, ETV Ethiopia, NBC Namibia and Bop TV of Bophuthatswana, a South African Territory. TPA Angola, NTA Nigeria and ZBC Zimbabwe each produced two reports and one was contributed by SLBS Sierra Leone and by RTT Tunisia.

Framing of events

This category deals with the way a story is made globally comprehensible by selecting a specific international, national or local framework in which to present it. It also refers to the geographical frame of reference given to an event. Fifty-five of the 397 reports were presented in relation to a continent. The majority of reports were presented in relation to Western Europe (14), Central Asia (8), the Middle East, the United States, and South Africa (5), and Central Europe (4).

Table 35: Number and Categories of Each African News Organization

Station Count Row Percent Col. Percent	Politics Mili./Def Economy	Int.Aid H.Rights Liberation	Agricult. Environ	Culture Education	Social Services	Crime/ Victims	Religion	Science/ Tech.	Health/ Medicine	Sport	Human interest	Natural disasters	Tourism	Law	Row total
TPA, Angola	1 50.0% 10.0%							1 50.0% 50.0%							2 5.9%
ETV, Egypt	1 33.3% 10.0		1 33.3% 12.5%				1 33.3% 100.0%								3 8.8%
ETV, Ethopia	1 33.3% 10.0%	1 33.3% 33.3%		1 33.3% 16.7%											3 8.8%
GBC, Ghana	1 20.0% 10.0%		1 20% 12.5%	3 60.0% 50.0%											5 14.7%
NBC, Namibia	1 33.3% 10.0%	1 33.3% 33.3%	1 33.3% 12.5%												3 8.8%
NTA, Nigeria	1 50.0% 10.0%	1 50.0% 33.3%													2 5.9%
SLBS, Sierra Leone	1 100.0% 10.0%														1 2.9%
BOP TV, South Africa	1 33.3% 10.0%		1 33.3% 12.5%		1 33.3% 100.0%										3 8.8%
SABC, South Africa	1 11.1% 10.0%		4 44.4% 50.0%	2 33.3% 33.3%		1 11.1% 100.0%		1 11.1% 50.0%							9 26.5%
RTT, Tunesia	1 100.0% 10.0%														1 2.9%
ZBC, Zimbabwe											1 50.0% 100.0%			1 50.0% 100.0%	2 5.9%
Column Total	10 29.4%	3 8.8%	8 23.5%	6 17.6%	1 2.9%	1 2.9%	1 2.9%	2 5.9%			1 2.9%			1 2.9%	34 100%

Of the 55 reports on the issues of culture and education (33 on culture and 22 on education), 26 were presented from a local and 21 from a national perspective, underlining the fact that the majority of events in the fields of education and culture reported on took place either in a local community or a national context. Five of the reports presented multinational enterprises, such as literacy or training programmes initiated by the United Nations, and one report focussed on an international event.

The new journalism

Interactive journalism

This term applies specifically to regions in crisis since the sample reveals that it is in those regions that this new form of 'global' journalism most frequently takes place. Interactive journalism represents a way of communicating with other countries through *World Report* stories. Since in these regions of crisis, diplomatic and other political communication has ceased to exist, a programme such as *World Report* provides a forum for communication. In the reports analysed this interactive journalism is clearly to be seen in the cae of Cuba which interacts with the United States (for example, Florida), and Cyprus, which 'interacts' with Turkish northern Cyprus.

Reciprocal journalism

This type of journalism can be seen in the reports from countries which have a restricted, state-regulated broadcasting system, which are aired on *World Report* and thus broadcast back into the country of origin. These reports sometimes involve critical issues which are subject to restriction on the domestic market, but not when reported on CNN *World Report*.

Showcase journalism

This *World Report* journalism is a nonpolitical category. It covers reports which try to present unique local or cultural issues to a global audience. The intention is not to present political issues but to market specific local, particular issues globally (for example, to improve tourism).

Notes

1   M-Net has begun to expand into other African nations.
2   ABC owns WTN, with an 80 per cent share, CBS owns CBS Newspath, which offers CBS affiliates the resources and expertise of CBS News for exclusive news in their broadcasts.
3   This interactive program was originally invented for 'video-on-demand' service and has recently become an issue among news broadcasters in the US
4   The BBC WSTV program is produced by Cintex Airline News and is available on Lufthansa, Cathay Pacific, British Airways and Royal Brunei.
5   These are the Cayman Islands, French Guiana, India, and the Maldives, Vietnam, the Czech Republic and Slovakia, Iceland, Romania, Serbia,

Slovenia, Jordan, Syria, Yemen, Algeria, Benin, Botswana, Djibouti, Ethiopia, Liberia, Malawi, Morocco, Senegal, Sierra Leone, Tunisia and Uganda.

6   Besides these innovations, influences and effects, CNN appears in various popular-culture productions such as the films *Clear and Present Danger* and *The Flintstones.*

7   The 'pool suit', which Reagan encouraged by restricting the access of news organizations to 'presidential events' (Whittemore, 1990).

8   Among the first international broadcasters that cooperated on this basis with CNN was NHK Japan.

9   See the example of Kennedy's 1980 campaign in Bush, 1987.

10   TCI, one of the multisystem operators (MSO) in the US partly owns the Turner Broadcasting System.

11   As many other US cable operators gain for the international market.

12   CNN acquired a 27.5 per cent stake in ntv. It provides CNN with with an added news source on the German market.

13   Three weeks in 1982 were selected: August 16-20, October 4-8 and November 8-12. One hundred forty-three CNN stories and one hundred twenty two network stories were the basis of the content analysis (The Media Institute, 1983:3).

14   When interviews were conducted, the EBU was about to establish 'Euronews.'

15   For both see Wimmer and Dominick, 1987:187-188.

16   In May 1993 CNN added a slight change to the program by opening a new larger CNNWR studio. All other segments of the program remained the same. For this reason a comparison between these two time periods is possible.

17   They say, 'Welcome to CNN *World Report,* where we bring you the news from world broadcasters, reported from their perspective'.

18   Since more and more packaged programs are aired, these reports are regarded as elements of the sample, representing a totality.

5

Towards a Global Civil Society

The political media had already established themselves as a powerful 'fourth estate' within a civil society in the eighteenth century. Print media had gained considerable power within the emerging public sphere of modern societies by that time. With their ability to wield influence in political and state affairs the media have become a dominant agent of public life in our time. Whereas within the framwork of a particular society their power as a fourth estate is closely related to the construction of the surrounding political system, their power in relation to a global political community is more difficult to define because the globally available variety of systems as well as content flow is immense. The meaning of media-transmitted news and political content is different in differently organised societies, and so on.

In order to understand more precisely the sphere of mediation in which a global civil society unfolds, it is necessary to look into the issues surrounding the concept of civil society. These will deliver the evidence for the existence of such a global society and its extrasocietal communication structure. In this way we shall be able to define the new global spheres of political communication and – using the theoretical framework of a mediation approach – show that it has created new areas of political participation. Our approach will also involve an interdisciplinary view of the field of global communication and the (related) appearance of new global social structures.

Concepts of civil society and dualism

Whereas ideas of civil society had already been conceptualised in theories of the state (like that of Hobbes) involving a dualism of civil and political society, or of government and society (as in Locke), Hegel's concept of civil society was the first of a modern kind. Hegel distinguishes the dualism of state (policy) and nation (civilty). Furthermore, the concept of civil society involves the mediation of 'voluntary associations', the new egalitarian groups who are increasingly participating in policy-making in modern society. 'It is precisely the function of the associations of civil society (corporations, estates) to provide a context in which new forms of solidarity, collective identity and common interest can emerge. Their most important function is to mitigate the centrifugal tendencies of the system of needs, bind individuals together in a common purpose and temper the egoism of self-interest. This is why Hegel refers to the corporation as the 'second family''. (Cohen and Arato, 1992:628-629)

It is this transforming process, to which Hegel gave the term 'mediation', which bridges the dualism of state and nation, which translates in today's terms into the dualism of societal and global communities. Whereas in Hegel's terminology this mediation occurred within the structures of a 'closed' system of 'good behaviour' and ethos, global mediation seems to relate most closely to the modern dimensions of the concept 'the human condition'. The sphere of mediation involves the universality of the discourse and in this sense is based on the following principles: freely articulated, (Cohen and Arato, 1992:21) open to a multiplicity of perspectives and a 'regulative principle of a discursive process in and through which participants reason together about which values, principles, need-interpretations merit being instutionalized as common norms'. (Cohen and Arato, 1992:21) The dualism which is implied in various concepts of civil society in order to distinguish the civil sphere from the political has another meaning when related to the concept of a global civil society. Within such a concept it relates to the duality of nation/state and the globe but it also inserts the global viewpoint into the context of the nation/state, a reciprocal process that is possible because of the structure of global communication.

New issues of global citizenship

Recently these conventional concepts of civil society and citizenship have increasingly become an issue in sociology. Modern civil societies are characterized by a 'plurality of form of life, they are structurally differentiated and socially heterogenous', (Cohen and Arato, 1992:10) which implies that with this plurality the concept of civil society – of traditional citizenship – is being eroded as new social structures arise. These are, for example, the following.

The autonomous citizen

This concept involves a methodological shift from 'modern' sociology towards globalization and involves concepts of citizenship which strive for a definition of new civil communities both within a nation/state and globally. Reasons for this shift of perspective can be seen in the following arguments which bring current globalization issues into the debate on civil societies. Steenbergen (1994) argues, for example, that notions of citizenship are to be found in different global communities such as pop culture, social arrangements or an inter-national community. Gunsteren argues that modern society is no longer a 'civil society' of 'autonomous individuals' since 'large organizations and accumulations of capital are the main determinants of affairs.' Instead of using the term 'civil society, he proposes to speak of a 'corporate society'.

This involves a variety of 'communities', some of which remain in existence for a longer, some for a shorter period of time.

> Besides the familiar communities of nationality, religion, trade unions and corporate life, we now find a host of less familar and less established bonds that often play an important role in the lives of individuals, but that we cannot easily call communities. Government bodies, too, have lost their traditional place in modern society. The nation-state has become but one locus of authority amidst a field containing many others. (Gunsteren, 1994:43)

These authors and many others see results of this development in the increasing variety and instability of political and social identities. The individual – 'the substrate of the citizen' – is a 'bouquet' because he or she composes his or her own mixed identity out of various connections and bonds. (Gunsteren, 1994:43/44) 'This individual is not the natural bearer of civic-mindedness and civic virtue, nor is he/she naturally inclined ... to calculate all action in terms of his/her own wealth and power'. (Gunsteren, 1994:44) Gunsteren remarks that the increasing 'relatively homogeneous middle class' that used to form the backbone of the stable republic of citizens' is decreasing. (Gunsteren, 1994:44) The third consequence is a modified conceptualisation of citizenship. 'Planning of civil society is, today even less possible than it was in the past. From the point of view of those steering, society is less and less knowable'. (Gunsteren, 1994:44) This argument applies to the debate on information societies which are characterized by an information overflow. This inundation does not, as widely assumed, intensify a sense of direction; rather, it produces disorientation. However, this increasingly un-knowable society does point towards the global sphere of mediation as a growing source of global knowledge.

The concept of autonomous citizenship can also be related to theories of consumerism or consumer culture.

> Whilst the exercise of citizenship presupposes collective action in pursuit of equality and fraternity as well as of individual liberty, the ideology of consumerism encourages people to seek private solutions to public problems by purchasing a commodity. It urges them to buy their way out of trouble rather than pressing for social change and improved social provision'. (Murdock, 1992:19)

The communication system has implicitly been involved in concepts of civil society or citizenship simply because if people are willing to exercise their full rights as citizens, 'they must have access to the information, advice, and analysis that will enable them to know what their personal rights are and allow them to pursue them effectively' and to develop their opinions. Besides this, they must have access to the 'broadest possible range of information, interpretation and debate on areas that involve public political choices'. They have to be able to 'use communication facilities in order to register criticism and propose alternative courses of action' and they have 'to be able to recognise themselves and their aspirations in the range of representations on offer within the central communication sectors and be able to contribute to developing and extending these representatives'. (Murdock, 1992:21) It can be argued that the media in a global civil society also function as initiators of 'voluntary associations', not of a permanent kind but in relation to new particular collectives which have a global integrating function.

Global civil society

Citizenship in a global and international civil society has also been the subject of increasing debate. Dahrendorf remarks: 'If we want to think seriously about bourgeois society, there isno escaping the fact that we have to regard it as a society that does not end at the frontiers of our own country. The principle itself demands a universal application, in the sense of a worldwide bourgeois society'. (Dahrendorf, 1992) This view releases the concept of international citizenship from its connection to the nation and state.

Falk distinguishes five different types of global citizenship: 'global reformer', 'elite global businessman', 'manager of the world order'(in the sense of environmental problems), as well as the politically conscious 'regionalist' and the 'transnational activist'. (Falk, 1994) These different types do not refer to a nation and state nor specifically to an international context. They represent a truly autonomous citizenship of a global civil society. Other concepts related to fields of civil 'action' such as ecology and culture. This refers to global 'environmental citizens', such as 'earth citizens' (humans who participate in nature), and 'global environmental citizens' (who can be described as world citizens), for whom the environment is 'big science' and the planet an object of global management. (Steenbergen, 1994)

In the context of these new approaches to citizenship it can be argued that the concept of citizenship has to be related in some way to a political context. It is not possible to apply the term 'citizenship' to a 'type' or 'style' without political implications. Citizenship is a political category implying membership of and varying degrees of participation in a community where 'liberty' and 'freedom', are meaningful concepts. This political community of citizenship, in the traditional sense, implied 'the city' as the political environment and action field for a *citoyen*. However, the variety of these political communities is increasing, especially given the existence of a global civil society. In this diversification, citizenship is related, for example, to nationalism and to new notions of citizenship relating to constitutional patriotism, involving new models of multi-cultural and group-related citizenship, women's rights and pop culture or geo-political regions. All these tendencies indicate the decline of state sovereignty and thus the decline of state and nation citizenship in the era of increasing supranational political values. These examples can be regarded as the ones which begin to define citizenship beyond state and national perspectives, though they consider these new political communities more from a descriptive perspective than a structuralist view, which would involve new channels of discourse of the widened public sphere. Other advanced stages of citizenship are neo-republican citizenship, cultural citizenship, active citizenship, race-neutral and gender-neutral citizenship, global citizenship, European citizenship, and ecological citizenship.

Information versus knowledge

These types of (global) citizenship refer to special knowledge, and they 'update' information in order for civil rights to be exercised in a particular political or other framework. This information is subject to timeliness and actuality. Luhmann describes knowledge within a world society as follows:

> On a fairly concrete level of description we can point to the clearly ascertainable and immense growth in knowledge about the facts of living and the conditions of interaction between all people. This knowledge is not of course present in every individual consciousness but as the knowledge that the appropriate information is available if needed. (Luhmann, 1975:53)

This world knowledge is shaped not only by current and recent information but also by collectively experienced historical events. Collective memory determines the reconstruction of historical realities. Global knowledge also consists of 'common sense', as Hall remarks. 'What passes for 'common sense' in our society – the residue of absolutely basic and commonly-agreed, consensual wisdoms – help us to classify out the world in simple but meaningful terms'. (Hall, 1977:325) Here what Gurevitch and Blumler describe as communicator and audience systems can be applied: the network of particular and universal news establishes new social commonsense communities. Knowledge as a component of citizenship is also relevant to media transmitted 'pseudo' news events. In Luhmann's view, scientific knowledge especially is spread within a global communication network. Besides this knowledge within a closed communication network, Luhmann proposes the existence of a something like 'general opinion', global public opinion, which 'takes up themes under the aspect of news and translates them into premises for the further interpretation of experience'. (Luhmann, 1975:54)

In connection with global communication Gurevitch and Blumler identify different styles of media reception which are: 'the partisan'– seeking a reinforcement for his existing beliefs, the 'liberal citizen' – seeking guidance in deciding how to vote – the 'monitor' – seeking information about features of the political environment – and the 'spectator' – seeking excitement and other affective satisfaction. (Gurevitch and Blumler, 1977:276)

They develop their argument by suggesting that these audience roles are matched by similar orientations among the political and professional communicators. In Robertson's perspective, globality 'appears increasingly to permeate the affairs of all societies and multitudes of people across the world'. (1992,132) For this reason, because of international communication processes, the field of political action is enlarged and the national boundaries of individual societies are opening up morally and even politically towards something like a global field of reference or an as yet diffuse notion of a global civil society. The 'human condition' approach could be applied globally to the right to free speech and the right to communicate.

One perspective to be considered in order to 'map the global condition' of worldwide political communication consists of specifying the political participation, the global and international omnipresence of political 'actors', and of globally distributed and universally recognisable political forums of action (such as the peace talks in the Middle East and the former Yugoslavia) and reaction (such as the UN and the North Atlantic Alliances of NATO), of public spaces for global political articulation.

The second perspective to be integrated here is the currently highly dynamic restructuring sphere of global political communication in which specific types of news channels and news programmes contribute to a global media sphere of 'political news' and 'political information', as opposed to the traditional public sphere. The active participants include various types of media-related organizations (commercial, private, state-run, and under public law) and the audiences they affect are diverse, and spread throughout the world. Their activities mediate the diverse global 'worlds' of ideas and create a new mediating sphere with various models of participation: symbolic, representative or real. World-wide news services, especially their professional systems for selecting events, their important part in global communication are still unsurveyed. A theoretical framework for these globally expanding political communication processes could make use of the existing models of civil society seen from the viewpoint of Robertson's concept of globalization. In this way we should arrive at a definition of global civil society (at least in some of its elements) in the context of global communication.

The problem of describing a global civil society can be seen in different models of the state across the globe, which are reached simultaneously by the same political information. Because of their different societal structures, 'civil society' means different things to different states: a fact reflected by their diverse access to the global mediation sphere. This access can be seen simply as taking part in and using this mediation sphere, but on a a more reflective level there is the notion that the 'world is watching.' Cohen and Arato also argue that the concept of civil society is 'particularly relevant to the West', since it is guaranteed by rules of law, civil rights, parliamentary democracy, market economy, etc (Cohen and Arato, 1992:15), and they argue that because of the revival of civil societies in Eastern Europe, some new aspects of civil society can be added.

> This revival goes beyond the model of the historical origins of civil society in the West, such as conception of self-limitation, the idea of civil society as comprised of social movements as well as a set of institutions, the orientation to civil society as a new terrain of democratisation ... is not necessarily identical with the creation of bourgeois society but rather involves a choice between a plurality of types of civil society. (Cohen and Arato, 1992:15)

The idea of civil society is a combining element in communication theory across the borders of different state systems. One cannot deny or avoid the challenge of framing the impact of global communication on diverse societal systems. The moral category of the 'human condition' (in Montaigne's term) or 'the promise of a new moral world' (Mattelart 1992) has become the first 'medium' of a global collectivity, of 'world society'.

From a theoretical standpoint the 'traditional' models of a civil society, as described by Cohen and Arato, do not exist in the global sphere, where what we have is a mixture of these models and new nonstate structures which are predominantly established by media. These crosscultural communication set new reference points beyond the state and nation and widen the field of political action from the state to the region, to world representatives (such as the UN). The question is, how the global civil society can connect with existing models and how communication across the world (and across these models) allows space for new models of global civil society (see also Cohen and Arato, 1992:4).

Robertson argues that in recent world history the universalism-particularism issue has come to constitute something like a 'global-cultural form, a major axis of the structuration of the world as a whole'. He suggests, rather than simply viewing the theme of universalism 'as having to do with principles which can and should be applied to all', and that of particularism as referring to that 'which can and should be applied only "locally", ... that the two have become tied together as part of globewide nexus.' Robertson argues that these dimensions 'have become united in terms of the universality of the experience, and increasingly, the expectation of universality'. Particularisation of universalism 'involves the idea of universal being given global-human concreteness; while the former - the universalisation of particularism – involves the extensive diffusion of the idea that there is virtually no limit to particularity, to uniqueness, to difference and to otherness'. (Robertson, 1992:102) Robertson describes this as the 'two-fold process', involving the 'universalisation of particularism and the particularisation of universalism', employing the themes of 'society and community', which in Robertson's view are becoming ever more closely linked to the 'discourse of globality'. (Robertson, 1992:pp.102)

Bibliography

Adorno, Theodor (1967) *Kulturindustrie*. Frankfurt: Suhrkamp.

Aggarwala, Narinder (1979) 'What is Development News', *Journal of Communication*, 29:180-181.

Agh, Attila (1994) 'Citizenship and Civil Society in Central Europe', in Steenbergen, Bart van (ed), pp.108-126.

Anderson, Benedict (1983*) Imagined Communities. Reflections on the Origin and Spread of Nationalism*. London: Verso.

Ang, Ien (1990) 'Culture and Communication: Towards an Ethnographic Critique of Media Consumption in the Transnational Media System', *European Journal of Communication*, 5, (June) 2-3:239-260.

Ansah, Paul A.V. (1992) 'Foreign Intervention is a Sensitive issue', *Intermedia*, 20, 6:33.

Ansah, Paul A.V. (1994) 'Communication Research and Development in Africa - An Overview', in Hamelink, Cees/Linne, Olga (eds), pp. 229-247.

Ante, Titi (1992) 'Ghana' , *Intermedia*, 20, (August-September) 4-5:22.

Appadurai, Arjun (1990) 'Disjuncture and Difference in the Global Cultural Economy', in Featherstone, Mike (ed), pp. 295-310.

Ball, Michael S./Smith, Gregory (1992) *Analyzing:Visual Data*. London, Newbury Park: Sage.

Barber, Benjamin,R. (1994) 'Zwischen Dschihad und Mc World.', *Die Zeit* Nr.42, (14.Oktober), p. 64.

Barker, Chris (1997) *Global Television*.Oxford:Blackwell.

BBC World Service (BBCWSS) (1993) *Global Audiences* (see Mytton).

Beck, Ulrich (1986) *Risikogesellschaft. Auf dem Weg in eine Moderne*. Frankfurt/Main: Suhrkamp.

Beck, Ulrich (1992) ' How Modern is Modern Society?', *Theory, Culture & Society*, 9:163-169.

Bittner, John R. (1982) *Broadcast Law and Regulation*. Englewood Cliffs, New Jersey: Prentice Hall.

Boorstin, Daniel J. (1971) 'From News-Gathering to News-Making: A Flood of Pseudo Events', in Schramm Wilbur (ed), *The Process and Effects of*

Mass Communication. Urbana, Chicago, London: University of Illinois Press.

Boventer, Hermann (1994) 'Muckrakers. Investigativer Journalismus zwischen Anspruch und Wirklichkeit', in Wunden, Wolfgang (ed), *Öffentlichkeit und Kommunikationskultur.* Hamburg, Stuttgart: Westdeutscher Verlag, pp. 215-230.

Boyd-Barrett, Oliver (1977) ' Media Imperialism: Towards an International Framework for the Analysis of Media Systems', in Curran, James/Gurevitch, Michael/Woollacott, Janet (eds), pp. 116-141.

Burns, Tom (1977) 'The Organization of Public Opinion', in Curran, James/Gurevitch, Michael/Woollacott, Janet (eds) , pp.44-69.

Bush, Gregory W. (1987) 'Edward Kennedy and the Televised Personality in the 1980 Presidential Campaign', in O'Connor, John E. (ed), *American History/American Television.* New York: Ungar, pp. 328-362.

Business Central Europe, 1994 (February), 'The Big Picture', pp. 28.

Chomsky, Noam/Herman, Edward (1988) *Manufacturing Consent. The Political Economy of the Mass Media.* New York: Pantheon Books.

Chomsky, Noam (1991) *Media Control: The Spectacular Achievements of Propaganda.* Westfield, New Jersey: Open Magazine Pamphlet Series.

CNN World Report Contributors Conference 1994, Atlanta, Georgia: Turner Broadcasting System.

CNN World Report Information (1993) (August). Atlanta, Georgia: Turner Broadcasting System.

CNN World Report Information (1993) (January). Atlanta, Georgia: Turner Broadcasting System.

CNN World Report Kit (1990) (January). Atlanta, Georgia: Turner Broadcasting System.

Cohen, Akiba/Adoni, Hanna/Bantz, Charles (1990) *Social Conflict and Television News.* London, Newbury Park, New Delhi: Sage.

Cohen, Jean L./Arato, Andrew (1992) *Civil Society and Political Theory.* Cambridge, Ma., London, England: M.I.T. Press.

Cooley, Charles H. (1900, 1912) *Social Organization. A Study of the larger Mind.* New York: Scribener.

Curran, James (1990) 'Rethinking the media as public sphere', in Dahlgren, Peter/Sparks, Colin (ed), pp. 27-57.

Curran, James/Gurevitch, Michael/Woollacott, Janet (eds) (1977) *Mass Communication and Society.* London: Edward Arnold.

Dahlgren, Peter/Sparks, Colin (1991) *Communication and Citizenship: Journalism and the Public Sphere in the New Media Age.* London: Routledge.

Dahrendorf, Ralf. (1992) 'Wege in die Irrelevanz. Schwierigkeiten mit der Bürgergesellschaft', in *Frankfurter Allgemeine Zeitung*, (28.10.), p. 33.

Davison, Phillips W. (1965) *International Political Communication*, New York, Washington, London: Longman.

Dayan, Daniel/Katz, Elihu (1992) *Media Events. The Live Broadcasting of History.* Cambridge, Ma., London, England: Harvard University Press.

De Fleur, Melvin L. (1970) 'Mass Communication and Social Change', in Tunstall, Jeremy (ed), *Media Sociology.* Urbana, Chicago, London: pp. 58-78.

Dirlik, Arif (1996) _The Global and the Local', in Wilson, Rob/Wimal Dissanayakee (eds) *Global/Local. Cultural Production and the Transnational Imaginary.* Oxford: Blackwell.

Dizard, Wilson P (1966) *Television. A World View.* Syracuse, New York: Longman.

Durkheim, Emile (1963) *Primitive Classification.* London: Cohen & West.

Eapen, K.E. (1994) 'Communication and Development: The Latin American Challenge', in Hamelink, Cees/Linne, Olga (eds), pp.277-289.

Eisenstadt, Samuel N. (1975) 'The Changing Vision of Modernization and Development', in Schramm, Wilbur/Lerner, Daniel (eds), *Communication and Change. The last ten Years - and the next.* Honolulu, Hawaii: East-West Centre Press, pp.31-48.

Ekecrantz, Jan (1987) 'The Sociological Order of the New Information Society', in Daryl Slack, Jennifer/Fejes, Fred (eds), *The Ideology of the Information Age.* Norwood, New Jersey: Ablex Publishing Corporation, pp. 78-94.

Elliott, Philip (1986) 'Intellectuals, the 'Information Society' and the Disappearance of the Public Sphere', in Collins, Philip et al. (eds), *Media, Culture and Society. A Critical Reader.* London, Newbury Park, New Delhi: Sage, pp. 105-115.

Falk, Richard (1994) 'The Making of Global Citizenship', in Steenbergen, Bart van (ed), pp. 127-140.

Featherstone, Mike (1990) 'Global Culture: An Introduction', in Featherstone, Mike (ed), pp.1-14.

Featherstone, Mike (1991): *Consumer Culture and Postmodernism.* London, Newbury Park, New Delhi: Sage.

Featherstone, Mike (ed) (1990) *Global Culture. Nationalism, Globalization and Modernity.* London, Newbury Park, New Delhi: Sage.

Ferguson, Majorie (1990) 'Electronic Media and the Redefining of Time and Space', in: Ferguson, Majorie (ed), *Public Opinion. The New Imperatives.* London, Newbury Park, New Delhi: Sage.

Financial Times, (1992) (Weekend October 3/4) 'A Revolution on the Russian Airwaves'.

Financial Times, (1994a) (December, 24) 'S African groups plan global pay TV network'.

Financial Times, (1994b) (December, 24) 'BSkyB and Reuters on verge of partnership'.

Fiske, John (1987) *TV Culture.* London, New York: Methusa.

Fitzgerald, Anne (1989) 'The News Hole: Reporting Africa', *Africa Report*. (July-August):59.

Flournoy, Don M. (1992) *CNN World Report: Ted Turner's International News Group* London: John Libbey. Revised edition.

Flournoy, Don M. & Stuart, Robert K *CNN: Making News in the Global Market* Luton: John Libby Media 1967.

Foote, John/Amin, Hussein (1992) *Global TV News in Developing Countries: CNN's Expansion to Egypt*. Paper presented to the Association for Education in Journalism and Mass Communication, Montreal, Canada August, 5-8, 1992.

Frankfurter Allgemeine Zeitung, (1992) (18.12.): 'CNN steigt beim Nachrichtenkanal N-TV ein'.

Friedman, Jonathan (1990) 'Being in the World. Globalization and Localization', in: Featherstone, Mike (ed), pp. 311-328.

Friedman, Jonathan (1994) *Cultural Identity & Global Process*. London. Newbury Park, New Delhi: Sage.

Galtung, Johan/Ruge, Mari Holmboe (1965) 'The Structure of Foreign News', *Journal of Peace Research*, 2:64-91.

Gargan, Edward A. (1994) 'Home Grown Business News in Asia', *New York Times*, (September, 5) p. 35.

Gerbner, George/Gross, Larry (1976) 'Living With Television: The Violence Profile', *Journal of Communication*, 26, 2:178-201.

Gerbner, George/Siefert, Marsha (eds) (1983) *World Communications: A Handbook*. New York, London: Longman.

Giddens, Anthony (1990) *The Consequences of Modernity*. Cambridge: Polity Press.

Gitlin, Todd (1991) 'Bites and Blips: Chunk News, Savy Talks and the Bifurcation of American Politics', in Dahlgren, Peter/Sparks, Colin. (eds), *Communication and Citizenship: Journalism and the Public Sphere in the New Media Age*. London, New York: Routledge

Greenfeld, Liah (1992) *Nationalism. Five Roads to Modernity*. Cambridge, Ma., London, England: Harvard University Press.

Griswold, William F./Swenson, Jill D. (1992) 'Development News in Rural Geogian Newspapers: A Comparison with Media in Developing Nations', *Journalism Quarterly*, 69, 3:580-590.

Gunsteren, Herman van (1994) 'Four Conceptions of Citizenship', in Steenbergen, Bart van (ed), pp. 35-48.

Gurevitch, Michael/Jay G. Blumler (1977) 'Linkages between the Mass Media and Politics: a Model for the Analysis of Political Communication Systems', in Curran/Gurevitch/Wollacott (eds), pp. 270-290.

Habermas, Jürgen (1992) *The Structural Transformation of the Public Sphere*, Cambridge, Ma., London, England: M.I.T. Press.

Habermas, Jürgen (1994) 'Citizenship and National Identity', in Steenbergen, Bart van (ed), pp. 20-35.

Hachten, W. (1987) *The World News Prism*. Ames, Iowa: Iowa University Press.

Hall, Stuart (1977) 'Culture, the Media and the 'Ideological Effect'', in Curran, James/Gurevitch, Michael/Wollacott, Janet (eds) 1977, pp. 315-348.

Hamelink, Cees J. (1994) 'Communication Research and the New International Information Order: An Essay on a Delicate Alliance', in Hamelink, Cees/Linne, Olga (eds), pp. 385-398.

Hamelink, Cees J./Linne, Olga (eds) (1994) *Mass Communication Research. On Problems and Politics*. Norwood, New Jersey: Ablex Publishing Corporation.

Hancock, Alan (1992) 'Communication Planning Revisited', *Monographs on Communication Planning* 5. Paris: Unesco Press.

Hancock, Alan (1994) 'Communication Policies, Planning, and Research', in Hamelink, Cees/Linne, Olga (eds), pp. 21-37.

Hannerz, Ulf (1990) 'Cosmopolitans and Locals in World Culture', in Featherstone, Mike (ed), pp. 327-252.

Hegel, Georg F. (1967) (original 1820) *Philosophy of Right,* translated by T.M. Knox. Oxford: Oxford University Press.

Höhne, Hansjoachim (1977) *Die Geschichte der Nachricht und ihrer Verbreiter*. Baden-Baden: Nomos Verlagsgesellschaft.

Hudson, Heather E. (1990) *Communication Satellites. Their Development and Impact*. London, New York: The Free Press.

(IHT) International Herald Tribune, (1993a) (Jan, 20) 'CNN Battles New Competition for International Viewers'.

(IHT) International Herald Tribune, (1993b) (March, 31) 'CNN Weighs up Implications of BBC-ABC-Deal'.

Jamieson, Neil L. 'Communication and the New Paradigm for Development', in Casmir, Fred L. (ed), *Communication in Development*. Norwood, New Jersey: Ablex Publishing Corporation, pp. 27-50.

Kant, Immanuel (1795, 1881) *Zum ewigen Frieden*. Leipzig: Reclam.

Kato, Hidetoshi (1976) 'Global Instantaneousness and Instant Globalism - The Significance of Popular Culture in Developing Countries', in Schramm, Wilbur/Lerner, Daniel (eds), pp. 253-258.

Katz, J. (1991) 'Covering the Gulf War: Collateral Damage to Network News', *Columbia Journalism Review,* March/April, p. 29.

Kavanaugh, Andrea (1986) 'Star WARCs and New Systems. An Analysis of US International Satellite Policy Information', *Telecommunications Policy,* June: 93-105.

Kerlinger, F (1973) *Foundations of Behavioral Research*. (2nd edition), New York.

Kivikuru, Ullamaija (1988) 'From Import to Modelling: Finland - An Example of Old Periphery Dependency, *European Journal of Communication*, 3:9-34.

Larsen, Peter (1992) 'More than Just Images: The Whole Picture: News in the Multichannel Universe', in: Skovmand, M./Schroder, K. (eds), *Media Cultures: Reappraising Transnational Media*. London, New York: Routledge.

Le Monde (Le Monde Radio Television) (1992) 'Chaines d'information la BBC, rivale planetaire de CNN', (21 au 27 septembre).

Lechner, Frank J. (1989) 'Cultural Aspects of the Modern World System', in Swatos, W.H. (ed), *Religious Politics in Global Perspective*, New York, pp. 11-28.

Lent, John A. (1991) 'Telematics in Malaysia: Room at the Top for a Selected Few', in Sussman, Gerald/Lent, John A. (eds), pp. 165-199.

Lerner, Daniel (1958, 1962) *The Passing of Traditional Society. Modernizing the Middle East*. Glencoe, Ill.: The Free Press.

Lichter, Robert S./Rothman, Stanley/Lichter, Linda (1981) *The Media Elite. America's New Powerbrokers*. New York: Hastings House.

Liebes, Tarmar/Katz Elihu (1990) *The Export of Meaning. Cross Cultural Readings of Dallas*. New York, Oxford: Oxford University Press.

Lippmann, Walter (1922) *Public Opinion*. New York: Macmillan.

Long, Theordore E. (1991) 'Old Testament Universalism: Prophetic Seeds on Particularistic Soil', in Roland Robertson/Garrett,William R. (eds), *Religion and Global Order*. New York: Paragon House Publishers, pp 19-34.

Luhmann, Niklas (1975) *Soziologische Aufklärung*, Vol. 2. Köln: Westdeutscher Verlag.

Luhmann, Niklas (1982) 'The World Society as a Social System', *Journal of General Systems*, 1982, 8: 131-138.

Mancini, Paolo (1991) 'The Public Sphere and the Use of News in a 'Coalition' System of Government', in Dahlgren, Peter/Sparks, Colin. (eds), pp. 137-154.

Mannheim, Karl (1964) *Wissenssoziologie*. Berlin, Neuwied: Luchterhand.

Marvin, Carolyn (1987) 'Information and History', in Daryl Slack, Jennifer/Fejes, Fred (eds), *The Ideology of the Information Age*. Norwood, New Jersey: Ablex Publishing Corporation, pp. 49-62.

Matson, Floyd (1976) 'The Global Village Revisited', in Schramm, Wilbur/Lerner, Daniel (eds), pp. 259-261.

Mattelart, Armand (1992) *La communication-monde. Histoire des idees et des strategies*. Paris.

McClellan, Steve (1994) 'News Networking pays off', *Broadcasting & Cable*, 10, 10:56.

McLuhan, Marshall (1964) Understanding Media: The Extensions of Man New York: McGraw-Hill.

McNeil, Alex (1991) *Total Television. A Comprehensive Guide to Programming from 1948 to the Present.* London: Penguin Books.

McQuail, Dennis (1987), *Mass Communication Theory,* London, Newbury Park, New Delhi: Sage.

McQuail, Dennis/Siune, Karen (1986) *New Media Politics. Comparative Perspectives in Western Europe.* London, Beverly Hills, New Delhi: Sage.

Melody, William H. (1990) 'Communication Policy in the Global Information Economy? Whither the Public Interest?', in Ferguson, Marjorie (ed), *Public Communication. The new Imperatives.* London, Newbury Park, New Delhi: Sage, pp.16-39.

Merrill, John C. (1983) *Global Journalism. A Survey of the World's Mass Media.* New York, London: Longman.

Mickiewics, Ellen (1988) *Split Signals. Television and Politics in the* Soviet *Union.* New York, Oxford: Oxford University Press.

Morgan, Michael (1990) 'International Cultivation Analysis' in Morgan, Michael et al.: (eds), *Cultivation Analysis.* London, New Delhi: Sage, pp. 225-247.

Mowlana, Hamid (1993) 'The new global order and cultural ecology', *Media Culture and Society,* 15:9-27.

Mowlana, Hamid (1994): 'International Communication Research in the 21st Century: From Functionalism to Postmodernism and Beyond', in Hamelink/Linne (eds), pp.351-368.

Mowlana, Hamid/Wilson, Laurie J. (1990) *The Passing of Modernity. Communication and the Transformation of Society.* New York, London: Longman.

Moynihan, D. P. (1993) *Pandaemonium. Ethnicity in International Politics.* Oxford, New York: Oxford University Press.

Murdock, Graham (1992) 'Citizens, Consumers, and Public Culture, in Skovmand, Michael/Schroder, Kim Christian (eds) *Media Cultures: Reappraising Transnational Media.* London: Routledge, pp. 17-41.

Murdock, Graham/Golding, Peter (1977): 'Capitalism, Communication and Class Relations', in Curran, James/Gurevitch, Michael/Woolacott, Janet (eds), pp. 12-43.

Mytton, Graham (ed) (1993): *Global Audiences. Research for Worldwide Broadcasting 1993.* London, Paris, Rome: John Libbey.

Negrine, R./Papathanassopoulos, S. (1990) *The Internationalization of Television.* London: Pinter.

Neumann, Russell W. (1991): *The Future of the Mass Audience.* Cambridge, New York, Port Chester, Melbourne, Sydney: Cambridge University Press.

Newsweek, (1993) (Jan., 25) 'Eyes of the World. Two European TV Services challenge the Dominance of America's CNN'.

Nordenstreng, Kaarle/Schiller, Herbert I. (eds) (1979) *National Sovereignty and International Communication.* Norwood, N.J.: Ablex Publishing.

Nordenstreng, Kaarle (1994): 'The Unesco Expert Panel with the Benefit of Hindsight' in: Hamelink, Cees /Linne, Olga (eds), pp. 3-19.

Noticias Argentine (1994) (June) 'CNN en vivo' (Translation:CNN Live - Seven Days in the Turner Operation).

Parsons, Talcott (1961) 'Some Considerations on the Theory of Social Change', *Rural Sociology*, 26, 3:219-239.

Parsons, Talcott (1978) *Action Theory and the Human Condition*. New York, London.

Pearce, Barnett W. (1989) *Communication and the Human Condition*. Carbondale and Edwardsville.

Porter, Vincent (1991) *Pluralism, Politics and the Marketplace: the Regulation of German Broadcasting*. London.

Potter, James W. (1991) 'Examining Cultivation From a Psychological Perspective', *Communicative Research*, 18, 1: 77-102.

Pye, Lucian (1983) Models of Traditional, Transitional and Modern communication Systems, in: Pye, Lucian (ed), communication and Poltical Development. Princeton , New Jersey: Princeton University Press,

Raboy, Marc/Dagenais, Bernard (1990) *Media, Crisis and Democracy. Mass Communication and the Disruption of Social Order*. London, Newbury Park, New Delhi: Sage.

Rahim, Syed A. (1984) 'International communication Agencies: an Overview', in Gerbner, George/Siefert, Marsha (eds), pp. 391-399.

Rao, Lakshmana (1966) *Communication and Development. A Study of Two Indian Villages*. Minneapolis.

Ratzel, Friedrich (1923) *Politische Geographie*. Munich, Berlin: R. Oldenbourg.

Revault, Rene-Jean (1987) 'The Ideology of the Information Age in a Senseless World', in Slack, Daryl/Fejes, Fred (eds), *The Ideology of the Information Age*. Norwood, New Jersey: Ablex, pp. 178-199.

Richter, Emanuel (1992) *Der Zerfall der Welteinheit. Vernunft und Globalisierung in der Moderne*. Frankfurt, New York: Campus.

Riggins, Stephen, H. (1992) *Ethnic Minority Media*. London, Newbury Park, New Delhi: Sage.

Robertson, Roland (1992) *Globalization. Social Theory and Global Culture*. London, Newbury Park, New Delhi: Sage.

Robertson, Roland (1990) 'Mapping the Global Condition: Globalization as the Central Concept', in Featherstone, Mike (ed), pp. 15-30.

Robertson, Roland (1992) 'Globality and Modernity', *Theory, Culture & Society*, 9:153-161.

Ross, Robert W. (1991) *Remarks at Medien Forum Nordrhein-Westfalen/International Television Conference* Cologne, Germany, (June, 10).

Schiller, Herbert I. (1976) *Communication and Cultural Domination*. White Plains, NY.: International Arts and Science Press.

Schiller, Herbert I. (1979) 'Transnational Media and National Development', in Nordenstreng, Kaarle/Schiller Herbert I. (eds),. *National* Sovereignty *and International Communication*, Norwood, New Jersey: Ablex Publishing Corporation, pp. 21-32.

Schiller, Herbert I. (1991) 'Not Yet the Post-Imperialist Era', *Critical Studies in Mass Communication*, 8:13-28.

Schiller, Herbert I. (1992) 'Fast Food, Fast Cars, Fast Political Rhetoric', *Intermedia*, 20, 4-5: 21.

Schlesinger, Philip (1986) 'In Search of the Intellectuals: some Comments on recent Theory', in Collins, Philip et al. (eds), *Media, Culture and Society. A Critical Reader*. London, Newbury Park, New Delhi: Sage, pp. 84-104.

Schmidt, Siegfried J./Weischenberg, Siegfried (1994) 'Mediengattungen, Berichterstattungsmuster, Darstellungsformen', in Merten, Klaus/Schmidt, Siegfried J./Weischenberg, Siegfried (eds), *Die Wirklichkeit der Medien*. Opladen: Westdeutscher Verlag, pp. 212-236.

Schramm, Wilbur (1959) *One day in the World's Press*. Stanford, California: Standford University Press.

Schramm, Wilbur (1964) *Mass Media and National Development. The Role of Information in the Developing Countries*. Stanford, California: Stanford University Press.

Schramm, Wilbur (1969, 1972) 'Communication and Change', in Lerner, Daniel/Schramm Wilbur (eds), *Communication and Change in the Developing Countries* Honolulu, Hawaii: East-West Centre, pp. 5-32.

Schramm, Wilbur/Lerner, Daniel (eds) (1976) *Communication and Change. The last ten Years - and the next*. Honolulu, Hawaii: East-West Centre.

Sepstrup, Preben (1990) *Transnationalization of* Television *in Western Europe*. London, Paris, Rome: Academia Research Monograph.

Servaes, Jan (1983): *Communication and* Development: *some theoretical Remarks*. Leuven: Ablex Publishing Corporation.

Servaes, Jan (1991) 'Toward a New Perspective for Communication and Development', in Casmir, Fred L. (ed), *Communication and Development*. Norwood, New Jersey: Ablex Publishing Corporation, pp 51-86.

Shields, Rob (ed) (1992) *Lifestyle Shopping. The Subject of Consumption*. London, New York, Routledge.

Smith, A. D. (1992) 'Is there a Global Culture?' *Intermedia*, August/September, Vol 20, No.4-5.

Smith, Anthony (1977) 'Technology and Control: the interactive Dimensions of Journalism', in Curran, James/Gurevitch, Michael/Woollacott, Janet (eds), pp. 174-194.

South China Morning Post, (1994) (May 8) 'China to go it alone in cable TV'.

South China Morning Post, (1994) (May, 8) 'TV's Splitting Images'

Spinner, Helmut (1994) *Die Wissensordnung: ein Leitkonzept für die dritte Grundordnung des Informationszeitalters.* Opladen: Leske und Budrich.

Steenbergen, Bart van (1994) 'The Condition of Citizenship: an Introduction', in Steenbergen, Bart van (ed), *The Condition of Citizenship.* London; Thousand Oaks, New Delhi: Sage, pp. 1-9.

Stephens, Mitchell (1988) *History of News. From the Drum to the Satellite.* New York: Viking.

Stevenson, Robert L./Cole, Richard R.(1984) 'Patterns of Foreign News', in: Stevenson, Robert L./Shaw, Donald Lewis (eds), pp 37-69.

Stevenson, Robert L./Shaw, Donald Lewis (1984) *Foreign News and the New World Information Order.* Ames, Iowa: Iowa State University Press.

Sussman, Gerald (1991) 'The Transnationalization of Philippine Telecommunications: Postcolonial Continuities', in Sussman, Gerald/Lent, John A. (eds), *Transnational Communications: Wiring the Third World.* London, Newbury Park, New Delhi: Sage.

Sussman,Gerald/Lent, John A. (eds) (1991) *Transnational* Communications: *Wiring the Third World.* Newbury Park, California: Sage.

Szecskö, Tamas (1994) 'Games Media People Play Changes in the Mass Communication System of Hungary', in Hamelink/Linne (eds), pp. 73-93.

The Independent (1994) (7, September) 'CNN: it's more news, folks'.

The Media Institute (1983) *CNN vs. The Networks: is more News better News?.* Washington/DC: The Media Institute, Media Research Series.

Tobenkin, David (1994): 'New Life for local TV News' in *Broadcasting & Cable,* 10, 10:68-70.

Tomlinson, John (1991) *Cultural Imperialism.* Baltimore: Johns Hopkins University Press.

Tönnies, Ferdinand (1887, 1963) *Gemeinschaft und Gesellschaft. Grundbegriffe der reinen Soziologie.* Darmstadt: Wissenschaftliche Buchgesellschaft.

Tunstall, J. *The Media are American: Anglo-American Media in the World.* London.

Turner, Bryan S. (1992) 'Weber, Giddens and Modernity', *Theory, Culture & Society* , 9:141-146.

UNESCO (1980) *Many Voices,* One *World.* Paris: Unesco Press.

Variety (1994) (March, 23) 'Global Report: The Latin Americas'.

Virilio, Paul (1989) *Der negative Horizont: Bewegung-Geschwindigkeit-Beschleunigung.* München.

Volkmer, Ingrid (1991a): 'In Thirty Minutes around the World: CNN and the Globalization of Knowledge' Paper presented on the *Annual Conference of the American Popular Culture Association,* San Antonio, Texas.

Volkmer, Ingrid (1991b): 'Die Entstehungsgeschichte von CNN' Paper presented on the *International Television* Conference, Cologne, Germany, (June, 10).

Volkmer, Ingrid (1992) 'Hic et nunc' Of Global News Generations: The Phenomenological Category of Da-sein. In the Perspective of Communication Theory, Paper presented on the 10th Anniversary Conference of *Theory, Culture & Society*, Pittsburgh.

Volkmer, Ingrid (1993) 'Feldherr im Bilderkrieg. Ted Turner - The World's News Leader', *Bertelsmann Briefe*, 130:33-36.

Volkmer, Ingrid (1997) 'Universalism and Particularism: The Problem of Cultural Sovereignty and Global Information Flow', in Kahin/Nesson (eds) *Borders in Cyberspace. Information Policy and the Global Information Infrastructure*, Cambridge: MIT Press, pp.48-83.

Wallerstein, Immanuel (1974) *The Modern World-System*. New York: Academic Press.

Wallis, Roger/Baran, Stanley (1990) *The Known World of Broadcast News: International News and the Electric Media*. London, New York: Routledge.

Warner, Malcolm (1970) 'Decision-Making in Network TV News', in Tunstall, Jeremy (ed), *Media* Sociology. Urbana, Chicago, London, pp. 158-167.

Werben & Verkaufen (1993) (29.10.) 'Medien als Machtfaktor, Subventionen als Stütze', 43: 200.

West Africa (1987(a)), (August) 'Culture of Silence'.

West Africa (1987(b)), (16, February) 'The Press and its Freedom'.

West Africa (1988), (2, March), 'From Apologies to Praises. Ajoa Yeboah-Afari says Ghana's Television Service is vastly improved'.

West Africa (1989), (24, April) 'Call for new order'.

White, Robert (1994) 'The Public Sphere as an Intergrating Concept for Development Communication', in Hamelink/Linne (eds), pp. 249-265.

Whittemore (1990) *CNN- The Inside Story*. Boston, Toronto, London: Little Brown and Company.

Wilhelm, Donald (1990) *Global communication and Political Power*. New Brunswick, London.

Wilke, Jürgen/Rosenberger, Bernhard (1991) *Die Nachrichtenmacher*. Köln, Weimar, Wien: Böhlau.

Williams, Frederick (1982) *The Communication Revolution*. Beverly Hills.

Wimmer, Roger D./Dominick, Joseph R. *Mass Media Research*. Belmont, California: Wadsworth Publishing Company.

Wilson, Rob/Wimal Dissanayake (eds) (1996) *Global/Local. Cultural Production and the Transnational Imaginary*. Durham/London:Duke University Press.

Worldbank (ed) (1994) *Weltentwicklungsbericht 1994. Infrastruktur und Entwicklung*. Bonn: United Nations Publications.

Zelizer, Barbie (1992) 'CNN, the Gulf War and Journalistic Practice', *Journal of Communication*, Vol. 42, 1.